ROWLAND HILL
Victorian Genius and Benefactor

THE EDUCATIONIST

On this admirable system of education the brightest hopes of the human race may anchor. The system has commenced its career; it must go on; it will become universal; we may share its triumphs; we cannot prevent them.

The Westminster Review, 1823

THE POSTAL REFORMER:

. . . . his great plan ran like wild-fire through the civilized world, and never, perhaps, was a local invention . . . and improvement applied in the lifetime of its author for the advantage of such multitudes of his fellow creatures.

William Ewart Gladstone, 1879

ROWLAND HILL
Victorian Genius and Benefactor

Colin G. Hey

QUILLER PRESS
LONDON

For
Phyl, Alison and Anthony

ISBN 1 870948 32 7

First published 1989
by Quiller Press Ltd
46 Lillie Road SW6 1TN

Copyright © 1989 Colin Hey

Phototypeset by Galleon Photosetting, Ipswich
Printed in Great Britain by Camelot Press plc

Contents

Acknowledgements

The author is very conscious of the generous assistance given to him from far and wide during his research on this book, and in particular he offers his grateful thanks to the following:

The Marc Fitch Fund
The Birmingham Reference Library
The Birmingham Museum and Art Gallery
Bruce Castle Museum, Tottenham
The Bodleian Library, Oxford
The Department of Education Studies, Oxford
The Royal Library, Stockholm
The Library of Congress, Washington
The Alderman Library, University of Virginia, USA
The Libraries of the Australian and West Australian Commissions, London
The Librarian, University College, London
The Temple Library, Rugby School
The National Postal Museum
The Post Office Archives
The School of Education Library, University of Birmingham
The Westwood Library, University of Warwick
The Brighton Railway Circle
The Brighton Central Reference Library
The Philatelic Bulletin
The National Portrait Gallery
The Science Museum, South Kensington
The County Library, Warwick

The author owes a special debt of gratitude to the following for the practical help they have given so readily:

Lord Stechford; Dr Frank H. T. Rhodes; Dr I. D. Hill; Mr Paul Morgan; Mr H. Parry; Mr Eric Goodliffe; Mr Percy Blandford; Mrs Jean Farrugia; Mr M. J. Cruttenden; Mr John Minnis; Miss Gillian Ledger; the late Professor Donald H. Hey, FRS, and to the many senior officials of the Post Office without whose enthusiastic and generous support this book might not have seen the light of day.

List of Illustrations

Foreword

by
Lord Butterfield of Stechford, OBE, MD, FRCP

Formerly Regius Professor of Physic, Master of Downing College and
Vice-Chancellor in the University of Cambridge

Having sat at Colin Hey's feet as a schoolboy, I feel I know him well
enough to commend this study of Rowland Hill to a wide range of readers. Like me, Rowland Hill was born and nurtured in the Midlands and
in his story I can see how characteristic he was of the drive, originality
and enterprise that Great Britain's industrial hub displayed to the world
in the nineteenth century.

When I first moved from Medicine to become Vice-Chancellor of the
University of Nottingham, I took some pains to study and understand
the circumstances of the great ferment of educational reform that the
nineteenth century had launched upon our country. In Nottingham this
was reflected by the establishment of the Mechanics' Institute in 1837
and in 1877 the University College, where D. H. Lawrence studied,
worthy foundations for the University of Nottingham inaugurated after
World War II.

In my readings I was drawn immediately to Rowland Hill's unusual
and pioneering School, Hazelwood, which had been founded almost
on my childhood doorstep. I saw at once that here were the seeds of a
new concept of secondary education to come into fruition in the years
ahead. I could grasp how Hazelwood School came to attract pupils from
Greece, Switzerland, France, Norway, Sweden and even South America
and the West Indies: to the world at large, Hazelwood carried a new
educational message for the new age emerging – relevance.

But it was not until I read Colin Hey's present book that I realised
the full extent of Rowland Hill's originality and the great range of
his talents, extending as they did far beyond the field of education –
for example his admirable work organising the colonisation of South
Australia, his brilliant direction and dramatic rehabilitation of the
London and Brighton railway, and, of course, his protracted battle with

the Establishment to give his country and the world in general the great boon of a cheap efficient postal service starting with the legendary penny black postage stamp!

First and foremost this book is a 'good read'. Rowland Hill's story is incredibly broad in its ramifications and world-wide in its connections. The book is written with a lightness of touch and sharpness of vision that rivet the reader's attention as the narrative moves along. I am sure it will give many readers the pleasure and satisfaction that it has given me.

John Butterfield,
December 1988   Cambridge.

Foreword

by
Dr Frank H. T. Rhodes, President, Cornell University, Ithaca, New York

This splendid book provides a lively account of the life of Rowland Hill, whose influence is traced through a series of four major events in Victorian history. The book, which is plentifully illustrated, and has extensive notes and a bibliography, traces the background of the Hill family and gives a detailed account of the experiment that they conducted together in the Hazelwood School at Birmingham and at Bruce Castle near London. The Hazelwood Experiment, which attracted pupils and interest from all over the world, occupied the first twenty-five years of Hill's professional life. Here he pioneered all that we would now regard as best in secondary education. In contrast to the rigidity of the public schools of the earlier nineteenth century, whose curriculum was narrowly classical, Hazelwood offered a curriculum that was uncompromisingly liberal, a self-imposed system of discipline, high idealism, extensive athletic facilities, and practical wide-ranging field work. Most of these reforms preceded by decades others – such as those of Arnold of Rugby – that are now better known.

The influence of Hill's schools extended far beyond the school system itself. The George Junior Republic, and similar 'democratic' institutions for delinquent youth spread across the eastern United States. Jefferson was interested in the experiment and based some aspects of the curriculum and honor system of the University of Virginia upon Hill's work.

The author gives a graphic account of Hill's astonishingly skilful supervision of the colonisation of South Australia and of his decisive direction and rescue of the near bankrupt London and Brighton Railway.

In spite of these successes, Hill is best remembered for his introduction of penny postage and for his creation of the modern postal service. That he did this, initially without any formal administrative responsibility, and in the teeth of sustained and organised opposition from those in positions of seniority, only adds to the significance of his achievements.

Colin Hey's book represents the first comprehensive biography of this remarkable man for over a century. Through the book, Rowland Hill emerges as a man of immense creativeness, painstaking attention to detail, consummate administrative skill, profound civil and religious convictions, and a tender concern for others.

This lively book is one to be read and cherished. It establishes Rowland Hill, not only as a great Victorian, but also as a great human benefactor, both through his imaginative dedication to education, and through his gift to the world of cheap communication, which has done so much to increase human understanding.

Frank H. T. Rhodes
1988   President, Cornell University

Author's Preface

This book does not presume to be a full-bodied biography of Rowland Hill; rather is it a selective study of the main episodes of his life, more in breadth than depth, taking in the halo of circumstance that inevitably envelops his history. Naturally his twenty-five years as a teacher and educational reformer, and his twenty-one years with the Treasury and Post Office claim the major portion of the book. This latter phase of his career is a difficult and complex story, and the account given here is no doubt too simplistic and naïve. One has only to read Dr M. J. Daunton's recent book *Royal Mail; the Post Office since 1840* (Athlone Press, 1985) to realise the mammoth task entailed in unravelling the tangle of controversy and statistics to achieve any degree of objectivity in assessing Rowland Hill's part in the story. In the final resort the present rather sketchy account may give a truer picture of Rowland Hill's experiences in the Post Office than that given by the statistical minutiae of Dr Daunton's scholarly study. By picking out the more dramatic moments of the story, and by questioning some of Dr Daunton's more speculative interpretations of events, the present work may possibly be closer to the facts and probably be more readable. I hope that it will be recognised that my concluding chapter – A Final Assessment – provides convincing proof, point by point, that most of Rowland Hill's suggestions of hostility, duplicity and non-co-operation on the part of many Post Office officials and contemporary politicians were real and not the subjective delusions they are often made out to be. Hence, as far as Rowland Hill's career in the Post Office is concerned, my book is presented as a corrective to the distorted views that have appeared elsewhere. It is particularly unfortunate, for example, that in some recent articles in the quarterly *Postal History* in 1986 the author, Mr Edward C. Baker, former Archivist to the Post Office, attempts a similar denigration of Rowland Hill's work in the Post Office, but once again the evidence he adduces is far from convincing.

Quite deliberately the book does not follow the traditional biographical stereotype; the reader will find, for instance, that the main narrative is complemented by an unusually enriched section of Notes and Comments. This represents the halo of circumstance mentioned above, and includes much incidental chit-chat, *obiter dicta*, biographical snapshots and other marginal matter that help to inspire the narrative with the breath of life. If we reflect on our grasp and feeling of past history, most people would admit that they have derived it more from the peripheral writers than from academic historians – from the historical novelists, the diarists, essayists and letter writers. How would *we* recapture the spirit of the seventeenth, eighteenth and nineteenth centuries without the observations and comments of such writers as Defoe, Pepys, Evelyn, Addison, Fanny Burney, Horace Walpole, Lamb and Hazlitt? It is hoped, therefore, that the spirit of our particular period may be recaptured and illuminated by the variety of Notes and Comments provided. They certainly unveil an impressive gallery of the leading contemporary reformers who were the very fount of the great liberal upsurge that occurred in the nineteenth century. Among them, of course, was a good sprinkling of cranks, pseudo-philosophers, starry-eyed philanthropists and unbalanced fanatics, but they all combine to convey the true flavour of the age.

The four main periods of Rowland Hill's varied career are dealt with in some detail. Firstly his twenty-five years as an innovative educationist and teacher at Hazelwood and Bruce Castle schools; secondly the best part of six years covering his work in organising the colonisation of South Australia; thirdly his three years spent in re-establishing the fortunes of the London and Brighton railway, and fourthly his work on postal reform – his three years temporary appointment with the Treasury from 1839 to 1842, and his real work as a permanent official of the Post Office from 1846 to his retirement on grounds of ill-health in 1864.

It is the story of a self-educated genius, a rank outsider who in his post office days was disparagingly referred to as 'that man from Birmingham'. Yet by sheer perseverance and faith in his ideas he achieved national and international fame for his postal reforms. Society at home and abroad immediately recognised his genius; to his contemporaries he was clearly a very eminent Victorian. There is concrete proof of this; in 1846 he was presented with a testimonial of £13,000 raised by public subscription; in 1857 he was elected Fellow of the Royal Society; in 1860 he was knighted by Queen Victoria; in 1864 at his retirement he was given his full salary as a pension for life as well as a Parliamentary Grant of £20,000. In the same year he was awarded an honorary DCL of the University of Oxford. On his deathbed in 1879 he was visited by a deputation under the City Chamberlain who presented him with the Freedom of the City of London. His final honour in the same year was a state funeral and burial in Westminster Abbey.

In the face of this and other evidence submitted later in the book the modern fashion of denigration must surely carry little weight. Those who were closest to the actual events spoke up in no uncertain terms. Typical were the words of a former Postmaster General, Mr Shaw-Lefevre, MP who at the Penny Postage Jubilee Dinner in 1890 declared:

> Every possible objection was raised to every part of the scheme. They maintained that uniformity would be unjust and impracticable; that payment in advance was impossible; and that the charge by weight could not be entertained. Sir Rowland not only carried his great scheme, but gave a great blow to the obtuse and ignorant and prejudiced officials from which it has, I rejoice to think, never recovered. It survived in fact for a time; but Sir Rowland inspired the Department with a new spirit, and founded a new school of officials.

The story I tell takes in Rowland's career in a broad sweep, seeing the wood rather than the trees, believing there is no profit or enjoyment playing academic cowboys and Indians amid the undergrowth in an attempt to score paltry debating points in minor issues. The nation and the world, I feel sure, prefer to see Rowland's life story in a similar manner, so I hope that my account will be received in the same spirit. In my effort to give the true story of Rowland Hill's role in Post Office history I have been mindful of Hamlet's dying utterances:

> ... What a wounded name,
> Things standing thus unknown, shall live behind me ...
> ... Horatio, I am dead;
> Thou livest; report me and my cause aright
> To the unsatisfied.

I should like to believe that I have performed a similar pious service for the name of Rowland Hill.

ROWLAND HILL, KCB, DCL, FRAS, FRS

BIOGRAPHICAL SUMMARY

1795   Born at Kidderminster on 3 December.

1802   His father, Thomas Wright Hill, bought a school in Lionel Street, Birmingham.

1803   School moved to larger premises at Hill Top, Birmingham.

1807   Rowland became a pupil teacher at the school.

1819   The new Hazelwood School opened in Birmingham, designed by Rowland.

1822   Rowland and his eldest brother, Matthew, published *Public Education*. It won excellent reviews and soon gained international fame.

1827   London branch opened at Bruce Castle, Tottenham, directed by Rowland and Edwin. Arthur and Frederic remained at Hazelwood.

1832   Rowland published a paper, *Home Colonies; a Plan for the Gradual Extinction of Pauperism and the Diminution of Crime*. A copy was sent to Lord Brougham, the Lord Chancellor.

1833   Hazelwood closed in Birmingham. At Bruce Castle Rowland, after twenty-six years of schoolmastering, was advised to retire on grounds of ill-health, leaving Arthur as Headmaster.

1833–1839   Rowland became interested in the move to colonise South Australia, and in 1835 became Secretary to the South Australian Commission appointed by the government to organise the colonisation programme.

1835   With his brother, Edwin, he patented their Rotary Printing Press.

1837–1838   Published four editions of his famous pamphlet, *Post Office Reform: its Importance and Practicability*.

1839   On 17 August the Penny Postage Act received Royal Assent.

1839   In September Rowland was given a two-year appointment at the Treasury to assist in the implementing of the Act, but he was denied any executive authority. His appointment was extended a third year.

1840   10 January; uniform Penny Postage was introduced.

1840   On 6 May the famous Penny Black stamp and stationery came into use.

1842   On change of government Rowland's appointment was terminated. Widespread public indignation was shown.

1843–1846   Became Director and later Chairman of the London and Brighton Railway.

1844   Awarded the Freedom of Aberdeen.

1846   In June presented with a testimonial of £13,000, raised by public subscription.

1846   In November he was appointed Secretary to the Postmaster General.

1854   In April he was appointed to the top post of Secretary to the Post Office on the promotion of Colonel Maberly to another department.

1857   Elected to a Fellowship of the Royal Society.

1860   Knighted by Queen Victoria.

1864   Awarded an Honorary DCL of the University of Oxford.

1864   In March he was forced to retire on medical advice. He was given a life pension of his full salary and a special Parliamentary grant of £20,000.

1865   He recovered enough to serve on the Royal Commission on Railways.

1879   Granted the Freedom of the City of London.

1879   On 27 August he died at his home in Hampstead.

1879   4 September; State funeral and burial in Westminster Abbey.

THE HILL FAMILY

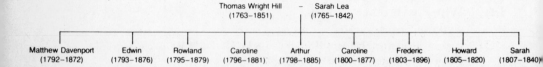

Thomas Wright Hill (1763–1851) – Sarah Lea (1765–1842)

Matthew Davenport (1792–1872) | Edwin (1793–1876) | Rowland (1795–1879) | Caroline (1796–1881) | Arthur (1798–1885) | Caroline (1800–1877) | Frederic (1803–1896) | Howard (1805–1820) | Sarah (1807–1840)

[I]

The Hazelwood Breakthrough

THIS account of the life of Rowland Hill brings to light areas in his career that are unknown to most people. The vast majority think of him as the great postal reformer, and even this is often narrowed down to the man who invented adhesive stamps. The strange fact is that when in 1846, at the age of fifty-one, he was granted his first permanent appointment with the Post Office he had already spent more than thirty-two years of his working life in other quite different occupations.

For the best part of six years he was associated with, and finally in 1835 became the Secretary and chief executive officer of the South Australian Commission,[1] responsible for the organisation of a substantial emigration programme to South Australia – a task he carried out with outstanding efficiency and great humanity. Some years later, for a period of just under three years, he proved to be a very successful Director, and later Chairman, of the London and Brighton Railway Company,[2] lifting the company from near bankruptcy to gratifying profitability and much appreciated operational efficiency. Detailed accounts of both these episodes are given in later chapters.

Far more important than these secondary episodes is the fact that Rowland spent twenty-five years of his life, from 1808 to 1833, as a schoolmaster and a very remarkable educational reformer. For much of the time he was Headmaster of Hazelwood School, Birmingham; then, in 1827, he left the Midlands to open the London branch of the school at Bruce Castle, Tottenham, where he and his bride, Caroline, established their first married home.

During these years he looked upon education as his real mission in life, and sure enough, before 1825 his unusual originality and striking administrative ability brought sudden world-wide fame to his work at Hazelwood. It was well deserved, for looking back over the whole field of educational development in Britain we can say that at Hazelwood, Rowland Hill conducted the most remarkable experiment in secondary education that Great Britain has ever seen, but by some strange quirk

[1]

of fate his achievement has been almost completely forgotten. It has certainly not been given its proper due in the various educational history books. Even so, it is clear that the achievements of Hazelwood have played a significant part in shaping the climate of opinion in which subsequent educational and social reforms were able to take place. This is demonstrated in some detail later.

An early assessment of the work and influence of Rowland Hill's educational achievement is to be found in the *Encyclopedia Britannica* – 9th Edition, 1875 – where we read:

> Rowland Hill, as an educationist, is entitled to a place side by side with Arnold of Rugby,[3] and was equally successful in making moral influence of the highest kind the permanent power in school discipline.

This verdict may surprise us today, but though it is a fair and just assessment as far as it goes, it omits half the story: it should have continued:

> But he was far more successful than Dr Arnold in broadening the curriculum beyond all recognition and in devising new and appropriate teaching methods to match the expanded content of education. Rowland Hill, in fact, radically re-shaped our whole concept of secondary education, and his pioneering work undoubtedly paved the way for the dramatic improvements that were later to take place in both the independent and state sectors. That these did not occur in the state system until *A. J. Balfour's Education Act*[4] of 1902 only goes to show how long it takes for new ideas to filter through.

The Hazelwood experiment really began in January 1803 when Rowland's father, Thomas Wright Hill, opened his private school, first in Lionel Street in central Birmingham, then a few months later at Hill Top, Birmingham, just a mile south-west of the town centre. Thomas Hill was a sincere Unitarian, a man of ideas and high ideals. Besides being the manager of a rolling-mill, he also worked as a teacher in Dr Joseph Priestley's Sunday School,[5] but soon decided that teaching was to be his true career. He made his rather novel philosophy of education clear in his opening Prospectus of Hill Top School in 1803 when he stated that he was more concerned with moral training and 'the virtues of the heart' than with the dispensing of random scraps of knowledge. He aimed to do this by firmness and kindness and not by authoritarian rules and fear of punishment. In its day this was decidedly revolutionary.

The Hills' educational ventures are unique in that they were all conducted by members of the family working closely together as a team. Thomas Wright Hill had six sons,[6] all of whom received their education in the family school; when they reached the age of thirteen or so most of the sons worked as pupil-teachers under their father. They had a complete unity of purpose and a profound conviction in the validity of their values and methods, and this spirit of unity remained with them all their lives. It proved its strength when Rowland began his association with the Post Office, for Edwin Hill gave up a successful career as an engineer to help his brother in the design and production of stamps, and later Rowland's younger brother, Frederic, likewise abandoned his career as a Barrister and Inspector of Prisons to work under Rowland. Both brothers accepted lower salaries in order to give their support to Rowland.

At this point we need to look briefly at the situation prevailing in the world of education when the Hill family arrived to shake it up. The backbone of the English system was provided by the nine historic Public Schools that were offering what they considered to be education to the sons of the Upper and Middle classes. The only alternatives to these were a number of local endowed Grammar Schools, a few Dissenting Academies,[7] a multitude of 'Dotheboys Halls'[8] and the employment of private tutors. The Hills' school, a private establishment, catered mostly for middle class pupils, but also admitted the sons of successful Midlands manufacturers and business-class families – mostly as boarders. The school also took in a sprinkling of upper-class pupils, amongst whom was Henry Montagu Villiers, a younger brother of the Fourth Earl of Clarendon,[9] and soon to become Bishop of Carlisle and later of Durham. In 1846 he was the Guest Speaker at the Bruce Castle Prize Day. The Villiers family had a close friendship with the Hills, and Charles Pelham Villiers, another brother, was proposed by old Thomas Wright Hill when he won his seat in the Commons in 1835 for Wolverhampton. The Earl himself visited Hazelwood School. But the values and quality of education that Hazelwood and the earlier Hill Top stood for were light-years ahead of what the Public Schools and other establishments could offer.

For three-quarters of the nineteenth century the nine authentic Public Schools were Eton, Harrow, Winchester, Westminster, Charterhouse, St Paul's, Merchant Taylors', Rugby and Shrewsbury which were all to a lesser or greater degree authoritarian communities of harsh brutality, where bullying and corporal punishment at the hands of masters and prefects were the order of the day, and where coarseness and debauchery made life nasty and brutish. If any moral training was discernible it was concealed in a compulsory, hell-fire type of Christianity which owed nothing to the ethics of the Sermon on the Mount. In the content, methods and range of their studies they were hopelessly narrow and out of date; their staple diet was the Classics, and this meant the endless construing of Greek and Latin texts backed up by largely meaningless grammar drills dictated by the ubiquitous *Eton Grammar*.

Such schools were becoming more and more irrelevant to the rapidly changing conditions of the world of the industrial revolution and of the Reform Act of 1832. In Birmingham the Hills were living at the very heart of these profound changes and they deliberately fashioned their curriculum and methods to meet its needs. On the discipline and moral training side they evolved a simple system of democratic, representative self-government for their older boys that anticipated the spirit of the impending Reform Act. In teaching methods they broke away from the rote learning that dominated the educational scene up and down the country and introduced novel, self-motivated procedures in tune with the wider and more practical curriculum they had introduced.

A very brief survey of the innovations introduced at Hill Top and Hazelwood will give some indication of the enormous step forward made by the Hill family.

At Hazelwood corporal punishment was abolished in 1818 and a Jury-court was established in which the boys administered their own disciplinary code. In place of a traditional prefect system the school, a few years later, had 'circles' of ten boys of different ages under the benign guidance of a 'guardian'. An internal metal currency took the place of marks, and classroom and social activities of every kind, including what was called 'voluntary labour' in all sorts of fields, contributed to the boys' 'aggregate rank'. This was expressed numerically, but was entirely non-competitive and only partly included academic achievement.

The curriculum was spectacularly wide and included at appropriate levels, Penmanship, English (including spelling and parsing), Elocution, Geography, History, Mathematics, French, Italian, Spanish, Latin and Greek (as options), Gymnastics, Art, Music, Woodwork, Metalwork, and Science. Mathematics was approached practically and led up to surveying and astronomical applications with the older boys. Modern languages, as well as Latin and Greek, were taught as far as possible by direct method. Speech and Drama formed an important aspect of work in English, and short plays in French and Latin were staged in Big School.

In its general amenities the school at Hazelwood, designed by Rowland himself, had a large assembly hall with stage and at least six ordinary classrooms, all heated by a central air-duct system. It was probably the first school to be lit by gas. In addition there was a whole range of craft-rooms, a library, one of the first school science laboratories to be built, a gymnasium, some studies for the older boys, a canteen, an observatory in the grounds, a swimming pool, a rented sports field and a school band. Many of these amenities became possible after the school

[4]

moved into the new Hazelwood premises in 1819, but innovations had been taking place throughout the years at Hill Top.

Rowland was his own architect[10] in designing the new building. It broke away completely from the traditional Big School in which half a dozen different classes were carried on at the same time and, as we have seen, provided a whole range of smaller classrooms and practical rooms appropriate for the wider curriculum and freer methods. When in July 1818 the footings were due to be pegged out, Rowland and his younger brother, Frederic, with their father camped out all night on the site in order to determine the building's orientation – true north and south – with astronomical precision. As a result the building line differed slightly from that of adjacent buildings on the Hagley Road. Further extensions were added in the early 1820s, following a serious fire.

All these extended facilities were first available in 1819, yet all the history books insist that Rugby School built the first school laboratory in 1859, and that Edward Thring of Uppingham School pioneered the provision of Craft rooms and studies for the older boys at about the same time. Actually, as we have seen, Hazelwood pre-dated them by some forty years. With these improved facilities the numbers at Hazelwood rose to 150 by 1826, at a time when Rugby School, two years before Dr Arnold's advent, numbered only 135.

By this time the Hills knew that they had achieved an educational breakthrough and decided the moment had come for them to tell the world about it. So with the help of his elder brother, Matthew, then just beginning his distinguished career at the Bar, Rowland published in 1822 the whole story in his book, *Plans for the Government and Liberal Instruction of Boys in Large Numbers, Drawn from Experience.* It burst like a bomb-shell on the educational world and a second edition was demanded in 1825. The title was then slightly changed by prefixing it with the phrase, *Public Education* and continuing *Plans for the Government etc.* The book is now more conveniently referred to as *Public Education* for short.

Almost immediately, beginning in the autumn of 1822, a whole spate of remarkably favourable reviews appeared in the serious journals of the day, beginning with the *National Register,* the *Guardian* and the *Eclectic Review.* Then in 1823 more followed in the *Monthly Review,* the *Traveller* and the Benthamite *Westminster Review,* a powerful organ of reform. The latter concluded its critical review in an exceptional burst of enthusiasm, claiming that if the Hazelwood system were generally adopted,

> the improvement which would immediately take place would be universal and without any bound which it is possible to fix. On this admirable system of education the brightest hopes of the human race may anchor.

> The system has commenced its career; it must go on; it will become universal; we may share its triumphs; we cannot prevent them.

Today we may smile at this rosy optimism; it is similar to what mankind felt at the birth of the League of Nations and the United Nations Organisation.

More support continued to pour in, for early in 1824 a notable fourteen page article appeared in the influential imperial-orientated review, the *Oriental Herald and Colonial Review*, written by its editor, James Silk Buckingham,[11] a leading traveller, writer and reformer. He was greatly impressed by the Hills' originality and strongly urged that the Hazelwood system should be introduced forthwith into India and the Colonies. He demonstrated his faith and sincerity by immediately sending his son to Hazelwood. Gradually bigger guns joined in the fray. In May 1824, Thomas De Quincey, the well-known contemporary author, wrote a powerfully supportive article of thirty-six pages in the *London Magazine* extolling the many merits and novel features of the Hazelwood system devised by this 'very original thinker on the science of education'. He concluded:

> In the hands of its founder we are convinced that it is calculated to work wonders; and so strong is the impression which his book conveys that he is not only a man of very extraordinary talents for the improvement of the science of education, but also a very conscientious man, that, for our part, we should confide a child to his care with that spirit of perfect confidence which he has described. . . There is an air of gentlemanly feeling spread over the book which tends still further to recommend the author.

In January 1825, one of the most famous journals of the day, the *Edinburgh Review*, printed a comprehensive twenty page critique which proclaimed that the Hazelwood venture represented a major advance in the science and art of education – a new conception of the nature of a school community. The article concluded:

> It must surely lead to most important consequences, and cannot now fail, whatever be its issue, to furnish valuable hints to all those engaged in the arduous business of education.

The one journal of which all progressives stood in awe was the formidable *Blackwood's Review*, the hard-hitting Tory publication which flayed every manifestation of Whiggery and Radicalism without mercy, with a sarcastic and cutting whip. In April 1825, *Blackwood* seems to have been caught off balance when it set out to review the Hills' book. The article starts off predictively in launching its usual attack on Benthamite ideas of all kinds, but, to its credit, finds itself forced to praise

[6]

the Hills for not slavishly following 'the gimcracks of Jerry Bentham[12] and company'. Clearly bewildered by the novelty of the Hills' ideas, the reviewer hesitates to criticise too sharply something he was not well acquainted with, and with unaccustomed generosity concludes:

> I should be sorry that any observations of mine should hurt the feelings of such evidently zealous and industrious men as the conductors of this establishment, and I wish them every success, if for no other reason, yet for the kindness and affection which they display to the precious charges committed to their care.

Even the vitriolic *Blackwood* seems to have capitulated; the roaring of the lion is as gentle as any sucking dove.

Most of the above critics, when they first read *Public Education*, were somewhat bewildered and out of their depth; they found it difficult to accept as gospel truth the remarkable events that the book revealed. So, many of them took the first opportunity to see it all with their own eyes; this certainly was the case with Dr Southwood Smith[13] of the *Westminster Review*, De Quincey of the *London Magazine*, James Silk Buckingham of the *Oriental Herald* and Captain Basil Hall[14] of the *Edinburgh Review*, who visited the school on behalf of its founder and editor, Francis Jeffrey.

James Silk Buckingham was not the only one wishing to export the Hazelwood system overseas – in his case to India and the Colonies. The redoubtable Jeremy Bentham invited Matthew Davenport Hill to 'a hermit's supper' one evening in June 1822 after reading *Public Education*, and told him he was anxious to introduce the Hazelwood system into Portugal, for which country he was then acting as constitutional adviser. He was engaged on working out a new constitution for the Cortez and realised that revolutionary changes of ideas, such as introducing the principles of democracy, had to begin at school level. This he observed to be happening in the unusual self-governing society of Hazelwood.

At this moment many countries in Europe, the Americas and in the Caribbean were just achieving independence, usually from Spain and Turkey. Anxious to join the ranks of the new self-governing democracies, they seized upon the Hazelwood system as the answer to their prayers. This was a more international and a more potent magic than the parochial variety purveyed by Dr Thomas Arnold some years later. John Bowring,[15] for instance, (who was a close associate of Bentham) was already negotiating to open schools in Greece following the Hazelwood principles, and Lord Byron's death in 1824, when supporting the fight for Greece's independence, added a richer lustre to

Hazelwood's radical message. This was not all, for there was a move by the French, working with a 'radical Bey' to set up schools on the Hazelwood pattern in Egypt. Haiti in the West Indies was also showing an interest, and Tripolitania in North Africa, and even Persia expressed a wish to send boys to Hazelwood to be inoculated with the doctrines of a new age. At this point Rowland tells us that he thought he would have to build a Mosque in the school grounds to provide for an influx of Moslems. We already know that the Argentine, Mexico, Portugal, France and Greece had sent boys to Hazelwood.

This surge of overseas' interest came about largely as a result of an article on, and a visit to, Hazelwood in September 1822 by one of France's leading educationists, M. Marc Antoine Jullien, editor of the influential international journal *La Revue Encyclopédique*. M. Jullien had been Secretary to the revolutionary leader, Robespierre, and was especially interested in education. He had studied the work of Pestalozzi[16] and Fellenberg[17] in Switzerland at first hand, and was in touch with most progressive developments in Europe; as such he was recognised as a filter and disseminator of advanced European educational and political thought. So impressed was he by what he saw and had read about Hazelwood that he promptly transferred his own son from Pestalozzi's school to the Hills' establishment in Birmingham, and wrote his comprehensive and appreciative account of the Hills' dramatic breakthrough in the next issue of his *Revue* in June 1823. Perhaps the strangest sequel to all this was the opening in June 1830 of a school in Stockholm, Sweden, modelled almost exactly on the Hazelwood pattern. In honour of the Hills it was called the Hillska Skola, and a brief account of it is given in Appendix B.

Apart from the fundamental innovations of the Hazelwood system in self-government, moral training and curriculum reform – which were the magnet that attracted world attention (and which we shall shortly deal with in detail), there was a whole range of varied activities that showed inventive thinking. The school magazine gives us some very vivid accounts of many of these, the magazine itself being a striking example of rare enterprise and originality. It was written, type-set and printed as an educational craft by the boys themselves, under the professional guidance of Arthur Hill, a former apprentice-printer, and it regularly contained etchings and lithographs produced by them. It is doubtful whether any school in Great Britain came anywhere near this in skill and originality, for at that time very few schools even thought of producing a magazine. The Hazelwood effort first appeared in its printed form in 1822 and was supported by at least sixty 'outsiders', including the philosopher Jeremy Bentham – a faithful and devoted admirer of the school; John Bowring, FRS, MP, founder of the *Westminster Review* and an active reformer, and William Hone, a well-known bookseller, writer of political pamphlets and a contributor to the *Penny Magazine*.

Among the major activities that must have astonished these 'outsiders' were the excursions indulged in by the *Franks*, a privileged group whose special status was obtained by all-round good work, especially when it contributed to the community as a whole. School outings and educational visits are commonplace today, but in the 1820s they were rarely to be found operating on the scale developed at Hazelwood. These excursions occupied a whole day or more, and took in such places as Hagley Hall (Sanderson Miller's[18] essay in the Palladian style); Worcester town and cathedral; William Shenstone's[19] famous *'ferme ornée'*, the Leasowes, near Halesowen; Dudley, Kenilworth and Maxstoke Castles and so on. The details of such a visit to Worcester in the summer of 1829 make particularly interesting reading. The boys rose at 4.00 am and boarded a canal boat at the Old Wharf in the centre of Birmingham. Soon they were clear of the town making for the famous Lapal tunnel which goes for some miles beneath a hill. Here the boat was 'legged' by the bargees lying on their backs and pushing with their feet against the roof of the tunnel. Among the party that day was a group of bandsmen who had brought their instruments with them and made fine sounds in the echoing tunnel.

After negotiating some thirty locks the party reached Worcester at 7.00 pm and stayed the night in a hotel. Next morning they were up early exploring the town before breakfast, and making a visit to the Cathedral. After breakfast the band gave an impromptu concert much to the astonishment of the natives. Early in the afternoon they embarked for the return journey, reaching Hazelwood by 1.00 am.

Another memorable feature of the school's wide variety of activities that would appeal to parents and interested outsiders by its originality, range and quality was the annual Exhibition or Open Day. On these occasions a cross-section of the school's activities was put on display. The whole school was open for inspection, and special displays were mounted to show the range of the school's interests. The Big School – the main assembly Hall – was the setting for a varied selection of the boys' work, mostly carried out as voluntary labour. These included maps, plans, elevations, mathematical diagrams (mechanical drawing), botanical collections, art work including landscapes, portraits and ornamental fabrics, craftwork in wood and metal, including lathe-work or turnery, and models – some being mechanical. Some of the latter were on display in the Science Laboratory where other experiments and demonstrations were taking place.

[9]

Here is the actual programme of the events that took place on the stage of Big School on 16 June 1824:

1. Musical introduction by the school band –
   4 flutes, 4 clarinets, 2 Kent bugles, 2 French horns, 1 trumpet, 1 bassoon, 1 drum.
2. Mental arithmetic demonstrations
   (revealing a knowledge of Tables up to 49 × 49 and finding the square of 952 and 54¼)
3. Dramatic performances:
   (a) In Latin – a considerable portion of the *Aulularia* by Plautus.
   (b) In French – a playlet, *Gil Blas.*
   (c) Scenes from Shakespeare: *Coriolanus.*
   (d) Foote's imitation of *Le Médicin Malgré Lui.*
   (e) Scene from Sheridan's *The Rivals.*
   (f) An original play in Latin – *School Adventures.*
   (g) Pyramus and Thisbe from *Midsummer Night's Dream* – Shakespeare.
4. Verse readings from Pope, Byron, etc.
5. Concluding address by a pupil on *The Greek Cause.*
6. A few words by Thomas Wright Hill.
7. God Save the King – played by above band.
8. A Collection taken by Joshua Scholefield Esq. and W. Blakeman Esq. in aid of the Greeks. (The sum of £60 was collected in two evenings)

Ambitious Exhibitions similar to this had been customary for many years. In June 1816 Maria Edgeworth's[20] play *Eton Montem* was performed, for which Rowland and his team of boys designed and painted some impressive scenery. Matthew Hill's task was to rehearse the actors and produce the play, which ran to packed houses for four nights. Two years later, on 17 June 1818, the whole of the *Captivii* of the Latin comic poet and dramatist, Titus Plautus (254–184BC) was performed in 5 Acts in Latin – 'astonishingly perfect' was Rowland's comment. Scenes from two French plays were also staged, as well as recitations in Latin and French.

All these things were taking place over 160 years ago.

We have dealt so far with the general life of the school; with its out of school activities and with the impact made far and wide by the Hills' book *Public Education.* But the central core of the Hazelwood system is to be found first in its experiments in democratic self-government and moral training, and secondly in its reformed·curriculum and teaching methods. Because of their fundamental importance we need to examine these aspects of the system in some detail. The first we can connote under the term Discipline.

Discipline

The key principle was to leave as much power as possible in the hands of the older, responsible pupils. To this end an elected school committee was formed to draw up a simple constitution with its code of laws – the school rules. The rules or 'laws' laid down by this committee – the legislative body – were enforced by the Judiciary, consisting of the Jury-court presided over by a Judge, and a minor court presided over by a Magistrate. Both courts had democratically elected Officers, changed monthly, each with his prescribed duties. The main Officers were:

> Chairman of Committee
> Secretary
> Judge of the High Court
> Clerk to the Court
> Magistrate of the Lower Court
> Two Constables of the Court
> Sheriff
> Attorney General
> Solicitor General
> Keeper of the Records
> Prosecutor General
> Defender General
> Custos Depositorum
> Silentiary

Rewards and Sanctions

Traditional sanctions such as corporal punishment, impositions and public disgrace had long been abandoned at Hazelwood. The sanctions now were the awarding or taking away of certain privileges. The key to the system was what was called *'Aggregate rank'*: this was assessed weekly by marks awarded for school work, voluntary labour, embracing every kind of activity in and out of school, and for conduct. In other words Aggregate rank combined moral and intellectual performance, and it conferred not only personal privileges but credit to

[11]

the individual's 'Circle' as well. The assessment of school work or classroom performance ingeniously contained a variable factor: one week it might be based on mathematics throughout the school; the next week Latin; then woodwork – and so on. Every talent or skill had its day.

Moral rank was determined on a numerical scale by a method that closely corresponds to modern psychological techniques of personality and character assessment as reviewed in a *Symposium of Personality* published in the *British Journal of Educational Psychology* in 1945.

Two kinds of marks were employed, Personal and Transferable. The latter were the more important and consisted of a range of metal tokens used as a kind of school currency: these were the basis of daily rewards and penalties or fines. These coins could be acquired in various ways:

(a) by superiority in class work
(b) by filling public offices – in the Court system and elsewhere
(c) by voluntary labour of many kinds

The metal tokens or coins were first used at Hill Top as early as 1803 when the school originally opened, and they usually carried a motto like *Persevere and Excel* or *No effort is Lost*. The coins in circulation were:

Prime	1
Triad	3
Pentad	5
Decad	10
Demi-cent	50
Cent	100
Quingent	500
Chiliad	1000

The Chiliad was also awarded as a prize-medal, minted in silver, for outstanding Voluntary Labour exceeding a hundred hours work. A few actual examples of Voluntary Labour include such tasks as:

1. Four books of Virgil's *Georgics* translated into blank verse.
2. Cardboard model of Hazelwood School building made in about 1827 by William Bowman[21] and John Dent Goodman,[22] both 12 years of age. The former became Sir William Bowman, FRS, FRCS, and the latter rose to become the first Chairman of the BSA Company and Chairman of the Midland Bank.
3. Magic Lantern show at 15 marks per boy.
4. Voluntary 'fagging' – brushing and pressing clothes; tidying desks and classrooms.

[12]

5. Helping in the Library or Laboratory.
6. Looking after games and gymnastic kit and apparatus.
7. Acting as news-reader at supper time or while boys were doing remedial physical exercises.

The Jury Court

This was established between 1810 and 1816 and consisted of six boys chosen by ballot from a shortlist of eligible candidates. No oaths were taken as it was an axiom of the school that only the truth was spoken. At a trial the defendant could conduct his own defence, or secure the services of a friend, or engage the services of the Defender General who had to be paid a fee in transferable marks – the metal coinage. Court fines were also paid with the coinage. If a defendant felt he had suffered an injustice he could refer his case to the main School Committee which acted as a Court of Appeal. Such appeals were very rare; only nine cases went to appeal during a period of nine years, out of more than six hundred cases. The Hills were not too starry eyed as to forget that on occasions boys will fight, but very precise procedures were introduced to prevent casual personal brawls, and in the last resort a pair of quarrelling boys were allowed to settle their differences by a superior 'trial by combat' or licensed boxing match. Rowland's records show that only two such combats took place in four years, between July 1821 and April 1825. This is typical of Rowland's meticulous keeping of statistics, a habit that remained with him throughout his career. His almost morbid passion for precise time-keeping and statistical records first appears in his Hazelwood days when bells and bugles had to keep to seconds. It influenced his work with the *South Australian Commission*, as it did with the running of the *London and Brighton Railway*. Finally it really came into its own when he embarked upon his work with the Post Office; the very validity of his Plan rested on his statistical data, and its day to day efficiency depended upon the punctuality of nationwide collections and deliveries. Even within months of his death in 1879 he used to keep exact records of the time his coachman reported for duty each morning, then subjecting the unfortunate fellow to a weekly lecture on the number of times he had been late and by how many minutes. He finally cured him by insisting on a written explanation of his lateness instead of the usual lame verbal excuses; the coachman found it much easier to be punctual in future.

The whole elaborate rigmarole of self-government, the Jury Court and the awarding of marks and fines seems at times to pass over into

[13]

the realm of fantasy, but no one can challenge its effectiveness in making Hazelwood a friendly, fair-minded and peaceful place in comparison with the Public Schools of the time. There bullying and beatings were everyday occurrences and hideous fist fights were as common as they were vicious. At Eton in 1825, for example, a savage fight with bare knuckles lasted for sixty rounds, encouraged by a howling mob of spectators. It resulted in the death of one of the contestants, the Hon. F. A. Cooper, age fifteen. Ironically he was a scion of the humane, idealistic Shaftesbury family who had long championed the cause of young people against cruelty and oppression.

The above account describes very briefly Rowland Hill's aims and achievements in implementing his new conception of discipline and moral training, which in the opinion of the *Encyclopedia Britannica* in 1875 put him side by side with Thomas Arnold of Rugby among the educationists of the nineteenth century. It explains why the leading intellectual journals of the day considered the tone and human relationships of Hazelwood to be unique, and why reformers throughout the world made pilgrimages to the school, in person or in spirit, and sought to imitate its magic. But the magic was perhaps more in the Hills than in their system, as many would-be imitators found to their cost. As with his later postal reforms Rowland Hill never claimed to be the sole originator of the ideas of self-government in education; he merely took over a progressive idea that had been dabbled with in a modest way from time to time. He just developed the idea ingeniously in a hundred ways, more thoroughly than had ever been imagined possible.

We now come to the second field of innovation in which Rowland Hill eclipsed what Arnold later achieved at Rugby, and which the *Encyclopedia Britannica* unfortunately overlooked – the *Curriculum*.

Curriculum

The following summary of the Hills' innovations in the curriculum and teaching methods shows how far ahead they were of their contemporaries.

English

From the earliest stages in the teaching of reading Rowland Hill and his brother, Matthew, were advocates of the 'sentence method', breaking away from the traditional phonic system that was to dominate infant

[14]

schools right up to modern times. In a letter to Lord Brougham[23] in the 1820s Matthew made very clear his progressive outlook on Infant education:

> I think the leading object of such a school should be to make the little pupils healthy and happy . . . at a period of life when joy gushes forth at every step. . . . With regard to literary instruction I would not even give it a second, but only a third place – the second rank being given to the education of the organs, the eye, the ear, the voice and above all the hand.

Such an advanced view as this could well have been written by Friedrich Froebel[24] or Maria Montessori.[25]

Out-of-school reading on a voluntary basis was strongly encouraged; it was closely guided and meticulously checked, and covered a wide range of subjects such as Travel and Geography, History, Natural History, simple Economics and Philosophy and, particularly, Science. In the Taunton Report of 1868 a similar practice was claimed as a noteworthy novelty in the field of Science by Harrow School – some forty years later.

Within the English syllabus Drama and Verse-speaking played a big part, as a reference to any of the Exhibitions will show.

Languages

Latin and Greek were taught as options, but most emphasis was placed on modern languages – French, Spanish, German and Italian, and they were all – even Latin and Greek – taught by Direct Method, anticipating the well-publicised work of Dr W. H. D. Rouse[26] of Perse School, Cambridge, by some eighty years. One unusual novelty at Hazelwood was that Geography in the top form was taught entirely in French, and that French had to be spoken at certain meal-times.

History and Geography

Visual aids were extensively used and Geography in particular was approached as practically as possible, finally linking up with mathematics in large scale survey work extending throughout the adjacent counties. For one ambitious piece of work involving triangulations throughout the county, the boys established their datum line in the centre of Birmingham by getting up at 3.00 am for three consecutive mornings

[15]

before traffic interfered with their measurements. Their calculated distance from the Barr Beacon triangulation point to Wolverhampton Church spire was only 7 feet different from Colonel Mudge's original survey when he was working on his Ordnance Survey maps a year or so earlier.

Mathematics

This comprised a well-constructed syllabus, very practical in its early stages, leading up to advanced work at University level. Rowland and his father had a high reputation in this field, and coached sixth form boys from the classically orientated King Edward VI School, Birmingham, for entrance to Oxford and Cambridge. Amongst these pupils were B. H. Kennedy, the famous grammarian, later to become Professor of Greek at Cambridge, and Edwin Guest, later Master of Caius College and Vice-Chancellor of the University.

Physical Education

This subject or activity was more advanced on the continent; Rowland studied their methods and also consulted the works of the family's Unitarian friend, Dr Lant Carpenter,[27] whose book *The Principles of Education; Intellectual, Moral and Physical* was published in 1820. Hazelwood was able to offer a wide range of activities – Rugby football[28] (before 1828); cricket[29]; gymnastics; athletics; wrestling; swimming; fencing and dancing. Somewhat surprisingly a drill sergeant was employed once a week and some kind of Cadet Corps was established when fears of a French invasion persisted. This fact shows that the Hills had a genuine patriotism and were in no sense subversive Jacobins as many believed.

The whole concept of education as envisaged by the Hills is best summed up in a letter Matthew Davenport Hill sent to Thomas Jefferson[30] on 28 March 1825, still preserved in the Library of Congress, USA:

> Education seems to be generally under the curse of pauperism. If it were placed on the liberal footing on which a gentleman puts his stables and dog-kennels, there would be little to wish for. Every school worthy of the name ought to have an ample library; there should be a good collection of philosophical apparatus; as this is pre-eminently a manufacturing country there ought to be a workshop well supplied with tools and materials, and

a laboratory. There should be a Gymnasium, and for the purposes of our system, where so much of the knowledge which boys gain of language is obtained through the drama, a permanent theatre would be a most useful addition to the usual buildings. There should be opportunities for learning to ride, to swim, to row, to guide the sail-boat.

It is chastening to recollect that it was not until the *Butler Education Act* of 1944 – over a hundred years later – that new secondary schools, Grammar, Technical and Modern, began to be built under an ambitious programme to provide most of these facilities for the secondary school population as a whole.

Science

This was the field in which Rowland Hill's innovations were most radical and most spectacular. They rested on Rowland's conviction that it was through science and technology that Britain's primacy in the economic world could be maintained. His aim, therefore, was to introduce science as a compulsory cultural subject for every pupil to follow. In this he was fortunate to attract a very brilliant scientist to help him work out his plans. This was Edward Brayley who joined the staff at Hazelwood in 1829 when he was twenty-seven years of age: he was an authority on meteors and a respected scientist in many fields, being a founder member of the *Zoological Society* and of the *Chemical Society*, and a popular lecturer at the *Royal Institution*. He was later elected FRS.

Rowland and Edward Brayley officially launched their new venture in a public lecture at Hazelwood on 26 October 1831, just two years before it closed and transferred to join its sister establishment at Bruce Castle. Brayley's views were later published in a pamphlet of 117 pages under the ponderous title, *The Utility of Knowledge of Nature, considered with reference to the introduction of instruction in the Physical Sciences into the General Education of Youth.*

The following outline indicates the wide scope of the Hazelwood science syllabus. It is here reproduced exactly as it appears in the pamphlet, a fact which accounts for the occasional unusual nomenclature and the curious groupings of subjects.

1. CHEMISTRY – ORGANIC AND INORGANIC
    Pneumatic, Vegetable and Animal Chemistry
    Heat
    Electricity
    Electro-chemistry

2. NATURAL PHILOSOPHY
   Light
   Acoustics
   Pneumatics
   Hydrostatics
   Mechanics

3. NATURAL HISTORY
   Mineralogy
   Geology
   Meteorology
   Botany – General principles
   Zoology – General principles

4. PHYSICAL GEOGRAPHY

5. MAGNETISM
   Electro-magnetism
   Thermo-magnetism

6. ASTRONOMY

The above is an outline of the whole science syllabus; it is now appropriate to give an example of how the subject was worked out in detail, so what follows shows how one section, Pneumatic Chemistry, was treated. This is only one third of the whole Chemistry syllabus.

Pneumatic Chemistry

As a lead in to the study of Science in general, three introductory lectures were given to the three upper classes. The course itself included demonstrations and practical laboratory work, and covered the following topics:

Experimental study of the nature of air; experiments in combustion; the burning of phosphorus in a confined atmosphere of air. Oxidation; heating mercury and lead to produce red oxide of mercury and red lead. The preparation of Oxygen, using a gas-jar, pneumatic trough, beehive-shelf etc. Analysis of air. Respiration. Mixtures and compounds explained. Chlorine, iodine and bromine – experimentally prepared and discussed. Chlorine's bleaching action; its use as a disinfectant. Liquefaction under pressure. Similar treatment of iodine; its medicinal use. Reference to iodine in the Spa-waters of Bath, Leamington, Matlock and Buxton. The spontaneous combustion of iodine and phosphorus.

The preparation of Hydrogen by the action of sulphuric acid on zinc. Demonstration of a balloon filled with Hydrogen. The history of its discovery by Mayo, Hales and Cavendish. The composition of water. Sulphur and its compounds. The study of Carbon; graphite, anthracite and diamonds.

The three lower classes apparently followed the syllabus of Vegetable Chemistry.

The importance given to science is shown by the amount of time allocated to its study. At Bruce Castle we are told that originally eleven hours per week were devoted to science; at Hazelwood it was twelve or thirteen hours. This makes an astonishing contrast with what other schools were doing at the same period of time and even during the next hundred years or more, in spite of the efforts of various government Commissions and Committees to bring science into its rightful place within the education system.

It is almost unbelievable that as late as 1936 the *Science Masters' Association*, the official professional body, could only suggest a minimum of three hours per week for pupils up to sixteen years of age. It is not surprising that the consequence of this indifference was the emergence of our disastrous 'two-culture' dichotomy so painfully exposed by C. P. Snow's[31] analysis. It accounts, too, for Britain's eclipse in science and technology by countries like Japan and Germany, not to mention the United States. Economically speaking we in Britain are beginning to be spoken of as being on a level with countries of the Third World. And we have brought it upon ourselves.

Ironically enough the rot began at Bruce Castle itself. Rowland Hill's far-sighted aim was to provide all his pupils from about thirteen years of age upwards with a coherent background of General Science before specialised sections of the subject were studied by the more advanced pupils. But his plan was thwarted by the ignorance and prejudices of the school's conventional middle-class parents. This rebuff undoubtedly brought on Rowland's breakdown in health and forced him to abandon schoolmastering for good, releasing him, by a strange turn of fate, for an even more illustrious career in the outside world.

But Rowland Hill's ideas on the place of science in education refused to die. His case for a broad-based education in General Science found a champion in the works of the versatile Victorian philosopher, Herbert Spencer (1820–1903) and in the teachings of the eminent scientist, Thomas Henry Huxley (1825–95) whose *Physiography* in 1869 expounded his views with convincing vigour.

By a curious coincidence a grandson of Matthew Davenport Hill was destined to play a major part in the rehabilitation of science teaching

[19]

in our schools. This was another Matthew Davenport Hill[32] who was Biology master at Eton College for over thirty years and had amongst his pupils Aldous Huxley and his brother, later familiar to us as Sir Julian Huxley, FRS. It was the latter who wrote an appreciative obituary in *The Times* on the death of his former teacher at the ripe old age of eighty-seven or so. He recounts the occasion when M. D. Hill, with the quirky individualism characteristic of the Hills, rode up to school one day mounted on the back of a llama, much to the astonishment of the natives and scholars of Eton.

The strange thing is that this Matthew Davenport Hill knew practically nothing of his forebears' pioneering work in the teaching of science, but in his own way he carried aloft the family torch. He was the founder and chairman of the *Association of Public Schools' Science Masters*, later to become the broader-based and still thriving *Science Masters' Association* which covers every type of secondary school in the country. He was also Secretary of the *Neglect of Science Committee* set up in 1916 under the chairmanship of Sir Ray Lancaster, FRS. Its watchword, ironically, was Hazelwood's lost cause – *Science for All*. At that moment of time during World War I we had our backs to the wall, and were beginning to realise that our neglect of science could quite easily lose us the war.

In the hope of remedying this educational weakness once and for all the Prime Minister set up a special committee under the chairmanship of the very distinguished physicist, Professor Sir J. J. Thomson. The *Thomson Report* was published in 1918 and its preamble has a familiar ring:

> Not for the first time our educational conscience has been stung by the thought that we are, as a nation, neglecting science. . . .

The report pleaded for a self-centred course of General Science for all pupils from twelve to sixteen years of age, recommending 4½ hours per week for the small group who wished to pursue some aspects of the work to an advanced level. In 1919 Sir Richard Gregory made a similar appeal to the *British Association for the Advancement of Science*. But in spite of all these pressures and the active support of bodies like the *Science Masters' Association* and the *Nuffield Foundation* the net result has been disappointing. In our schools we are still not within a mile of what Rowland Hill and Edward Brayley were actually achieving at Hazelwood and Bruce Castle back in the 1830s. Consequently we are still perpetuating the fatal schism to which our attention was drawn by C. P. Snow.

The full significance of what Rowland Hill and his colleagues achieved in the teaching of science is difficult for us to appreciate today; it quite stunned even the latter day Matthew Davenport Hill, as the present author found when he visited him in his retirement near Ledbury in 1954, shortly before his death. After reading a fairly full account of his forebears' work he wrote:

> It is veritably a remarkable achievement. . . . I had no idea that the Hills were such pioneers in the teaching of science in schools. What I have read almost takes my breath away. . . . The science teaching at Hazelwood and Bruce Castle that you describe is truly a revelation.

A prophet is without honour, it seems, even in his own family.

To conclude this section we cannot be more effectively reminded of the magnitude of Rowland Hill's achievements in the teaching of science than by a brief flash-back to what Dr Thomas Arnold was doing at Rugby at about the same time – in what was then deemed to be the most progressive of the Public Schools. In 1836 Arnold was insisting that science had to be subordinate to moral subjects, by which he meant the Classics and Divinity. Rather than give science any priority he declared that he would 'rather have his son think that the sun went around the earth'. But by 1840 uneasy doubts began to intrude and in a letter to his biographer, Dr Stanley, he goes so far as to declare, 'It is not right to leave boys in ignorance of the beginnings of physical science'. Even so, in practice he still clung to his meagre two hours per week for mathematics, leaving science in the hands of his peripatetic bagman, D. F. Walker, with his barrow load of scientific goodies to illustrate the twelve two-hour lectures he gave over a period of three years.

Against this melancholy story of our national neglect of Science and Technology over the centuries, it is encouraging to note that the current (1988) Minister of State for Education, Mr Kenneth Baker, is now making a desperate attempt to put matters right by his novel scheme of establishing twenty new City Technical Centres in or near large urban areas under direct Ministry control. The first to be opened is at Solihull, Warwickshire, barely sixteen miles from the site of Rowland Hill's Hazelwood School, and appropriately near to the heart of the industrial midlands, just as Hazelwood was. Baker's new College or Centre specialises in Craft Design and Technology, linked with basic General Science, Mathematics and Physics. This is a courageous and timely development, but it is no more than a modern re-hash of the Hazelwood formula of 1830 – woodwork, metalwork, technical drawing and design, mathematics and science, not forgetting the humanities.

Whether the idea will succeed or not, or go the same way as the Technical Schools envisaged in the tri-partite pattern of the Butler Education Act of 1944 (a much undervalued piece of legislation) remains to be seen.

[II]

The Hill Family

NO study of Rowland Hill's achievements can fail to mention the enormous debt he owed to the family; they were his inspiration and his advisers all through his career. They were his father, Thomas Wright Hill, and his four brothers, Matthew (b. 1792); Edwin (b. 1793); Arthur (b. 1798) and Frederic (b. 1803). A younger brother, Howard (b. 1805), died of tuberculosis when he was fifteen, and there were two sisters, Caroline (b. 1800); and Sarah (b. 1807). Together they formed a 'family council' which was always consulted in all important matters.

But more than that, Rowland's brothers all contributed very substantially to the creation and development of Hazelwood School, not only as class and specialist teachers, but also as truly innovative thinkers. It would be difficult to find a family with a more united front and a deeper interdependence in the cause of reforms of all kinds. Under Rowland's guidance and inspiration they made a breath-taking impact in the field of education; then, when Rowland eventually embarked upon his work in the Post Office, two of the brothers, Edwin and Frederic, eventually joined him, sacrificing their more lucrative professions to do so, and contributing richly to the success of Rowland's reforms. In a sense, therefore, the story of Rowland Hill is the saga of a very remarkable family, originating with the father, Thomas Wright Hill.

Thomas Wright Hill

Thomas Wright Hill, the *pater familias*, was born in 1763. He received a modest education on traditional lines, but his special talent and interest was to be found in mathematics and science, much of which he taught himself. He was apprenticed to a brass-founder and in 1787 became manager of a rolling-mill in Wolverhampton. Education and the world of ideas had always interested him, and in his spare time he taught in the famous Dr Joseph Priestley's Sunday school, for he, like Priestley, was a deeply sincere Unitarian. In 1802 when he was thirty-nine years of age with five children on his hands, he purchased a small school in Lionel Street, Birmingham, which was transferred a year later to larger premises called Hill Top, just a mile or so south-west of the town centre. Here the school remained until 1819, developing its original ideas and winning the confidence of the townspeople. In that year it moved to much more imposing custom-built premises in the Hagley Road.

Known as Hazelwood School, its fame was soon to spread in a remarkable way all over the world. In 1827 a London branch was opened in the prestigious Bruce Castle in Tottenham, overlapping with the Birmingham Hazelwood School until 1833 when the latter was finally closed. Though Rowland was the effective Headmaster of both these establishments, his father continued as an active teacher, particularly in mathematics, until quite an advanced age. He is also credited in 1819 as the originator of the principle of proportional representation by means of the single transferable vote.

Throughout his life Thomas Wright Hill was highly respected in Birmingham and the Midlands as a man of outstanding integrity and talent. He was ingenious and original in his thinking, liberal, wise and generous-spirited, but a little unworldly. He took his family responsibilities very seriously, inculcating sound learning, high moral standards and a rare sense of family loyalty and unity. As a devout Unitarian he naturally brought up his family in that creed, but he was no zealot and was content to communicate his faith by quiet reason and example.

For many years he gave lectures and demonstrations in science at the Birmingham Philosophical Institution with his sons Matthew, Edwin and Rowland as his assistants. Quite naturally science formed an important part in the school's curriculum and this was strikingly developed by Rowland in the years ahead. He was one of the senior Fellows of the Royal Astronomical Society and in 1845, at the age of 82, he delivered an unusual paper at a meeting of the British Association at Cambridge outlining a novel system of mathematical notation. As a young man he had devised an original system of shorthand, evolved a new method of curing stammering, and had written a useful short book on penmanship and spelling, later to be shamelessly plagiarised in America.

Thomas Wright Hill had lived through one of the most exciting periods of British history. He had witnessed the infamous 'Church and King' riots in Birmingham in 1791–2, when Dr Priestley's house and Meeting Place were sacked and burnt, and had courageously rescued some of Priestley's books and scientific apparatus under the noses of the rioters. He took an active interest in the Reform Bill agitations in the years leading up to 1832, and back in 1819 he participated in the famous mass meeting when the townsfolk of Birmingham, denied legal representation in Parliament, took it upon themselves to elect a 'legislatorial attorney' to make the town's views known. Although the town had grown in little over fifty years from a population of some 70,000 in 1770 to a teeming industrial community of 180,000 in the 1830s, it still suffered the penalties of not being a corporate borough and of being without Parliamentary representation. With the passing of the Reform Act in 1832 Thomas Hill had the honour of proposing Thomas Attwood as the first member of Parliament for Birmingham. But this happy conclusion was not achieved without bitter struggles typified in the highly provocative 'legislatorial attorney' incident in 1819.

This piece of impudence led to the trial of the notorious Major John Cartwright,[1] a very active reformer, on a charge of sedition in which Matthew Davenport Hill, the eldest of the sons, recently called to the Bar, helped materially in the defence of the accused. In 1838, six years after the passing of the Reform Act, Thomas Hill rejoiced to see his former Hazelwood pupil, William Scholefield,[2] become the first Charter Mayor of Birmingham on its elevation to the status of a corporate borough, and in 1847 to become Liberal MP for the town.

It delighted the old man to see his Hazelwood chickens coming home to roost, for one of the first acts of the new Charter Mayor in 1839 was to secure the appointment of Matthew Davenport Hill QC to the high legal office of Recorder of Birmingham, and to organise a mammoth petition to Parliament urging the immediate adoption of Rowland Hill's measures for postal reforms. This was one of an avalanche of similar petitions which materially helped to secure the passage of the Penny Postage Act in 1839.

During these troubled years the leaders in the battle for political rights – and the Hills were numbered among these – were deemed to be Jacobins, roughly equivalent in our own day to Trotskyites or ultra left-wing extremists. Yet such was the respect in which the Hill family was held, particularly Thomas Wright Hill, that this opprobrious label failed to alienate even deep-dyed Birmingham Tories and staunch Anglican families who continued to send their sons to Hazelwood despite the political taint. Indeed, in the year 1826, at the height of the Reform Bill agitations, Hazelwood was booming; it had more pupils on its roll, mostly as boarders, than either the long-established and prestigious King Edward VI Grammar School, Birmingham or the famous Rugby School – just two years before Dr Thomas Arnold appeared on the scene.

This, then, was the background of the eight children of Thomas and

Sarah Hill, and it throws a good deal of light on the attitudes, characters and progress of their offspring whose careers we shall recount, beginning with the eldest, Matthew Davenport Hill.

Matthew Davenport Hill

Matthew Davenport Hill (1792–1872), the first-born, received his education under his father at Hill Top school, and in 1805, at the age of thirteen, he assisted his father in the teaching, helped three years later by Rowland, the third son. In 1814 Matthew, with ambitions beyond schoolmastering, enrolled for the Bar at Lincoln's Inn, but did not start his terms until two years later. Meanwhile he turned his hand to journalism, writing articles for the *Midland Chronicle* on matters of social and political reform. He was clearly a chip off the old block. While studying for the Bar in London, at Lincoln's Inn, he earned money by writing reports on proceedings in the House of Commons, and as a contributor to John and Samuel Steer's *Sunday Review*. He was called to the Bar in 1819, just as the new Hazelwood building was being opened on the Hagley Road, and almost immediately returned to Birmingham to practise on the Midland circuit. But he retained a close interest in the school, and with his brother, Rowland, planned ambitious developments in the years ahead. This bore fruit, as we have seen, in the publication of their book, *Public Education*, in 1822.

The book attracted widespread interest and its revolutionary ideas brought Matthew and Rowland into contact with many of the leaders of radical thought in this country and beyond. Jeremy Bentham, the world-renowned Utilitarian philosopher, showed an immediate interest and was an enthusiastic supporter of Hazelwood for the remainder of his life. He even sent two young Greek refugees[3] to the school at his own expense, and contemplated recommending the adoption of some of the Hills' ideas into the reformed constitution of Portugal on which he was advising the Cortez. Further afield, as we relate elsewhere, Thomas Jefferson, former President of USA, specially requested a copy of the book, which Matthew duly sent off accompanied by a six page letter – still to be seen in the Library of Congress.

In 1826 Matthew and Rowland became founder members of the *Society for the Diffusion of Useful Knowledge*, a venture launched by Henry Brougham and the publisher Charles Knight.[4] It seems very likely that at its committee meetings the Hills must have met Dr Thomas Arnold about the time he moved to Rugby. The Society did much to spread literacy and knowledge, and one of its greatest successes was the publication of the famous *Penny Magazine*, whose name was suggested by Matthew and which achieved a circulation of some 200,000 copies per issue; this was followed by the *Penny Encyclopedia* with equal success.

Matthew Hill did much to mitigate the harshness and ineffectiveness of the existing criminal law. His views and influence in this field can be seen in his book *'Suggestions for the Repression of Crime'*, published in 1857. In this field of law reform he was closely associated with his younger brother Frederic, also a barrister, who worked for many years as Inspector of Prisons, mostly in Scotland and the north of England. In 1853 Frederic had published a book that became a legal classic, *Hill on Crime*, which developed reforms parallel with the thinking of his brother Matthew. Having handled boys for many years at Hill Top and Hazelwood, Matthew saw juvenile crime in a more sympathetic light than most of his contemporaries. It appalled him that young boys of ten and thirteen were hanged for quite trivial thieving, and that there were over two hundred crimes punishable by the death penalty. Through the efforts of Matthew and Frederic Hill and others of similar sympathies only fifteen capital offences remained on the Statute book by 1837.

In 1851 Matthew was appointed Commissioner of Bankruptcy for Bristol, while functioning as Recorder in Birmingham. Characteristically he was an active member of the *Social Science Association*, and he took a very practical interest in the Co-operative movement and in the boarding out of pauper and abandoned children. In association with Mary Carpenter[5] he helped to establish Industrial and Ragged schools and the setting up of Cottage homes for homeless, deprived and delinquent children, as an alternative to the normal barrack-like reformatories. In the treatment of criminals his belief was 'by good conduct and work alone the prisoner was to earn indulgences and liberation'. This was a procedure that had worked well in a slightly different context at Hazelwood and Matthew never forgot it.

Matthew Davenport Hill was by any standard a really good man who left the world far better than he found it. Though he had wide sympathies with the less fortunate of his fellow men, he appears to have been rather a stern, humourless character, conceited and arrogant in the Hill manner. In legal disputation he was devastatingly logical and he could display a mordant and biting wit. As an MP for Hull he was not a great success, for like an opinionated schoolmaster he talked too much and too dogmatically for his fellow members' liking. Throughout his life he remained very close and loyal to his brothers, particularly to Rowland to whom he acted as scribe and trusted adviser right to the end.

As a distinguished QC Matthew mixed with the leading politicians and public figures of the day – influential people like Lord Brougham, Lord Lansdowne, Lord Truro, Lord Monteagle, Sir Francis Baring and W. E. Gladstone to name but a few – and there is little doubt that he used these contacts to further his brother Rowland's plans for postal reform. Matthew, with his wide experience of public life and keen legal mind, was always a key figure in the Hills' family council. Rowland was in no doubt about this and a few years before his death he wrote a very touching and generous letter to Matthew, dated 10 February 1870, in which he says:

> You, as the eldest, most intelligent and in all respects the best qualified to lead, are the real head of the family, and though we have all assisted more or less, it is to you the greatest advancement of the family is mainly owing.

One outstanding example of Rowland's reliance on the judgment and personal concern of his brother occurred when, following the passing of the Penny Postage Act in August 1839 (which implemented the essentials of Rowland's plan), the Chancellor of the Exchequer, Francis Baring, summoned Rowland to the Treasury and offered him a temporary appointment for two years at a salary of £500 per annum. Not surprisingly Rowland was taken aback; he was earning that with the Emigration Commission, so he was inclined to reject it out of hand or even to volunteer his services to the Post Office without salary. But he told the Chancellor that he would consult his advisers before making any decision. That same afternoon he took the stage coach to Leicester to consult his brother Matthew who was appearing there as counsel on the Midland circuit. On arrival that evening Rowland hurried to his brother's lodgings where he found Matthew resting on his bed after a tiring day in the court. When Rowland told his story, Matthew leapt up furious that his brother had been so insultingly treated, and forthwith wrote a long, carefully worded letter of indignant protest for Rowland to deliver to the Chancellor next day. Not standing on ceremony Rowland called at Downing Street on the following day and requested an interview with Mr Baring. The Chancellor received him most courteously, read the letter, made some encouraging remarks and asked Rowland to call on him in the morning. By that time the Chancellor had had time to reflect on the quality of the people he was dealing with and promptly revised his salary offer to £1,500. It was to remain a temporary appointment for two years with no guarantee of renewal. But Rowland had complete confidence in his ability to win a permanent appointment at the end of the two years, so he accepted the offer. Little did he dream of the trouble that was to follow. The incident shows what a tower of strength Matthew proved to be at a moment of crisis. He died in Bristol

[27]

in June 1872 at the ripe age of eighty, an outstandingly gifted member of the Hill family, and indefatigable worker for social, educational and legal reform.

Edwin Hill

Edwin Hill (1793–1876), the second son, was educated at Hill Top but instead of remaining as a full time pupil teacher he worked part-time in the Birmingham Assay office and later became an engineering apprentice and in time was appointed manager of a rolling-mill, where he became familiar with business administration as well as with engineering. He was a gifted and original engineer and when Rowland left Birmingham to open Bruce Castle in 1827, Edwin decided to join him and develop woodwork, metalwork and practical engineering skills at the school.

The craft of printing had long been part of the curriculum at Hazelwood. The School Magazine from 1822 until February 1830 was actually typeset and printed by the boys themselves, guided by Rowland's younger brother Arthur who had been apprenticed to a printer in Birmingham, but who had joined the staff of the school in 1817. Rowland's interest and skill in art led to the incorporation of etchings and lithographs in the magazine a little later. When in 1826 the *Society for the Diffusion of Useful Knowledge* launched its famous *Penny Magazine* Rowland saw the need for a high-speed printing press. So he and his brothers gave years of thought and experiment to the problem. Eventually Rowland and Edwin produced and patented the first effective rotary printing press, registered as Patent No. 6762 with the Patent Office in 1835.

In 1840 Rowland secured a post for Edwin in the Stamp Department of the Inland Revenue where he served the Post Office with distinction for thirty-two years and made a lasting impact with his original ideas and practical engineering skills. He took the first steps in bringing the Post Office into the modern age of mechanisation. At the time his devices gave an impression of wizardry that bewildered and dazzled the uncomprehending Victorians, and at the same time gratified his employers by saving the country large sums per annum.

At home he amused himself by installing a device by which he could open and close his bedroom curtains by remote control, and another by which, by pulling a cord, he could remove or add a blanket on his bed. Apart from inventing an envelope folding machine, his modernisation of the transporting, sorting and stamping of letters has a flavour of twentieth century automation about it as the following contemporary comment shows:

> Once fairly underground, it is as if we were in the cave of an amiable magician. Doors open of their own accord; stamps of fabulous value are created out of waste-paper by a wave of the hand; wooden arms and limbs are moved by unseen agencies and classify documents with inconceivable rapidity and unfailing rectitude. Bundles of valuable deeds . . . walk gravely into the room unaided and present themselves silently to be stamped. Other mysterious contrivances for lessening human labour abound . . . all ingenious inventions of the Comptroller of the Stamp Department.
>
> The *Daily News*, 3 September 1871

A characteristic incident revealed his very kindly outlook. When he discovered that the porter at the Wellington Street entrance to Somerset House (where the Stamps and Taxes office was housed), suffered from bronchitis and rheumatism, Edwin specially designed and installed some wind-proof doors for the unfortunate porter's protection. Such consideration for his colleagues won unstinted admiration. Although he wished to retire when he felt the infirmities of age creeping upon him, his employers persuaded him to carry on, permitting him to come and go as he pleased. Eventually when he was approaching eighty he used to arrive at 12 noon and leave at 2.00 pm. He died in 1876 in his eighty-third year.

Edwin, it would seem, had more common sense, a greater human warmth and less eccentricity than most of his brothers. He was an even-tempered man, a better mixer and more conventional in his dress and social habits, and, like his younger brother Arthur, was well-accepted by the people of Tottenham. He and his family even attended the parish church regularly.

Edwin possessed the same wide interests and intellectual gifts that his brothers had. Though basically a professional engineer he wrote papers and books on such topics as currency reform and crime – a special province of the Hill family. His writings were warmly received in America, and the papers and lectures he delivered to the *British Association for the Advancement of Science* and to the *Social Science Association* won wide acclaim for their originality and penetration.

Rowland Hill

We come now to the third son, Rowland, who was destined to become the most famous of the Hill family. He was born in Kidderminster in 1795. By a strange trick of fate he was led at a very early age to reflect on the shortcomings, and indeed evils, of the existing postal system. An ordinary domestic incident made a big impression on his childish mind and undoubtedly sowed the seed of his ideas for establishing a cheap, nation-wide postal service; it proved to be the main trigger-point of his whole career. One morning the postman or 'letter-carrier' of those days delivered a letter to the Hill household, but Rowland's mother did not have enough money in the house to pay the required postage, which at that time was payable on delivery. Rowland long remembered the indignation he felt at being sent into town with a bundle of old clothes in order to raise enough money to pay the postage. The incident also brought home to him very vividly and painfully what he called 'the terrible inconvenience of poverty'. No wonder Rowland soon cast himself in the role of a reformer.

Before he was eight years of age the little school his father had recently opened in Lionel Street, Birmingham, moved about a mile or so further south to Hill Top. Under his father's tuition Rowland made rapid headway in writing and arithmetic, but found difficulty with Latin – not surprising at eight years of age. For the time being he decided with his father's permission to drop the subject so as to concentrate on the subjects he would shortly be required to teach as a pupil-teacher in the school. He always regretted his decision, and unlike his brothers, never found time to resume his study of the language.

Rowland and his elder brother Edwin were early risers and took a pride in seeing that Hill Top was the first house in the neighbourhood to open its shutters each day. One summer morning the watchman on his round found the two boys in the street latching back the shutters at 3.00 am. One of the pleasant hobbies the two boys used to enjoy was to work in the little workshop their father had set up in an outbuilding. Here, with a range of tools, a workbench, a vice and a little forge all the Hill brothers learnt the rudiments of craftsmanship, a skill that they enjoyed and found useful throughout their lives. On one occasion, half as a boyish prank, Rowland and his eldest brother Matthew sold home-made hot-cross buns in the streets of Birmingham on Good Friday. Another time they sold bunches of horehound (then widely used as a remedy for coughs and colds) that they had grown in their little garden. By these means they were able to raise a small amount of pocket-money, but, more than that, such activities taught them self-reliance and independence.

Throughout his boyhood Rowland used to undertake all sorts of household duties, going errands, helping with the cleaning and general household chores and doing all sorts of repairs and maintenance. Thus from an early age he learnt how to co-operate for the common good, to

1. Sir Rowland Hill (1795–1879), by J. A. Vinter.

2. Thomas Wright Hill (1763–1851), 'Paterfamilias'.

SIR ROWLAND HILL KCB
POSTAL
REFORMER
RESIDED
AT NUMBER 68
OPPOSITE
1802 to 1803
1795 to 1879

3. Plaque marking Lionel Street School, 1802–3.

4. Hazelwood School in mid 1820s by Samuel Lines, Snr.

5. Bruce Castle School, Tottenham.

6. Plan of Birmingham showing school sites.

7. Hazelwood building in 1956, just before its demolition.

believe in the gospel of work and to exercise his initiative and ingenuity in tackling all sorts of daily problems. It is not surprising that he built these values into the Hazelwood system as it evolved over the years.

In 1810, when he was fifteen years of age and had been working as a pupil-teacher at Hill Top for two years, his father excused him one day a week to take on his brother Edwin's place as a part-time employee at the Birmingham Assay Office. Here he had to inspect and stamp silver articles with the Assay mark, as well as cleaning and taking care of the punches and keeping the duty-book up to date. He worked here for two and a half years gaining valuable first-hand experience with metal-working and engineering processes in general. About this time Rowland also acted as assistant secretary to his father who was the official secretary and administrator of the *Birmingham Institute for the Education of Deaf and Dumb Children* founded by Dr de Lys. Rowland carried on this work for some years, earning a fee of £20 per annum for his pains, and it incidentally gave him an insight into some of the problems of special education. He was ready at all times to take on extra work in order to supplement the family income. In 1815, for example, he repaired an electrical machine belonging to Samuel Tertius Galton,[6] a neighbour not far away in Duddesdon, Birmingham. The Galtons were one of the leading intellectual families in England and Samuel's son Francis was the founder of the science of Eugenics and a cousin of Charles Darwin. Like the Hill family, the Galtons were non-conformists, not Unitarians, but members of the Society of Friends, and as fellow 'outsiders' they knew and respected each other in the Birmingham of those days.

Another means of augmenting the family income was by undertaking private coaching, and both Rowland and his father undertook this. An arduous coaching commitment Rowland undertook at this time was to teach navigation to a young midshipman living in Stourbridge. This involved Rowland in walking the 12½ miles to Stourbridge carrying a heavy Hadley's Quadrant, then returning the same distance later in the day. Also, of course, it involved some strenuous study on Rowland's part to acquire a thorough knowledge of the subject before attempting to teach it. No wonder his normal working day averaged twelve or thirteen hours for seven days a week.

When we come to study the details of Rowland's career – in creating and running Hazelwood School, in organising the logistical side of the colonisation of South Australia, in managing and directing the London and Brighton railway, and finally in implementing his reforms in the Post Office – we notice two recurring and dominating factors; his remarkable skill in meticulous, detailed administration, and his unusual capacity for long hours of hard, sustained work. He usually rose between

[31]

5.30 and 6.00 am and never ceased his toil until late at night. Wherever he worked he had the disconcerting habit of appearing in the office hours before his colleagues, much to the dismay of the early-morning cleaners.

Genius is sometimes defined as a capacity for taking infinite pains, and nowhere has this been better illustrated than in Rowland Hill's career. In his Post Office days, at the climax of his career, his work output was almost incredible. Long before the day of efficient short-hand typists, typewriters or tape-recorders he incessantly drafted and polished memoranda, reports and pamphlets and kept up a voluminous correspondence both personal and official in an unceasing flow, loading many of his documents with statistics and official returns which often took him weeks to unearth. They were invariably accurate. The only real help he had was that of his brothers and more immediately his dear wife, Caroline, his childhood sweetheart, who night after night and before the break of each dawn acted as his amanuensis, jotting down his dictation and preparing a written draft which he later polished and directed to its proper destination. Amongst the brothers it was Matthew and Arthur who made specially valuable contributions in committing to writing Rowland's many ideas and proposals.

How desperately he needed this family support and encouragement is evident when we recount Rowland's battles with the entrenched hierarchy of the Post Office and with the diehard politicians who derided his plan. It is a tale reflecting very little credit to the Post Office and Treasury Officials of the day, or to the unimaginative and ultra-conservative politicians involved. With real justification Rowland Hill can claim that he was the victim of snobbery, petty-jealousy and sheer obstructionism on the part of many of his colleagues and masters. Recent attempts to dismiss Rowland's complaints as being mostly imaginary grievances are effectively challenged in Chapter VIII – A Final Assessment.

From the start he was looked down upon as an intruder, a rank out-sider, a non-conformist of very suspect left-wing views, apparently self-educated and certainly not a product of the Public Schools or of Oxford or Cambridge. To his immediate senior colleague in the Post Office, the notorious Colonel Maberly,[7] Secretary to the Post Office, he was 'that man from Birmingham'. Maberly's attitude was unequivocal: here was this opinionated bounder who had never been behind the counter or window in the Post Office barging in at senior level, and cheeky enough to teach his grandmother to suck eggs. Right. We'll show him! But events were to turn out very differently. Within three years of the publication of his famous pamphlet in 1837 Rowland and his supporters were to see the passing of the *Penny Postage Act* and the actual implementation of its basic principles. In its historical and political context this was an outstanding achievement.

Apart from daily snubs and constant non-co-operation from many of his colleagues around him, there were at least four occasions when powerful cabals, as he says, formed against him to discredit and frustrate everything he attempted to do. Apart from Senior Post Office officials these cabals included Treasury officers and Tory politicians themselves. In writing up his memoirs in later life Rowland rarely mentions these unprincipled schemers by name; having finally won the day, Rowland, as a man of peace and reconciliation, preferred to forget his bitterness and resentment and show a charity that his detractors hardly deserved. Stubborn and ruthless though he could be on matters of principle, he always shrank away from vindictive personal conflict and sedulously avoided giving pain to the relations and friends of his attackers. This fundamental nobility of character is demonstrated time and time again, and on many occasions he gives fair-minded praise even to his arch-enemy, Colonel Maberly, for some of his actions.

At no other time in his long and varied career did Rowland Hill come up against such blind hostility; the other activities he indulged in brought him success and genuinely friendly admiration. There were four distinct periods in his career; firstly his pioneer work in education at Hill Top, Hazelwood and Bruce Castle schools from about 1808 to 1833; secondly his work between 1833 and 1839 in organising the logistical side of the colonisation of South Australia; thirdly his work as Director and Chairman of the London and Brighton Railway Company between 1843 and 1846 which followed the termination of his temporary appointment with the Treasury in 1842; and fourthly, of course, his real life's work as a Civil Servant when he was finally appointed Secretary to the Postmaster General in 1846 leading to the top post of Secretary to the Post Office in 1854. This position he held until his retirement on grounds of failing health in 1864.

In all these fields his outstanding administrative talents were exercised and this gift can be seen in action all through his career. 'Administration is my forte' he used to claim, and we first see him employing his skill even in his earliest days at Hill Top school, when he began to help as a pupil-teacher in 1808 at the tender age of twelve-and-a-half. Straightaway he made his presence felt under his rather easy-going father, the proprietor and headmaster, by addressing his attention to time-keeping and punctuality for which he always had a somewhat morbid passion. He laid down the precise times, almost to the second, and when the school bell should be rung on various occasions during the day, and imposed an automatic penalty on the bell-ringer for any default. This laying down of precise duties and imposing penalties for non-performance, with corresponding bonuses of various kinds for faithful service, was carried on right through his life. It brought the ship-charterers to heel during his work with the South Australian Commission; it kept the drivers, guards and signalmen on their toes on the London and Brighton railway, and it later promoted unheard-of efficiency among the sorters, letter-carriers, postmasters and guards of mail coaches, on road and rail, during his sojourn at the Post Office.

From his earliest days Rowland Hill displayed a determination and staying-power that were limitless; his unflagging industry and thoroughness were quite remarkable, all directed by a first-class analytical mind which reflected his very high intellectual talents. Not many people were able, as he and his father were, to debate abstract mathematical and astronomical problems with no less than the Astronomer Royal. He was conceited and egoistic as most men of genius are. When he discovered that the promises made to him about his promotion and status were being ignored, and that his superior officer, Colonel Maberly, the Secretary to the Post Office, was a permanent and fatal obstacle to his ideas on postal reform, Rowland coolly wrote to the Postmaster General and to the Chancellor of the Exchequer suggesting that the obstructive Colonel should be forthwith retired on full pay or kicked upstairs to a better-paid post in some other government department. By hook or by crook the Colonel had to be removed.

As early as 1820, when he was twenty-five years of age, this self-confident young man could write in his diary:

> . . . the combination of talent, energy and industry which exists in our family . . . may some time or other produce effects which will render our name illustrious in after ages. The more I mix with the world, the more insight I have into the proceedings and opinions of other men, the conviction is forced upon me that our family possesses talents, energy and devotedness to one subject seldom to be met with. . . .

The 'one subject' he had in mind at that time was the science of education, and his prophecy is true when we realise that in the Hazelwood experiment he achieved a radical breakthrough in educational thinking and practice, and created what is probably by far the most original and progressive school ever to appear in British educational history. Those who are well versed in the literature of this field will, after reading the whole Hazelwood story, have little difficulty in agreeing that this is a fact beyond contradiction, even though the international fame it brought Rowland Hill proved to be more enduring than the kudos he gained in his own country. The trouble was that he was blackballed as an outsider.

At this time he firmly imagined that Hazelwood was his life-work, towards the consummation of which he and his brothers toiled unremittingly, regularly working twelve or thirteen hours a day. Occasionally at times of crisis Rowland records working for eighteen hours for a long spell. It was here that Rowland acquired the habit of long hours of disciplined work and learnt the art of highly sophisticated administration. At Hazelwood he was creating a living community of astonishingly detailed complexity, but which ran smoothly and happily. Nothing was left to chance; he foresaw every difficulty and fashioned his little world with every conceivable check and balance to ensure its efficient running. By clever planning he often killed two birds with one stone, as De Quincey, a keen supporter of the school, discovered. He called it 'burning its own smoke'. For example he noted that in the top form Geography was taught entirely in French, and discovered that the writing of the activities of the boys' Jury-court constituted an English language exercise, and that a boy could earn mark-credits for reading national news summaries to the whole of the boarding house during meal times.

It was in 1820, at the age of twenty-five, that Rowland really took over the running of the school. Significantly he recorded in his diary:

> The school is now a very perfect machine . . . we are able to appropriate every minute of the day to its respective use. The bells ring, the classes assemble, break up, take their meals etc. with such clock-like regularity that it has the appearance of almost magic. . . . By far the greater part of the system is my own and I am not a little proud of its effects.

In a sense here we have the seeds of the school's failure to survive in its original form; it was too mechanistic, too inhumanly efficient, too legalistic in conception. This is a point made by a distinguished former pupil of Hazelwood, W. L. Sargant,[8] who declared:

> The thoughtlessness, the spring, the elation of childhood was taken from us; we were premature men. . . . The school was, in truth, a moral hot-bed which forced us into a precocious imitation of maturity.

Sargant incidentally goes on to point out that Dr Arnold's hot-house products at Rugby were similarly looked upon as prigs by their Oxford contemporaries. Nowadays we are wiser perhaps in presenting a little 'roughage' in our diet, culinary and educational.

In all sorts of ways Rowland's experience as boy and man at Hazelwood seemed to equip him for his later challenges, just as that other egotistical genius, John Milton, used his earlier poetry and prose works to lead inexorably to *Paradise Lost*. For instance, from his earliest days Rowland was happy when using his hands, for craftsmanship was in the air of the Midlands. As a young boy he had ready access to a well-equipped workshop where he was able to learn and practise the basic skills of woodwork and metalwork. As he grew up, he and his elder brother, Edwin, spent many hours devising and making engineering models to meet various needs, sometimes for the school's science courses, sometimes for demonstration purposes at lectures given by the Hill family at the meetings of the *Birmingham Philosophical Institution* and sometimes for pure research. In the light of this background it is not surprising that Rowland introduced craftwork of various kinds into the Hazelwood curriculum, which is one indication of the way he broke completely away from the old classical and purely cerebral form of education. Edwin went on, as we have shown, to introduce an early example of extensive automation in the Post Office when he held the position of Comptroller of the Stamp Department.

In his early days as a teacher at Hill Top and Hazelwood Rowland acquired proficiency in various unexpected fields; he was an able draughtsman, an artist of great promise, a competent and imaginative architect and highly skilled in navigation and surveying. He used to take his older pupils on considerable surveying expeditions, mapping and surveying large areas of Warwickshire and Worcestershire with considerable accuracy, emulating as we have seen some of the work recently carried out by Colonel Mudge in establishing the first Ordnance Survey of the country.

It was such inside knowledge as this that, many years later, enabled him to call the bluff of the group of surveyors sent out to South Australia to carry out surveys of the territory for the benefit of the emigration organisers. These surveyors, thinking themselves to be safe from Rowland Hill's critical eye, sent back exaggerated accounts of the problems, urging a vast increase in resources to enable them to make any headway in their task. Rowland examined the facts with his usual hard-headed thoroughness and, understanding at first hand the problems of conducting a survey, bluntly refused to be bamboozled into unnecessary expenditure. Instead he sent out a very competent, hard-working young officer from the Royal Engineers who duly cracked the whip and galvanised the work-shy young men into effective action without additional expense.

Another immense benefit Rowland derived from his days at Hazelwood was the expansion of his circle of friends and admirers which the fame of the school brought with it. Many of the leading Radicals and progressive thinkers of the day came to inspect this unusual venture and to meet its author and originator. These very people were to give him powerful support nearly fifteen years later when he was fighting to get his plan for postal reform implemented. Among the influential public figures who corresponded with him or actually visited Hazelwood and Bruce Castle around 1825 to 1833 were the following[9]: Jeremy Bentham, the famous Utilitarian philosopher and constitutional lawyer; Lord John Russell, one of the framers of the Reform Bill; Thomas Campbell, poet and reformer; William Wilberforce, anti-slaver; John Silk Buckingham, political writer and reformer; George Grote,[10] historian and pioneer of higher education; Bishop Maltby of Durham, reformer and educationist; Joseph Hume, MP, great reformer and leader of the Radicals; Charles Babbage FRS, early inventor of computers; Dr Dionysius Lardner FRS, great populariser of science; Thomas Malthus, the economist; Captain Basil Hall FRS, Robert Owen and his son Robert Dale Owen, Lord Lansdowne; Lord Auckland; Lord Clarendon (whose brother had been a former pupil); Sir George Napier, Lord Kinnaird; Sir George Pollock – all enlightened Liberals and active social reformers, many of them being acquaintances of M. D. Hill, QC. All these interested parties were progressive and liberal in their views and their names frequently crop up in Hansard, in public petitions and in letters to the newspapers and journals in support of Rowland's Penny Postage plan; they were his own unsolicited pressure group.

At Hazelwood, too, Rowland Hill had been able, as it were under a microscope, to study human behaviour and questions of motivation, rewards and penalties. He discovered the importance of rewarding good work and honest effort (not measured merely by academic standards) and saw the efficacy of immediate and inescapable penalties for indolence and default. This was a lesson he never forgot.

Though kindly and mild in manner he was unmistakably '*suaviter in modo, fortiter in re*'; he was a believer in self-discipline and self-motivation, but his pupils, and those in employment under him in later years, knew that in the last resort it was he who called the tune. He retained something of his schoolmaster manner throughout his life, and this, no doubt, contributed to his unpopularity among some of his colleagues at the Post Office. An amusing and characteristic incident occurred on the first occasion he summoned his corps of surveyors to meet him at St Martin's le Grand, his headquarters in London. These officials were his field officers, his inspectors, his eyes and ears, who were distributed up and down the country to send him up-to-date reports on the working of the postal system. On this occasion the dozen or so surveyors, including Anthony Trollope[11] the novelist, were awaiting Rowland Hill's entrance

[37]

and were indulging in lively quips and jests like a bunch of schoolboys. As he entered the room Rowland paused and looked them over until dead silence prevailed, then he said,

> Gentlemen, you have no doubt noticed that in the official communications I send you from time to time, it is customary for me to conclude my letter with the words, 'I am, Sir, your obedient servant', but please don't be misled by this, for in fact I am nothing of the kind. Now we may begin.

Incidentally Trollope and Rowland Hill did not get on very well together. Trollope admitted Rowland's phenomenal accuracy with figures and facts, but declared 'I never came across anyone who so little understood the ways of men – unless it was his brother Frederic'. He resented Rowland for squeezing out Colonel Maberly and for treating the Post Office employees like machines; he was too hard a taskmaster. On one occasion Trollope gave a lecture on the *Civil Service* to Post Office employees, no doubt treating the subject rather flippantly and critically. Rowland Hill, not appreciating Trollope's sense of humour, took great exception to a subordinate's *jeu d'esprit* and promptly told the Postmaster General that Trollope ought to be dismissed for improper conduct. No action was taken. Trollope's brother-in-law, John Tilley, originally also a surveyor, rose in due course to become Rowland's right-hand man and finally succeeded him as Chief Secretary. No doubt Trollope was kept well-informed of the goings-on at the Post Office and could have been a serious handicap to Rowland by associating himself with some of the cabals working against Rowland Hill, but there is no evidence of this. Trollope eventually resigned from the Post Office in 1867, a few years after Rowland's retirement. He showed his magnanimity by writing a very generous and warm letter of appreciation to Rowland when the latter retired.

As Trollope's literary reputation grew he became very much a man about town in the London society of the period and was much sought after. He had the right background, Harrow, Winchester and the hunting field and was able to grace any reception with wit and conversational ease. Rowland Hill was quite different and not the sort of person to choose for an evening out: like all his family he was frugal, austere and teetotal, never socially at ease. He and his brothers were notoriously individualistic and eccentric; even in dress they were grimly formal, black-suited, mostly bearded like patriarchs of old, addicted as a group to wearing dark, broad-brimmed, rather outlandish wide-awake felt hats, looking for all the world like a gaggle of Levantine Rabbis or a covey of Mormons straight out of Salt Lake City.

Intimidating a character he might be, but Rowland Hill always did his best for his employees. In the Post Office he established promotion by merit, giving every humble letter-carrier the opportunity to rise in the service. He looked after their health and safety by introducing stringent building regulations which ensured adequate space and ventilation and protection against the hazards of fire. Hours of work were progressively reduced and paid annual holidays were introduced. He encouraged prudent insurance and savings schemes and established a modest benevolent fund to help the sick and needy. It is not true to claim that human beings were to him merely cogs in a machine.

His marriage to his childhood sweetheart was a very happy one and his wife Caroline proved to be a tower of strength to him in giving moral and practical support at all times. They had four children, a son Pearson (1832–98) who joined his father in the Post Office, and three daughters. From his earliest days he was never self-seeking, but always tried to do whatever he could to ease the lot of his fellow men – particularly those who were poor. Few people have conferred richer benefits on the world than Rowland Hill and there is world-wide recognition of this simple fact. His native land was proud to confer upon him the highest honours possible. Very properly his impressive State funeral in Westminster Abbey expressed the gratitude felt by his fellow countrymen – he was laid to rest with the great.

Arthur Hill

Arthur Hill (1798–1885) was the fourth of the Hill brothers, and like his elder brothers, Rowland and Edwin, at the age of thirteen he worked part-time in the Birmingham Assay Office, spending the rest of his time as a pupil-teacher at the school. When he was about sixteen he entered upon an apprenticeship with the well-known printer, James Belcher, in Birmingham. In 1817 when the eldest brother, Matthew, left teaching at the school to study for the bar in Lincoln's Inn, Arthur abandoned his apprenticeship in order to replace Matthew at Hill Top. Here he made an intensive study of Latin to enable him to take over the subject in the time-table.

Arthur had the right temperament for a schoolmaster and he was the only one of the brothers to remain such for the whole of his career. In 1827, when the move to Bruce Castle took place, he and his younger brother Frederic remained in Birmingham to keep Hazelwood going while Rowland and Edwin established themselves in Tottenham. In 1833 when Hazelwood in Birmingham closed its doors he moved to Bruce Castle just at the moment when Rowland's breakdown in health forced him to give up all his school work. Arthur held the headmastership of Bruce Castle from 1833 to 1867 and even then continued some part-time teaching when his son, Dr Birkbeck Hill,[12] took over the school. He was an extremely gifted teacher with a remarkable moral influence over his pupils, and with a lively, well-stored mind, generous, kindly and wise. All who knew him regarded him as a great peace-maker and a man of sweet reasonableness. He had a fine literary taste and even at eighty years of age knew many Shakespearean plays by heart. At Bruce Castle it had long been his practice to recite a whole play to the boarders on Saturday evenings, without even a glance at the text. This is claimed to be a well-authenticated fact. When he was eighty-five years of age he translated Horace's *Ars Poetica* into blank verse, even though his sight was too feeble to read the text – for years he had known it by heart. A privately printed copy of this still survives.

Arthur Hill was one of nature's gentlemen, always considerate and kindly – he could not bear to see young servant girls at Bruce Castle carrying heavy buckets of coal about the house; invariably he carried the load for them.

On his retirement from Bruce Castle a considerable sum of money was raised as an appreciative testimonial by his pupils, parents and 'Old Boys' of the school. Characteristically he insisted on donating this to the *Royal National Lifeboat Institution* (founded in 1822) for maintaining a lifeboat at Fowey, Cornwall. Actually the boat carried his name; the first, formerly named *Rochdale and Catherine Rashleigh* was renamed *Arthur Hill* in 1879 and continued in service until 1887, in which year (two years after Arthur's death) a new lifeboat was named after him, and between 1887 and 1904 it was launched three times on rescue missions, saving four lives. No further information appears to be available.

Arthur lived a life of patriarchal simplicity and exerted an immense influence by his nobility of character. He died at the age of eighty-seven.

Frederic Hill

Frederic Hill (1803–96) was the fifth son; he also taught at the school from thirteen years of age onwards, at Hazelwood and finally at Bruce Castle. He had been reading for the Bar for some time and was 'called' at Lincoln's Inn in 1834. He was then appointed Parliamentary Secretary to Mr Serjeant Wilde[13] who later became Lord Truro and Lord Chancellor. Frederic no doubt achieved his appointment through the personal and professional friendship of his brother Matthew with Lord Truro. This association with the Hills resulted in Mr Serjeant Wilde becoming one of Rowland Hill's strongest supporters in the House of Commons for his postal reforms.

In 1835 Frederic was appointed to one of the first Inspectorships of Prisons under the Home Office and was assigned to the vast district of Northumberland and Durham and the whole of Scotland. Here he applied his keen and kindly mind to matters associated with the penal system and brought about many reforms of the system. In 1847 he was transferred to a district in England where he continued his good work. During these years he never lost interest in the wider educational field and he published *National Education; its Present State and Prospects* in 1836. This proved to be a valuable work as it provided a wealth of reliable educational and statistical data which later educational reformers were able to use with profit.

Frederic remained in the service until 1851 when Rowland, then struggling to implement his reforms in the Post Office, persuaded his brother to join him in his work. Rowland met serious resistance when he first raised the question, and after much wrangling with the Postmaster General and the Chancellor of the Exchequer he managed to get his brother appointed as his Assistant Secretary. The arguments hinged on expense as the appointment was a new one, but it is probable that Rowland's superiors were sufficiently concerned about the friction that Rowland was allegedly generating in the department to contemplate introducing another high-powered Hill into the system. However, the appointment was made and Frederic made a really important contribution to efficiency and development in the Post Office. His unswerving loyalty and confidence in Rowland is shown by the fact that he accepted a considerable cut in salary to join his brother in the post he held until his retirement in 1876.

The fraternal partnership worked harmoniously and went into action at once. Early in 1852 they together proposed a reform of the salary scales of small postmasters, numbering some 6,000. Then they gave their minds to a comprehensive revision of the whole structure of the Civil Service salaries. This led almost immediately to the setting up of a Commission on which Rowland gave evidence for eight days when he was questioned on the plans he and Frederic had put forward. When the Commission's report was published in 1854 its provisions closely reflected the ideas originally put forward by the Hill brothers. The essentials of their proposals were for the introduction of a regular incremental scale for employees who were giving satisfactory service; for promotion purely by merit and suitability, and for the elimination of patronage. In view of Rowland's feelings on patronage it is ironic to note that he was able to secure the appointment of his brothers, Edwin and Frederic, to senior posts in government departments and to find jobs for Edwin's son, Ormond in 1840, and for his own son, Pearson in 1850. In fact there was no question of favouritism; they all had to face a selection board, and very soon confirmed the board's judgment by showing their outstanding competence in the posts to which they had been appointed.

Frederic's most important contribution was his reorganisation of the Money Order department. This service fulfilled a widespread and popular need, from the highest to the lowest classes, and, working closely together, Rowland and Frederic vastly improved its efficiency and economic viability. Soon its efficiency was doubled and its costs halved. In office routine alone some seventy-eight laborious ledgers were scrapped, releasing sixty clerks from largely unnecessary duties. With their Hazelwood experience with printing they devised and printed smaller and simpler forms which alone saved £1,000 per annum, and eliminated the despatch of 46,000 unnecessary letters and invoices every week. Altogether they effected savings of more than £17,000 per annum. An interesting side-light on the value and popularity of the improved Money Order service is revealed by the fact that during the Crimean War (1853–56) the troops sent home more than £100,000 in Money Orders under special arrangements made by Rowland Hill.

In spite of the heavy responsibilities he carried in the Post Office, Frederic Hill never lost his interest in education and prison reform; all the Hills saw life whole in this way. Hence it is typical to find Frederic very actively involved with the *Law Amendment Society*, and the *Metropolitan Discharged Prisoners' Aid Society* and so on. In 1853 he published his very highly regarded book, *Crime, its Amount, Causes and Remedies* (Murray 1853) which was soon referred to as *'Hill on Crime'*; it was immediately hailed as a classic of 'penalogical science' and had considerable influence in Great Britain as well as in America. It is on record that Frederic's portrait was hung on the wall of the Governor's office in the infamous Sing Sing Prison in America, and in the Commandant's office in the American Naval Prison in Portsmouth, New Hampshire, as an inspiration and hope for all who worked there. In both these institutions the Governor had been Thomas Mott Osborne, a great American reformer and a fervent admirer of Rowland and Frederic Hill, and this was later to have surprising consequences for education in both America and Great Britain. Appendix A, *The American Connection*, relates the whole curious story.

An unexpected side-light on Frederic's character is revealed by the fact that he was a strong supporter of the first school established in England following the Froebel system. It was started by Herr and Frau

Ronge in Tavistock Place, London in 1854, and Frederic was the first English parent to send his children to the school.

Like most of the Hills, Frederic was not noted for his sense of humour. Sometimes, however, he could display a sardonic wit, as on the occasion in April 1855 when the Emperor Louis Napoleon passed the Post Office in a grand procession to a Guildhall reception. Frederic refused to join his colleagues on the roof to witness the cavalcade, commenting, 'I have been so long an Inspector of Prisons that the sight of a rogue has ceased to be any novelty to me'.

Frederic Hill died in 1896, in his ninety-fourth year. In an obituary notice *The Times* wrote:

> One satisfaction of his old age was to watch the adoption here and in the USA and on the continent of the principle which he had been almost alone in advocating in his classical and epoch-making work on *Crime*. To the last he was the Reformer.

William Howard Hill

William Howard Hill (1805–20) was the youngest of the six brothers, and to the great sorrow of the family he died of tuberculosis when he was just fifteen years of age. He had been educated at the school and on leaving the classroom at thirteen he followed the family practice of becoming a pupil-teacher at the school. He appears to have been a lively, likeable young man and the last we hear of him was when he was accompanying a party of Franks on a tour of London docks – a typically enterprising Hazelwood activity more to be expected in the livelier secondary schools of today than in a private school 160 years ago.

The Hill brothers had two sisters, Caroline (1800–77) and Sarah (1807–40) who were certainly taught alongside their brothers and other boys. Caroline, for example, took an active part in the school's play productions. Other girls appear in the records of Hill Top; there is still surviving a very striking Geography exercise book, consisting of forty-three most painstakingly drawn and coloured maps produced by Miss M. A. Plimley in 1815. There is no evidence of girls having attended Hazelwood and Bruce Castle schools in later years.

[III]

The Colonisation of South Australia

ROWLAND HILL was thirty-eight years of age in 1833 when he retired from schoolmastering for good, broken in health and bitterly disappointed with his failure to retain the support of the parents at Bruce Castle. They bluntly refused to accept the priority he was giving to science in the curriculum; to conventional, middle-class southerners the whole idea seemed crazy. So with the sympathy and support of the whole family Rowland packed his bags and departed for a long holiday in France.

Matthew, by this time highly successful at the Bar, strongly urged Rowland to make the break, declaring that there was no future for innovative ideas in the barren soil of the home counties. This was true, for the magnitude of the opposition Rowland had to face at Bruce Castle is revealed in the almost unbelievable confession made thirty-three years later by Dr George Birkbeck Hill who was Headmaster at the time. In giving evidence in 1866 to the Schools' Enquiry Commission (the Taunton Report) he declared that 'the teaching of science has been discontinued' (see items 17093/4/5). Even so, the greatly extended curriculum survived, so did the general principles of self-government that had been pioneered at Hazelwood. As for Rowland, all was not lost and he was by no means bound for the wilderness, for almost immediately an unexpected opportunity was presented to him in France. It was by pure chance that in Lyons Rowland came across Edward Gibbon Wakefield of whom he had heard as the author of a well-known pamphlet, Letter from Sydney, published in 1829. The document made a powerful case for what the author termed 'systematic colonisation' to take the place of the unscrupulous exploitation that had hitherto disgraced earlier emigration ventures. This had led to thousands of misinformed emigrants being shipped to Australia in appalling conditions only to find misery and catastrophe instead of the promised land they had been led to expect.

At this chance meeting in Lyons, Edward Wakefield, seeing how interested and enthusiastic Rowland was in the scheme, persuaded him to become associated with the venture, hinting at the possibility of employment as administrative secretary. Needing a new job of some kind, Rowland regarded this suggestion as a great opportunity to do something constructive and worthwhile for his fellow-men, and it appealed to him to be able to work with an enterprising man of similar vision and lofty ideals. He was already well aware of the distressing experiences of the thousands of decent men and women who had ventured to emigrate without any safeguards or guarantees. We, today, can hardly credit what the passengers endured on these earlier voyages. Conditions on the long 16,000 mile trip had been appalling, physically and morally, for the unfortunate travellers – not very different from those of the convict ships. Unseaworthy hulks were pressed into service, loaded to the gunwales with suffering humanity, ill-fed, packed like sardines in filth and squalor, bullied, robbed and molested. Many perished on the voyage and others succumbed shortly after landing; the killers were typhus, measles and scarlet-fever.

In spite of these earlier scandals, right up to the 1830s there was a strong body of opinion in England that still believed in the benefit of properly organised emigration to Australia. Many members of the government supported this view, and, influenced by Edward Wakefield's campaign, tabled a Bill to promote the founding of a colony in South Australia. A provisional committee was then formed of very respectable supporters, including seventeen MPs of both parties, to investigate the proposal more thoroughly. Then in 1834 the official *South Australian Association* was set up, consisting of twenty-nine members including Rowland Hill, Matthew Davenport Hill, Dr Southwood Smith, with George Grote the historian, as chairman. The two latter had always been enthusiastic supporters of Hazelwood and were well-acquainted with the talents of the Hill family. The aim of the Association was to publicise the proposed emigration scheme, explain its principles and objects and review the prospects for the new colony.

From the first the project had caught the interest of Rowland Hill, for in 1832 he had himself published a pamphlet on a similar, though more localised, scheme entitled *Home Colonies: a Plan for the Gradual Extinction of Pauperism and the Diminution of Crime*. This was based on a successful experiment carried out in Holland, which Rowland had studied. In the proposed South Australian project Rowland recognised a bold, praiseworthy attempt to cope with the same social problem on a much wider and more ambitious scale. When working on his own Home Colonies scheme, always ready to seek the support of powerful backers, Rowland had sent a copy of his pamphlet to Lord Brougham, the Lord

Chancellor and leading Whig politician. He knew Henry Brougham as a staunch supporter of progressive causes, for back in the mid 1820s he had shown a keen interest in Hazelwood school and had helped to found the *Society for the Diffusion of Useful Knowledge:* he was also destined to play a leading role later, in forcing through Parliament the *Penny Postage Act of 1839.* Rowland always cultivated his backers with far-sighted shrewdness.

In considering Edward Wakefield's and the Association's proposals, Rowland, as usual, set about doing his homework. He made it his business to study the causes of the disastrous happenings when an attempted colonisation of Western Australia had taken place a few years earlier. He soon discovered why the bid to found the *Swan River Colony* in 1829 had been doomed from the start. Inadequate surveys and misleading publicity had concealed from the would-be settlers that, far from establishing themselves in a fertile area of abundant opportunities, they were actually dumped on the edge of one of the biggest tracts of arid country in the world. It proved to be a land of 'sand, sorrow and sore eyes' and nothing else.

To Rowland Hill it was a horrifying story and a cautionary tale; it originated in the incompetent planning of Thomas Peel, a cousin of the then Home Secretary, Robert Peel. Though well-intentioned, Thomas Peel, the king-pin of the venture, had taken too much on trust and had skimped his research. Carried away by the dramatic annexation of the entire west coast of Australia by Captain C. H. Freemantle in 1829, Thomas Peel, with fame and fortune in mind, foolishly rushed into forming a syndicate of entrepreneurs to develop the territory. To their credit they renounced the usual policy of transporting convict labour from the United Kingdom to do the back-breaking jobs. Instead they planned to induce 10,000 small farmers, craftsmen, domestics and honest labourers to settle in the *Swan River* area (near present day Perth), offering 40 acres of land to every colonist who brought £3 with him.

Strangely enough in 1828 Thomas Arnold[2] himself, looking ahead to early retirement (though he had only just started at Rugby), seriously considered investing his first £1,000 in the purchase of land in the *Swan River* area, and even contemplated despatching his sons Matthew and Thomas to one or other of the colonies because he deemed them both to be lazy and work-shy! Clearly the lure of emigration was a potent force at this particular time, so it was not surprising that Thomas Peel found many trustful subscribers to his project. Alas, they set off in their thousands grossly ill-equipped to face the hazards that lay ahead. The result was that hundreds, if not thousands, of respectable, well-to-do families found themselves put ashore on barren beaches, surrounded by crates of their precious furniture, libraries, stylish clothes and even grand pianos. Bewildered and frightened they searched in vain for non-existent villages, even for any form of shelter, and soon running low on water and food they inevitably collapsed from exhaustion. Dysentry and scurvy took their toll, and such servants as they had brought with them soon deserted them and made for the nearest small haven or settlement they could find. Their masters and mistresses had to fend for themselves, working like lumberjacks and navvies to construct primitive shelters in order to survive. The hapless Thomas Peel was himself a victim of his folly and was soon to be seen wandering crazily, ragged and unkempt, among his destitute countrymen. The Governor tried to get help from the home country, but before it arrived many of the survivors had left for Tasmania (then called Van Diemen's land) where conditions were supposed to be better. The population of Western Australia soon dwindled from 4,000 to a mere 1,400, and eventually the ill-fated colony had to resort to convict labour to ensure survival, just as New South Wales and Tasmania had done from the start, with appalling consequences of violence, crime and debauchery.

This was what Edward Wakefield and Rowland Hill were determined to avoid. So in 1835 when Rowland was officially appointed *Secretary to the South Australian Commission*, the department set up by Parliament to oversee and organise the colonisation of South Australia, he knew a good deal about the problems facing him; in particular he saw very clearly the fatal blunders that had been made. Fortunately he had as his chairman the admirable Colonel Robert Torrens under whom he worked with complete confidence.

The principles of the Commission were clear and enlightened; all sailings had to be thoroughly organised, the accommodation on board had to be well provided, with reasonable space for each passenger. No convicts or paupers were to be carried. Land was to be offered for sale by the newly formed *South Australian Company* at £1 per acre, and the proceeds were to be used to promote and assist the emigration of suitable applicants. By October 1835 eager investors and would-be emigrants had supported the company to the tune of £50,000 on the strength of which a further 20,000 acres were put up for sale at 12 shillings per acre.

This was the point when Rowland Hill came into the picture; it was his responsibility to work out the details of the scheme, and lay down precise conditions for a humane and orderly emigration programme. It was just the sort of detailed administrative work that he had brought to intricate perfection during his twenty-five years at Hazelwood.

Rowland's meticulous administration can be detected in the criteria

[47]

laid down by him for the award of free and assisted passages; these were strictly limited to applicants who could contribute special skills to the community – agricultural labourers, shepherds, bakers, blacksmiths, braziers and tin-smiths. In addition it was required that men had to be married, of good health and with satisfactory character references. Free passage could be obtained by single women of good character, 'accustomed to farming and dairy-work, sempstresses, straw-plaiters and domestic servants'. Great care was taken to keep a balance between men and women. Each adult was allowed to take half a ton of luggage free, and had to have his or her own bedding, clothing, eating utensils, a pewter mug and the tools of his or her trade.

In commissioning the necessary ships Rowland deliberately sought small vessels, often not exceeding 300 tons. He knew he could have more control over the situation if the vessels were of modest tonnage and not too crowded with passengers. Prudently he struck a sensible balance between passengers and cargo, but he also despatched some ships carrying mostly cargo to meet the expressed needs of the colony.

Although the Commission ran into some difficulties and disagreements, Rowland Hill toiled away into the small hours checking the thousand and one administrative details that required attention. Characteristically he began with tightening up and improving the arrangements for chartering the necessary ships. He was tough and exacting with the various contractors he had to deal with, making sure they were left in no doubt as to what their obligations were. This was something disconcertingly new for the hard-bitten fraternity who had hitherto had to deal with easy-going government departments or profit-making speculators. With their new task-master they soon found they had no alternative but to toe the line and fulfil their contracts to the letter.

Traditionally, payment of ship-owners and officers such as captains, mates, surgeons and so on was based on the number of emigrants embarked, but Rowland insisted that payment in future should be calculated on the number of those who actually landed in Australia. This gave a real inducement to all concerned to exercise proper care and to provide wholesome food and hygienic conditions for those aboard the vessel. Rowland also laid down meticulous inspection check-lists to make sure that all his requirements as regards accommodation, food, water and medical care were being observed. By good fortune and careful administration not a single ship chartered by him was lost or suffered serious accident. As usual, his record-keeping was immaculate. The following statement, for example, signed by Rowland Hill, records details of the first fourteen vessels whose sailings were organised by him in 1836; one was with the co-operation of the Royal Navy and some were mostly for cargo:

No.	Name of Vessel	Departure Date (1836)	Registered tonnage	No. of emigrants
1.	John Pirie	Feb. 22	160	23
2.	Duke of York	Feb. 24	191	25
3.	Cygnet	Mar. 20	239	69
4.	Lady Mary Pelham	Mar. 30	207	24
5.	Emma	Apr. 21	160	18
6.	Rapid	May 1	130	17
7.	Africaine	June 28	316	52
8.	Tam O'Shanter	July 19	360	68
9.	HMS Buffalo	Aug. 4	850	136
10.	William Hutt	Aug. 18	260	1
11.	Coromandel	Sept. 3	662	140
12.	Isabella	Sept. 3	282	2
13.	Sarah & Elizabeth	Sept. 26	269	36
14.	John Renwick	Oct. 18	403	124

Total number of emigrants   735

Total cost for 735 emigrants   £10,482.
Average cost for emigrant   £ 14. 5. 2¾
Taken out by the above ships:
 Bedding and stores for the voyage.
 Tents, ironmongery for the Emigrants' Dept.
 36 Double Cottages.

The first of Rowland's emigrant ships to reach South Australia was the *Duke of York*, a small vessel of 191 tons (number two in his list), which anchored in *Nepean Bay, Kangaroo Island*, on 27 July 1836, after almost a five-month voyage. Most of the other vessels sailed up the gulf and dropped anchor off *Glenelg*, just south of the present day *Port Adelaide* and *Adelaide* itself, whose 'streets' had been hastily pegged out by Colonel William Light, the official Surveyor.

It is of interest to note that on board *HMS Buffalo* which had left England on 4 August was Governor Hindmarsh, who landed at *Holdfast Bay* and in a formal ceremony took possession of the colony in the name of King William IV on 28 December 1836. It was actually proclaimed *The British Province of South Australia* and was deemed to be something more than a mere colony. The eventual capital, *Adelaide*, commemorated Queen Adelaide and was handsomely sited on the *River Torrens*, named after Colonel Robert Torrens, first *Chairman of the South Australia Commission*. During the four years he worked as *Secretary to the*

Commission, Rowland Hill was responsible for chartering a total of 38 ships, carrying over 5,000 emigrants to South Australia.

The first of Rowland's settlers found conditions primitive in the extreme; most of them had to live in tents they had brought with them; the wealthier and more provident had brought special pre-fabricated wooden houses, purchased from Mannings of Holborn. But shortages of labour and transport caused all sorts of difficulties. Edward Stephens, the manager of the company's bank, had to leave behind his pre-fabricated house on the beach at *Glenelg* and make his way to Adelaide where, in a pegged-out, non-existent street, he pitched a large tent to serve as his bank and his bedroom. Likewise Governor Hindmarsh had perforce to set up his first seat of government and swear in his first Council in a similar tent at *Glenelg*.

Very soon more substantial commercial buildings and houses began to spring up and the new settlers adapted themselves to a simple, arduous but relatively congenial style of life in spite of swarms of flies and troublesome rats. Nearly every settler grew his own vegetables, and many kept poultry, sheep, cows and pigs. A competent blacksmith could earn a pound a day and live well on his income; a cabinet-maker from London, starting with nothing, wrote home to say that he now owned two large town blocks, and having built up a thriving wood-working business, offered jobs to any of his former workmates who cared to join him. By 1840 the population of South Australia had grown to 15,000, of whom 12,000 were settlers who had come out on free passages originally organised by Rowland Hill. This is the measure of the confidence the public had in the scheme he was administering.

One can imagine the conscientious attention he must have given to his task in sifting through piles of applications, interviewing and selecting the most suitable, processing their papers, contracting appropriate vessels, laying down very precise terms of hire for the services of captains, officers, surgeon and crew, and finally provisioning the ships for their long five month voyage. All this resulted in the colonisation of South Australia standing out as a model of what a planned emigration should be. There was no convict labour, and the emigrants arrived in Australia proud and confident after experiencing at first hand the decent standards and humane treatment they had received from the Commission and its servants. They had been spared the shocking experiences of the earlier settlers who, in their thousands, had suffered robbery on the high-seas, protection rackets, near-starvation, molestation, moral corruption amid indescribable dirt and squalor. Life on board Rowland Hill's vessels was conducted, relatively speaking, with the decorum of a Unitarian Sunday school.

Perhaps one of the most remarkable features of the story is the fact that, while Rowland Hill was heavily committed to the task in question, he was also working at his ideas on postal reform, and with his brother, Edwin, was putting the final touches to their revolutionary rotary printing press which was patented at the very same time – in 1835. Rowland remained *Secretary to the South Australian Commission* until 1839, during which time, in the year 1837, he published in January and February two editions of his famous pamphlet, *Post Office Reform: its Importance and Practicability*. Such was the interest shown by the public and politicians in his scheme that a third edition was published in November 1837, followed by a fourth edition in 1838.

The Post Office issue really came to the boil after the publication of his pamphlet, when the government began to take serious notice. Detailed examinations of Rowland's proposals were carried out by the *Post Office Commission* in February 1837 then, more thoroughly, by the special *Parliamentary Committee* in November 1837. The latter sat for sixty-three days, during which time Rowland was summoned as a witness and subjected to a prolonged grilling for many days. The Committee's report, published in July 1838, in general supported the plan, but rejected the penny rate and proposed twopence instead. It is not surprising that Rowland considered the year 1837 to have been the most important of his life: it saw the triumph of his youthful hopes and of his years of painstaking research and planning. Yet during all this time he had been involved in the day to day handling of the complicated affairs of the South Australian Commission.

When in August 1839 the *Penny Postage Act* was entered on the Statute Book, Rowland resigned his post with the Commission, fully confident that he would be offered a senior post in the Post Office to help in the implementation of his scheme. There is on record the letter he received from his Chairman, Colonel Robert Torrens, expressing the latter's 'deep gratitude for the exemplary zeal, energy and talent he had shown in carrying out so efficiently the arduous and complicated arrangements of the Department of Emigration'. An extremely happy sequel to Rowland's association with the Torrens family is the fact that Colonel Robert Torrens' granddaughter (Sir Robert Torrens' daughter) married Rowland's only son, Pearson. Their own first son was very appropriately named Rowland Torrens Hill.

After his four years' work as *Secretary of the South Australia Commission* and two earlier years' involvement with the *South Australian Association*, never earning more than £500 per annum, Rowland moved on to the task he had been waiting and preparing for since his earliest years. He was full of optimism and confidence, not dreaming of the hornets' nest he was about to disturb. Instead of being offered a senior Post Office appointment carrying the prestige and salary appropriate to a key-figure brought in to assist in the implementation of his major reforms, he was at first fobbed off with a temporary post for two years with the Treasury, without the authority or resources to initiate anything – and at the derisory salary of £500 per annum, no more than he had been earning with the South Australian Commission for the past four years. Not unnaturally he felt insulted and ignominiously slighted, and within twenty-four hours he had embarked upon his battle of attrition with the powers that be that was to occupy his mind for the next quarter of a century. This story will be told in a succeeding chapter.

[IV]

The London and Brighton Railway

THE three and a quarter years that Rowland Hill spent with the London and Brighton Railway (1843–46), first as a Director, then as Chairman of the Board, form only a small part of his adult life and the story does not take long to relate. The interlude, however, is interesting in that it shows his versatility, his abiding interest in the lot of the common man and his characteristic way of dealing with administrative problems. His philosophy of life remains consistent throughout his career. It inspires and unifies his work in all his spheres of activity; at Hazelwood School (approximately 1808–33); with the South Australian Association and Commission (1833–39); with the London and Brighton Railway Company (1843–46); and most strikingly with the Post Office (1839–42 and 1846–64). The various stages of his life are like the movements of a great symphony, coming together in a final movement as a grand summation of all that has gone before.

It was during the period of the 'railway mania' that Rowland Hill was invited to join the Board of the London and Brighton railway. In September 1842, following a change of government, he was dismissed from his temporary post with the Treasury. Despite a public outcry at the reformer's curt dismissal, Rowland found himself unemployed. Fortuitously the London and Brighton Railway Company offered him an appointment on their Board which he accepted with feelings of some relief.

Accordingly he took up residence at 11, Hanover Crescent, Brighton, and lived there until 1848 when he returned to London, having been appointed Secretary to the Postmaster General in 1846. Throughout the country at this time there was a tremendous enthusiasm for railway development and investors were queuing up to buy shares in these exciting new projects. The London and Brighton line was no exception but the eager public had little idea of the complicated procedures involved in establishing a new line. The railway was opened in three stages between May 1840 and September 1841, the culmination of

[53]

many years of complicated and difficult work in surveying the route, getting Parliamentary approval, completing scores of land deals, constructing embankments, cuttings, viaducts and tunnels, acquiring rails and signalling equipment as well as sufficient locomotives and rolling stock to begin operations. Finally, apart from recruiting and training the necessary employees, the Company had to come to some agreement with the existing London and Croydon Railway and the South Eastern Railway Company for the shared use of their tracks on certain sections of the route – in the latter case, between East Croydon and Redhill.

From 1837 to 1843 the Company was directed by its hardworking Chairman, John Harman, but it was not long before it ran into trouble; inexperience, inefficiency, breakdowns, accidents and delays provoked bitter criticism and even hostility among the shareholders and general public. The *Brighton Guardian*, long sceptical and antagonistic, reported these events with glee. In July 1842 even *The Times* drew public attention to the poor quality of the Company's management. The previous year there had also been the scandal caused by the Secretary, Mr Wood, who had absconded with company funds to the tune of £1,000.

In the face of criticism and discord on the part of the Board, John Harman resigned and his chairmanship was taken over by J. M. Parsons for a few months, followed by Captain Kelly, RN for an equally short period. It was at this moment in the autumn of 1843 that Rowland Hill stepped into the breach, first as a Director and later, in February 1845, taking over the vacant chairmanship. On joining the Board and being well aware of the situation facing the company he characteristically made a thorough investigation of the management and financial problems. This revealed all sorts of incompetence; the company had even declared a dividend of 20 shillings per share when there was actually no profit to disburse. No wonder that the company's £50 shares had slumped to £35. With sublime confidence in himself he had no doubt that he could run the line profitably; to this end he invested most of his savings in the company and persuaded his family and friends to do the same. They too had complete confidence in their man and by July 1845 the shares had risen to £75.

Rowland Hill possessed a very shrewd business sense and having abundant courage and determination he gladly accepted the challenge. He correctly assessed the great potential of an efficient London and Brighton railway and felt confident that he could develop it to be an outstanding success.

He pin-pointed areas of extravagance and waste, and soon realised that part of the Company's financial difficulties arose from not developing the third-class market. The Directors were apprehensive of a flood

[54]

of London's east-enders, who would impair Brighton's reputation as a 'superior' resort. Margate, on the other hand, had zealously cultivated the third-class market and had accordingly prospered.

A change in the social habits of the well-to-do was to be observed at this time in their growing preference for continental holidays rather than the traditional seaside vacations in Britain. This seriously affected Brighton, so Rowland boldly made a bid to attract more visitors to the town by reducing the fares and, most important of all, by extensively developing Excursion trains at weekends and on public holidays. It will be recalled that at Hazelwood School over twenty years earlier the idea of excursions for the pupils had been thoroughly exploited, even using boats on the canals. The success of this undoubtedly encouraged Rowland to extend the idea to railway excursions on the Brighton line.

Though some tentative experiments for Sunday excursions were tried out in May 1843 just before Rowland Hill joined the company, the first major excursion instituted by him is reported to have been run on Easter Monday, 1844, and an extraordinary sight it must have been. The train started from London Bridge with forty-five carriages drawn by four engines. At New Cross, just under three miles from London Bridge, six more carriages were attached with another engine. At the next stop, Croydon, just ten miles from the start, another six carriages and a sixth engine were added. The whole journey is reported to have taken four and a half hours, no doubt illustrating the dictum that it is better to travel than to arrive. But there was no doubt of the success of excursions; they had come to stay and greatly increased the earnings of the company. Rowland Hill himself was delighted by the success of the experiment, for it not only benefited the revenue, but, equally important, it did something to bring colour and pleasure into the lives of the poorer sections of the community. Throughout his life he held firmly to this principle and it was the driving force behind his zeal for postal reform.

But not everyone approved of the social consequences of these developments. The upper crust of Brighton still regarded the excursion trains and the cheapening of the fares with disapproval. Queen Victoria herself was not amused to see the Royal watering-place, Prinny's elegant playground, degenerating into a common seaside resort; so much so that she declared she would never visit the place again. Whether she actually stuck to this decision is not clear, but it would appear that she never forgave Rowland Hill for daring to interfere with her royal privileges. This is certainly how it struck the Hill family, for at the Palace Investiture in 1860, when Rowland received his knighthood, the Queen somewhat perfunctorily dubbed the kneeling reformer with her ceremonial sword and dismissed him without the normal word of greeting, congratulation or approval.[1] She did, however, give her support for the abolition of franking, and expressed approval of her likeness on the Penny Black stamp.

The worst fears, however, proved not to be justified, for Rowland's long-term aim was to induce more of the professional classes to consider the novel idea of living by the seaside and working during the week in London. This was a major step in popularising the practice of 'commuting'; no longer was a house in Hampstead or Wimbledon a sufficient symbol of success, when, with a ninety minute journey in a comfortable train, you could live by the sea in fashionable Brighton,[2] pavilioned in splendour and wafted in ozone. By reducing fares and ensuring the travellers' safety and comfort, the idea caught on and Brighton's population started to grow rapidly. To inspire confidence Rowland himself travelled to London at least three times a week, occupying, perhaps a little ostentatiously, his favourite 'coupé' facing backwards at the rear of the train. He was often accompanied by the Company's solicitor and by various fellow directors. He and the Company used every trick in the book to establish this first 'age of the train'; first class day-return tickets for £1 had already been introduced in 1843, and a monthly season, called a periodical ticket, was offered for £14. More spectacularly a Mr Mann of Brighton was granted an annual season ticket for £100, and a similar ticket was offered for Redhill for £65.

Rowland Hill joined the Company in time to add his weight to various proposals that had been under discussion for some time. He obviously approved of the decision to associate the London and Brighton Railway with the locomotive pooling scheme operated by the South Eastern Railway and the London and Croydon Railway. He was anxious to promote sensible co-operation or even amalgamation with such competing or overlapping companies, for he saw the inconvenience, unnecessary expense and actual dangers of existing *ad hoc* arrangements. Moreover, such moves would help to fend off threats of encroachment by rival Companies on their flanks. To this end the Company was given authority in July 1844 to build a line from Shoreham to Chichester – the Brighton and Chichester Railway – thus protecting its western flank. By acquiring an interest in the Brighton, Lewes and Hastings Railway the eastern flank was also protected.

The dangers of an uncoordinated railway system were very evident when the London and Brighton's trains had to use inferior quality track owned by other companies. Worse still, Rowland discovered by personal observation that on three stretches of line owned by three different companies, each laid down its own signalling rules. The wretched engine-driver had to remember exactly which stretch of the line he was on at any particular moment before he could interpret the signals correctly. It was a relief when, just before Rowland resigned from the Board, the shareholders agreed that the lines should be amalgamated to form the London, Brighton and South Coast Railway. This was formally implemented in April 1846. All through his service at Brighton it was characteristic of Rowland Hill to study problems on the spot. He frequently travelled on the footplate, stop-watch in hand, carefully observing the signals and recording the speeds and timings throughout the journey. No experience, he declared, was more exciting than travelling on the footplate at night.

All his varied experience with the London and Brighton Railway stood Rowland in very good stead during his subsequent career with the Post Office. There he met the very same problems writ large, but by this time he felt quite at home in the endless and complicated negotiations he had to conduct with major railway and steamship companies, as well as with foreign postal systems and governments. It is sad to relate that the only really stubborn, uncompromising and unscrupulous people he had to deal with during his whole career proved, alas, to be officials of the Post Office staff and the politicians in and out of government who ganged up against his postal reforms.

As an administrator Rowland Hill's thinking was always consistent and his judgment uncannily sound. He believed in the economic good sense of improving the service and reducing its cost, and followed this practice on the railway and in the Post Office. In both fields his judgement was correct; the public was pleased and the profits improved. But characteristically his decisions were always based on a thorough statistical analysis of the issue in question.

Before Rowland Hill joined the Board the finances of the Company, as we have seen, were in a serious state, and in May 1842 the Directors, as a means of economy, had reduced the traffic to six trains a day each way, but in May 1843, just before Rowland's arrival, a return had been made to seven services a day. Soon after this, fares were reduced on slow trains and Sunday services in the hope of attracting more passengers. Then in a feverish attempt to economise, this order was rescinded and rather ludicrously the number of railway policemen detailed to guard the Clayton tunnel was reduced from four to three! When Rowland arrived in the autumn he must have made his presence felt at once, for a minute of the Board meeting on 9 September ordered the clock in the Board room to be set at the correct time, not five minutes slow. This bears

Rowland's fingerprint, for it typically reveals his fetish for punctilious time-keeping; throughout his life he regarded lateness as virtually a sin against the Holy Ghost.

During Rowland's first years as chairman the Company gave notice of a revised time-table with reduced fares as from 1 May 1844. Various types of train provided seven services a day each way as the actual time-table clearly shows.

Almost at the same time Gladstone's Railway Act of 1844 established the right of third class passengers to travel at fares of 1 penny a mile as from November 1844. These were the famous 'Parliamentary trains' satirically referred to in the Gilbert and Sullivan operettas.[3] Rowland's fare reductions in May 1844 provided third class travel from London to Brighton for 5 shillings (60 old pence), and first class for 14 shillings. His Board of Directors complained that this was quite uneconomic, but Rowland, confident in his thorough statistical analysis, carried the day. During 1845 he reduced the fares still further, bringing the first class fare down from 14 shillings to 12 shillings and 5 pence, with corresponding cuts in the fares of other classes and categories. But Gladstone's 'Parliamentary train' fares in May 1845 prescribed a third class ticket from London to Brighton for 50 pence (i.e. a penny per mile), undercutting Rowland's first reduction by 10 pence. His further reduction in 1845 brought the third class fare down to approximately 53 pence, thus closely matching Gladstone's 50 pence.

Then the company made a special effort to win back traffic from the wealthier section of the community who were now increasingly taking their holidays on the continent. This was achieved by working in close co-operation with the Steam Packet Company who were running improved services from Shoreham to Dieppe and Le Havre. The railway time-table gave full publicity to this in the following announcement:

> The quickest route to Paris is by Railway to Kingston Wharf, Shoreham Harbour, and then by Steam Packet to Dieppe; Steam Packets also leave Kingston Wharf for Le Havre. These Packets call (weather permitting and during daylight only) at Brighton Pier half an hour after their departure from Kingston Wharf, Shoreham. Particulars of times of sailing are published in a separate bill.
>
> Trains leave Rouen for Paris six times a day, performing the journey in four hours. A *special* train for London is always despatched from Shoreham if the Packet arrives at Kingston Wharf too late to catch the scheduled connection.

This is typical of Rowland's meticulous attention to detail in communicating information. The company's records also show that between 6 April and 31 October 1844, a total of 11,054 railway passengers used the cross-channel service provided by the Shoreham Steam Packet, confirming the Directors' expectation of substantial revenue benefits to the company.

When Rowland Hill joined the Company in 1843, he inherited a reasonable working concern in spite of its lamentable financial state. The permanent way was fully established as far as Brighton, sufficient locomotives and carriages were available even though repairs and replacements were sorely needed. The whole system was working after a fashion, but like the rolling stock was clearly in need of an overhaul. In spite of some disillusion and grumblings on the part of shareholders and townsfolk there still existed a reservoir of good-will upon which the company could draw. The solid, prestigious railway station at Brighton always seemed to stand as a symbol of better things to come.

From the start Rowland Hill made it clear that he was concerned with three matters: safety, efficiency and revenue, the latter very much depending on the two former factors. Unfortunately he inherited some troubles that had to be cleared up before real progress could be made. The worst of these was the long-standing wrangle about an accident dating back to 2 October 1841, long before he joined the company. The 10.45 train from London carrying ninety-seven passengers in twelve carriages had been derailed at Copyhold Cutting near Haywards Heath with the loss of four lives – two firemen and two passengers. The immediate enquiry largely attributed the cause to the unsuitability of the four-wheeled locomotive. This was dealt with by a re-build which added a pair of trailing wheels, but disquiet remained and arguments continued, resulting in a serious loss of confidence in the line. This was aggravated in the same month by a collapse at the southern end of Patcham Tunnel and by further slips at Mersham and Earlswood. To make matters worse it was just after this that the Secretary absconded with £1,000 of company money.

On top of this legacy of trouble and lost confidence Rowland found himself faced with serious and expensive engineering problems because of the dangerous state of a number of the company's locomotives. This was happening, of course, in the early days of railway locomotives; it was only eighteen years since the first passenger train ran between Stockton and Darlington in 1825 and only fourteen years since Stephenson's *Rocket* first appeared on the Liverpool to Manchester line. Two of the early locomotives used by Rowland on the London and Brighton line in 1845 are herewith illustrated – the Jones and Potts Single, No. 39 and the Jones Single No. 121. As with most of these early locomotives they were later rebuilt and improved, and appear in subsequent engine-lists under different numbers, the above appearing as No. 115 (after

Craven's renewal) and No. 97 respectively. The illustrations show them in their rebuilt form, still without any protective cab for the engine-driver and his fireman.

Concerned about the unserviceability of their locomotives the Directors called in an expert, Thomas Cabry, the Chief Engineer of the York and North Midland Railway, whose report was presented on 2 October 1843, just as Rowland Hill joined the Board. A small number of the company's locomotives were declared unsafe and were recommended for urgent attention which was duly given at the very efficient New Cross Depot. In March 1845 Rowland and his directors appointed John Gray as Locomotive Superintendent. He came from the Hull and Selby railway with a reputation as a good practical engineer with some original locomotive designs which had proved successful in service. So it was that in September 1845 fourteen of Gray's latest models were ordered from Timothy Hackworth at a cost of £1,770 each, with the promise of seven more to follow. In his typical way Rowland insisted on a very precise contract: first delivery had to be guaranteed for February 1846 with a flow of two locomotives every three months thereafter. A characteristic penalty clause was added, specifying a fine of £100 for each month's late delivery. Alas, Hackworth did not realise that Rowland really meant it and disastrous consequences followed; only two locomotives were delivered by December 1846, by which time Rowland had resigned from the Company on grounds of ill-health and partly in response to the long-awaited summons from the government to resume his work in the Post Office.

This was not the sort of parting Rowland would have wished for, and he would have relished the impending encounter with the unreliable contractors; no one got away with defections like this when Rowland Hill was at the helm. Unfortunately for the railway, Rowland's first and only real love – his plan for postal reform – had the stronger claim and he had warned his fellow Directors many times that a recall to London was likely on a change of government. In the event, the unfortunate John Gray was given three months' notice and it took some years before the railway was able to proceed with its renewals and new locomotives as had been hoped.

It is curious how Rowland Hill's interests, skills and experience seemed to fit him perfectly for the very varied tasks he had to perform during his career. Although he joined the London and Brighton Railway Company as an administrator, he knew as much as most professionals did on engineering matters and he was particularly well informed on all aspects of steam engines. He was born in the Black Country and spent the first thirty years of his life in the heart of the industrial Midlands. The

Hills' schools at Hill Top and Hazelwood in Birmingham were hardly a mile or two from Matthew Boulton's famous Soho Manufactory and Foundry which was the largest in the world at that time. Here from 1775 onwards Boulton, James Watt and William Murdoch pioneered very important developments in the steam engine and Murdoch had actually built working models of steam locomotives. All this, of course, paved the way for the work of Richard Trevethick in Cornwall, and in the north, for George Stephenson whose famous *Rocket* appeared in 1829 when Rowland Hill was thirty-four years of age. Much of this pioneer work was going on right on Rowland's doorstep and he followed events with the enthusiasm of a fellow engineer, for this is what he was by inclination and by practice. Before he was sixteen he had constructed an early form of Wimshurst machine to generate static electric charges; he used this in ingenious science demonstrations at public lectures in Birmingham. About this time he also constructed working models of steam engines for demonstration purposes in the school science laboratory. Later, as we know, in conjunction with his elder brother, Edwin, he invented and patented the first effective Rotary Printing press. This up-to-date engineering background helped Rowland to make informed judgments on technical problems on the railway, and this talent was to serve him well in the later dealings he had with railway and steamship companies when he was implementing his postal reforms.

While working at Brighton Rowland was still giving considerable attention to his ideas on postal reform, but with his remarkable capacity for detailed, sustained work, he threw himself heart and soul into his railway tasks. One important innovation was the speeding up of the journey by changing locomotives at Redhill instead of waiting half an hour or so while the tender was replenished with water and a sufficient head of steam restored. This policy, we are assured, helped him to reduce the time of the express trains to 90 minutes each way. Another important administrative change was his policy (reminiscent of his Hazelwood days) of the strict enforcement of penalties for every breach of a rule, whether it led to an accident or not. When actual accidents occurred he insisted that a full report of what had happened and why it had occurred should be sent to every employee on the line. This was clearly good for morale: it assured every worker that he was an essential cog in the company's machine and stressed the company's concern for the safety and comfort of its passengers.

One significant step was taken by the Company, responding rather dubiously to Rowland's reasoned plea. This was to offer to carry Post Office mails between London and Brighton at a very nominal fee. Here was a clever coming together of Rowland's main interests – the railway and the Post Office. He reasoned that by providing a speedy and reliable postal service with London, the appeal of Brighton as a commuters' town would be vastly increased. Business and professional people living in Brighton could receive their post at breakfast before leaving for London; a letter posted in London during the late afternoon would reach Brighton the same evening and be delivered at 8.00 am the next morning. This cut the ground from under the feet of the querulous know-hows who claimed that a person commuting from Brighton daily to London would be handicapped by delays in communication and travel. Once again Rowland's judgment was correct; as he predicted, more and more businessmen elected to live genteelly by the sea. Other railway companies, unfortunately, turned out to be less ready to grasp the advantages of such a reciprocal deal when in later years Rowland put it to them this time on behalf of the Post Office.

There is general agreement that the London and Brighton Railway benefited greatly by Rowland Hill's direction and gained the reputation of being one of the best-run lines in the country. On his resignation in 1846 the *Railway Chronicle* wrote:

> Mr Hill's retirement will be felt by the Company and the public. Since he became Chairman, the Brighton Railway has increased more than 50% in value, and the public accommodation on the line in all respects – cheapness, speed, punctuality and a kind solicitude for the comfort of all passengers from the highest to the lowest – may justly be said to have been raised quite to an equality with that of the best-managed line in the kingdom.

This reputation persisted for many years and the line always represented something a cut above the ordinary. So much so that as late as 1895 in Oscar Wilde's delightful comedy *The Importance of Being Earnest* the leading male character, John Worthing's best claim to 'class' and gentility – in spite of beginning life as an abandoned infant found in a handbag at a London train terminus – was to insist that after all it was the left luggage department of the Brighton line!

The *Railway Chronicle*'s gratifying valediction to Rowland Hill's short career with the London and Brighton Railway would undoubtedly have pleased him. He enjoyed his years with the Company, for the task he had undertaken was clearly constructive and of real social value, and his colleagues in the service were friendly, fair-minded people. He appreciated the absence of friction, jealousy and disloyalty that had so dogged him in the Post Office and were to continue in the years to come, and he much enjoyed the tranquillity of the sea-side resort after his feverish years in London. So much so, in fact, that he continued to live at 11 Hanover Crescent for more than two years after resigning from

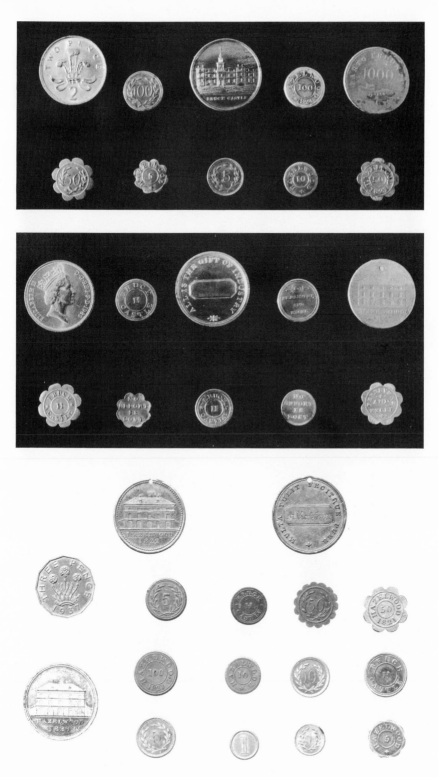

8. Hazelwood coinage for marks.

9. Model of school by Goodman and Bowman, 1827.

10. Mathew Davenport Hill, QC (1792–1872).

11. Edwin Hill (1793–1876)

12. Rowland Hill (1795–1879)

13. Arthur Hill (1798–1885)

14. Frederic Hill (1803–96)

15. Mathew Davenport Hill Jnr, science
master at Eton College.

A beach landing near Adelaide

The first seat of government Glenelg Dec.1836

A main street, Adelaide. circa 1840

Based on contemporary sketches

16. South Australia: the beginnings.

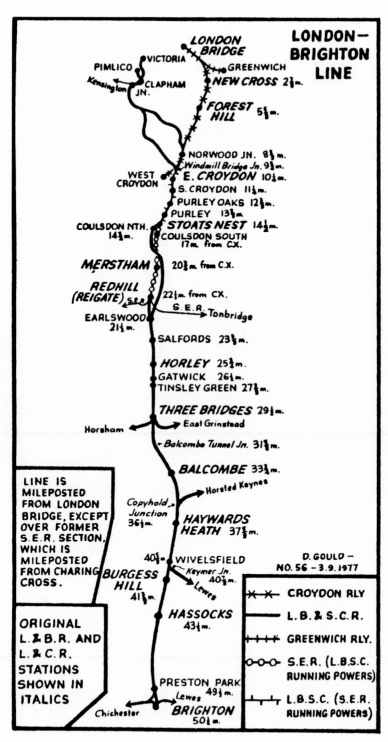

17. London–Brighton Line.

18. Brighton Railway Station.

19. Early locomotives.

the Company. When he finally left Brighton he was fifty-three years of age; and, astonishing to relate, had embarked upon the main part of his distinguished career, which was to occupy the next eighteen years. His triumphant success came after years of wearing and frustrating effort which finally broke his health. While still enjoying the comparative tranquillity of Brighton his services to the nation had already been publicly recognised and richly rewarded. In 1844 at the start of his railway career he was granted the freedom of Aberdeen; then just as he was leaving Brighton in 1846 he was given a nationally raised public testimonial of £13,000 to mark his inestimable work in initiating the penny post. Other even greater honours were to follow, but through it all, he always looked back with pride and gratitude to the kindness and opportunity given to him by the people of Brighton.

[V]

Rowland Hill's Postal Reforms

THE story of Rowland Hill's reforms of the Postal Service has been fully told many times, but in our comparatively brief account we are not so much concerned with the political and administrative aspects of his work in the Post Office (which would be the interest of the academic historian) as we are with the human side of the story, the personal drama – the struggle of a brave and noble spirit storming the forts of folly and challenging sloth and incompetence wherever he found it. There is no denying that he was a difficult man to work with; he was impatient and very determined, egotistical and uncompromising, but very sure of himself and genuinely concerned for the betterment of life for the less privileged of the world. To achieve his ends he drove himself relentlessly, never counting the cost.

From 1829 onwards when he was in charge of Bruce Castle school, the family began to be concerned about Rowland's deteriorating health; they knew that he had been working impossibly hard for a very long time. They realised that a complete breakdown could not be far away, so at least on three occasions the whole family council met to discuss a possible change of occupation for him. He himself felt confident that he could make a living as an inventor, an occupation that would remove him from the nervous strain of running a school with its relentless clamour of bells and boys. So in 1832, a year before he finally resigned from the school, he made a feasibility study of his possible future, listing the following ideas as possible lines of development, some of which are prophetically relevant to what actually happened:

1. Improvements in the design of steam engines.
2. Propelling steamboats by screws instead of paddles.
3. Improving the traditional Bramah Hydraulic Press.
4. A device for recording the speed of stage coaches.
5. Plan for the expeditious weighing of letters.
6. Plan for the sorting of letters in transit in Mail coaches.

7. Plan for a telegraphic system by air pressure.
8. Gas distribution in small-bore pipes under pressure.
9. Road making by machinery.

Nearly all these ideas are related to improving communications, and three of them are directly concerned with the postal service. At this time he was also very concerned about the excessive stamp duty levied on newspapers, and in his characteristic manner he ferreted out relevant statistical data to show how the duty could be reduced without sacrificing revenue.

The secret was to develop the revenue that was beginning to be attracted by Press advertising which would allow the government to recoup the loss of stamp duty by a tax on this growing source of newspaper income. Rowland even went with a deputation to present the case to the Chancellor of the Exchequer, Lord Monteagle,[1] who was so convinced that the stamp duty was forthwith reduced from 3½ pence to one penny.

Rowland never hesitated to go to the highest authority to plead his case, whatever it might be, and he was soon well-known in government circles as a very bright young man with novel ideas, sound judgment and dogged persistence. In this way not only did he become acquainted with many of the leading politicians and radical thinkers of the day, but he also had his first taste of official obstructionism – the brick-wall mentality of civil servants of those days and of government officials generally. This he first discovered painfully when in 1835 he tried to persuade the Treasury to adopt his newly patented rotary printing press. He pointed out that not only would the use of the new Press dramatically speed up the printing of papers, government Reports and circulars, but it could also automatically register the individual number of the Stamp Duty on each copy of a newspaper as it rolled through the press. This was the point that worried the Treasury officials; hitherto each copy of a newspaper had to have its stamp duty impressed and numbered individually at a vast expenditure of time and effort, and the Treasury could not believe that the operation could be performed mechanically with perfect safety and accuracy. Inevitably Rowland received the usual dusty official answer to his request to the Treasury to try out his device: . . . 'My Lords cannot accede to your request'. There was no question of a friendly discussion and demonstration; just the closed mind of officialdom with which he was soon to become much more closely acquainted.

In unfolding Rowland's life-story we can discern two unusual features; firstly his very early interest in the postal service, from about the age of eight, and secondly his singularly united family whose team-work created the international reputation of Hazelwood and Bruce Castle schools and later made possible Rowland's brilliant achievements in the Post Office which also won world-wide acclaim. It is difficult to find any parallel to this extraordinary family effort. We are well aware that dramatic advances such as Rowland Hill made, first in education at Hazelwood School, then in his postal reforms, do not suddenly emerge from virgin soil; in both cases we see a steady evolutionary process at work. When creating Hazelwood and writing about it in *Public Education* Rowland was fully conscious of the work of educational pioneers like Rousseau,[2] Pestalozzi, Fellenberg and the Edgeworths, and never hesitated to recognise his debt to them. Likewise he was well acquainted with the earlier pioneers in postal matters – the use of stage-coaches to supersede the horse-posts of the seventeenth and eighteenth centuries; the innovations of William Dockwra[3] in 1680 when an efficient penny post system, called the *London Penny Post*, provided almost hourly collections and deliveries within the city. He noted with interest the manifold advantages of the various penny-post systems that had been operating around many of the bigger towns from 1793 onwards, which, by the time he published his famous pamphlet in 1837, had already provided some 2,000 villages with a cheap and efficient postal service. This gave a further spur to his desire to extend the penny post throughout the whole country. It was not a question of a brilliant new idea, but rather a bold, nationwide extension of many successful local arrangements, supported this time by meticulous statistical evidence to justify the risk. And, of course, to Rowland it provided the opportunity of making a childhood dream come true.

Rowland was clearly well-informed about the evolution of the postal service; he had studied the past and had watched developments during his own lifetime. He was familiar with the peripatetic bellman who collected letters in the streets long before street letter-boxes were first introduced in Jersey in 1852 and he had long been an admirer of the enterprising contribution of Ralph Allen[4] of Bath as early as 1720 in extending communications by his cross-posts and in improving office procedures for recording all receipts and outgoings. He knew how Post Office revenue had almost doubled from £90,000 p.a. in 1688 to more than £150,000 in 1764, by which time the Exchequer had removed the service from contracting entrepreneurs to the control of the Chancellor himself for the benefit of the nation as a whole. He was equally aware of the long established milking of the postal revenue to provide pensions and gratuities for Royal favourites and others: the Earl of Rochester received £1,000 p.a.; the Duke of Marlborough £5,000 p.a.; Queen Anne's consort

£8,250 p.a.; Lord Somers £1,500 p.a.; the Duke of Leeds £2,635 p.a.; and in the late seventeenth century even the notorious Titus Oates was a beneficiary.

Nearer his own time, Rowland was much impressed by the pioneer work of John Palmer[5] in 1784 in introducing his handsome, well-made Mail Coaches which ensured that a letter posted in Bath by six o'clock in the evening would be delivered in London the next day. This innovation, Rowland must have noted with some apprehension, had at first been strongly opposed by the mandarins of the Post Office. Was it a hint of things to come?

He realised the significance of the contributions of Thomas Telford[6] and John McAdam[7] in improving communications by their fine roads, canals and bridges. Finally, in his own day, the tireless work of Robert Wallace MP for Greenock,[8] won Rowland's unstinted admiration; he openly declared that it was impossible for him to speak too strongly of his obligation to Wallace. It was Wallace who was responsible for securing the setting up of the important *Commissions of Inquiry* in 1829 and 1830 and in particular of the later *Select Committee* which published ten valuable Reports between 1835 and 1838 including Rowland's own evidence given to the Committee in person following the publication of his pamphlet, *Post Office Reform: its Importance and Practicability* in 1837.

It was Robert Wallace, incidentally, who, when Rowland was struggling to consult masses of Post Office and government documents, sent to Rowland's house a cab-load of official government *Blue Books* weighing more than two hundredweight – a generous and kindly gesture which also demonstrated to Rowland what was possible under the privileged franking system by which members of Parliament were exempt from postal charges. From a detailed study of these *Blue Books* Rowland was able to produce concrete facts and figures to support his own plan. He unearthed statistical evidence, for example, that when there had been a general reduction of tax and excise duties in 1823, the results were that the price of soap fell by one eighth; tea by one sixth; silk goods by one fifth and coffee by a quarter. At the same time the sales of soap increased by over 30 per cent; tea by 50 per cent; silks by 100 per cent and coffee by 300 per cent. These results confirmed Rowland's conviction that by reducing postal charges similar benefits would accrue to the Post Office and the nation as a whole; more jobs would become available to cope with the increase of letters; shorter working hours would become possible and an increase in wages justifiable – as indeed came to pass as Rowland's plan came into effect.

It is strange to look back to discover that the incident that triggered off Rowland's interest in the Post Office occurred in Birmingham when he was about eight years of age in 1803 – as was earlier related on page 30.

As he grew older he was struck by the waste and extravagance of the postal system, and realised that the high costs of postage not only cut off families from each other but were also handicaps to trade and business. As the years passed he began a serious investigation into the various extravagances, waste, malpractices and incompetence of the postal service and started amassing facts on which to build a case. He could see before his very eyes the appalling abuse of the 'franking' system, which was originally introduced to allow Members of Parliament and government officials to send letters free by 'franking' them with their signatures. In itself this was not an unreasonable privilege, but investigation showed how monstrously it was being abused. From 1836 onwards various committees and Rowland's own investigations began to reveal that something like £1,000,000 per annum was being lost to the Treasury by illegal franking. About that time records revealed that 'packages' like the following were franked: fifteen couples of hounds; two maid-servants; sides of bacon; a cow; a feather-bed; a horse and a piano. Many members of Parliament franked letters for their friends and relatives and gave franks as a bonus to their servants instead of additional wages. For years Parliament had been trying to eliminate these malpractices and as far back as 1771 the unfortunate Dr Dodd was hanged at Tyburn for the offence.

Another source of abuse and consequent loss of revenue followed from the regulation that letters were charged postage by the number of sheets, not by weight. Here again Rowland could see the ridiculous dodges that people adopted to avoid using a second or third sheet. To carry the cheapest postal rate a letter had to be written on one sheet; this resulted in the almost illegible but economical practice of 'cross-writing', which involved writing over the page at right angles to the original script. If a second, separate sheet was used, or even if the tiniest scrap of paper were enclosed, then the postage was doubled. If an envelope was used, it was held up for examination in front of a candle in a darkened room – a process called 'candling'. This at once led to dishonest practices for if the presence of a bank-note seemed to be indicated, the postal clerk could quietly extract it for his own benefit.

But the clerk had to do more than merely 'candling'; he had to check that the destination of the letter did not exceed the permitted mileage; if it did then the postal charge was increased. It was clearly a laborious, time-wasting and expensive use of manpower. To defeat the heavy cost of sending letters and business communications all sorts of cunning ruses were employed, and a whole army of smugglers and 'fixers' came into being. For example, London business firms often combined to send one large sheet of paper containing orders and correspondence from perhaps fifty different offices. This was sent at the lowest postal rate i.e. as for one sheet, to an agent say in Birmingham or Manchester, who would then cut out the separate items and despatch them to their respective destinations by local delivery-boys. Investigations revealed that five-sixths of Manchester's letters were thus illegally carried and delivered at a great loss to the Treasury. More startling still, it came to light that the first mail delivery to New York by steamship carried only five letters in the official bag, but ten thousand in illegal unofficial bags.

To Rowland Hill's sharp, questioning mind, postal regulations that made possible practices like these were unintelligent and stupid and were losing vast sums of revenue every year. The more he found out, the more eager he was to pursue his own investigations. For example, existing records had shown that it took the postman at least five minutes to knock at a front door, hand in a letter and receive and record payment. Commercial houses in London found this to be quite unacceptable; quicker deliveries were vital for trade. A test case provided astonishing evidence; it was found that it took a postman 1½ hours to deliver 67 letters when he had to wait for payment, whereas he could deliver 570 in half an hour if he did not have to wait at the door for the cash settlement. A further weakness of the prevailing system was that the handling of a considerable sum of money in the course of his round made the postman an easy victim to street-robbers and the like.

By studying statistical data in the Blue Books Rowland suddenly realised that the length of a letter's journey made no appreciable difference to the cost, which proved to him that a uniform postal rate was economically justifiable. This alone would save an enormous waste of time and labour as at one stroke some forty variations in postal rate based on distance were eliminated. From the evidence before him Rowland saw that his golden rule had to be simplification. For example, by introducing pre-payment of postage, thus limiting the postman's task merely to delivering letters, he was later led to the next logical step of requiring every house and all business premises to have a letter box. This simple step cut out any waiting on the doorstep on the part of the postman. Even a harmless innovation like this in due course brought an irate letter from a noble lord who objected to having to cut a hole in his expensive mahogany front door.

Conscious of the weight of evidence he had amassed, and sensing the rising strength of public feeling in support of his ideas, Rowland and his backers felt that the tide was running strongly in their favour and that the moment had arrived for vigorous action. So, following the publication of Rowland's pamphlet *Post Office Reform; its Importance and Practicability* in its four editions between January 1837 and 1838, a massive offensive was started on all fronts.

Inspired and initiated by William Scholefield, a former Hazelwood pupil who in 1838 had become the first Charter Mayor of Birmingham on its being granted corporate status, petitions began to pour into Parliament demanding the passing of Rowland Hill's *Penny Postage Bill*. They came from every quarter; town councils, Chambers of Commerce, the ancient Livery Companies, industrial establishments, Mechanics' Institutes, professional bodies and learned societies. On behalf of the city of London, the commercial heart of the nation, George Grote, the historian and for long a staunch supporter of Hazelwood and the talented Hill family, presented a petition of 1,200 signatures. Reflecting similar interests the newly formed but extremely influential *Mercantile Committee* of the city of London, conceived by Henry Cole (later Sir Henry Cole),[9] published a powerful broadsheet which was distributed throughout the land; 2,000 copies were sent to MPs; over a hundred thousand were sold or otherwise distributed, and 40,000 copies were sent out with the thirteenth instalment of Dickens' *Nicholas Nickleby* then the latest best seller.

The Times newspaper also came out in powerful support: in March 1839 its leading article claimed that all classes and all parties supported the Bill, but it was being blocked by a small coterie of placeholders in St Martin's le Grand.

In the event the *Penny Postage Bill* secured three readings in the Commons without much difficulty, as MPs knew that the country as a whole was ardently in favour of the measure. But there were fears that the ensuing passage through the House of Lords might be more difficult, so the influential *Mercantile Committee* got to work on members of the Upper House. Rowland was persuaded to write personally to the Duke of Wellington outlining his case, and in spite of earlier doubts and fears the Duke duly voted for the measure.

On the fateful day the Bill was presented to the assembled Lords and to everyone's relief it passed its first reading immediately. In due course the second and third readings were carried and on 17 August 1839 the Act received the Royal Assent.

After years of toil, helped and encouraged by his united family, including his wife Caroline who had often commenced her day at 4.00 am summarising and transcribing vital information from the Blue Books, Rowland finally achieved his greatest triumph; his *Penny Postage Act* was at last on the Statute Book. Alas, his troubles were about to begin.

[70]

Acting swiftly Rowland's staunchest supporters, Robert Wallace and Henry Warburton, both wrote personally to the Prime Minister, Lord Melbourne, urging him to appoint Rowland to a senior post in the Post Office so that he could start immediately to implement his plan. Within days the Chancellor of the Exchequer, Francis Baring, summoned Rowland to Downing Street where he received him most courteously and offered him a temporary appointment as a head clerk in the Treasury at a salary of £500 p.a. We have already read how Rowland and his brother reacted to this insult, with the result that a few days later a chastened Chancellor raised the salary to £1,500. In the following letter of confirmation it was made clear that Rowland, though a Treasury official, 'would have access to the Post Office', but would have to make all communications and comments through the Treasury, who would then pass on its instructions to the Post Office. It was also made clear that the appointment would be temporary for two years, 'with no claim or expectations of future employment'.

Smouldering with indignation Rowland accepted these humiliating conditions for he was confident that his talents and efficiency would be immediately recognised and that a permanent Post Office appointment would follow. So on 16 September 1839 he began his duties at the Treasury and the Chancellor himself accompanied Rowland on his very first visit to the exclusive and hallowed halls of St Martin's le Grand. Up to that moment he had always had a curt refusal to any request he had made to see something of the working of the Post Office.

Rowland realised that a visit by the Chancellor would have put the whole office on its best behaviour and that everything would be done to impress the august visitor. Quietly Rowland assessed everything he saw, soon noticing that the sorting of letters was carried out too slowly, largely because of the cramped conditions of work, even though the building was only ten years old. Brought up in the equable temperatures of the Hazelwood air-duct heating system he found the rooms unbearably hot and ill-ventilated; the temperature registered around 90°F. He discussed these and other matters with the Chancellor and suggested that an additional floor should be added to the building; this was eventually done. From his senior colleagues at the Post Office he received a cool but courteous welcome; after all, the Chancellor was present.

The next time Rowland entered the building to have a further look around it was at 6.00 am – much to the dismay of the office cleaners. More than two hours later the clerks and senior officers started to arrive, somewhat shaken by this unwonted visitation. Thereafter Rowland regularly began work at 7.00 am in his office at the Treasury but he made frequent visits to the Post Office to study methods and procedures.

[71]

His critical eye soon revealed the fact that there were actually too many sorters for the load of work; he would deal with that in due course.

Before the end of September Rowland was able to persuade the Chancellor that he needed more assistance to enable him to do the job properly, so his lively and dynamic friend, Henry Cole, the power behind the London *Mercantile Committee*, was appointed as his personal assistant. A clerk was also appointed at 30 shillings a week, though Rowland Hill had suggested the figure of 40 shillings. Nevertheless the Chancellor proved to be a good friend and a staunch supporter, for he soon arranged for Rowland to visit the French Post Office in Paris in the company of George Wynn, a clerk in the Inland Section of the Post Office, to widen his background. Rowland already knew something of French practices which in some respects were considerably ahead of Britain's, and when in Paris he looked particularly at their system of registered post for the safe transit of money and valuables and at their department dealing with Money Orders. This gave him some useful ideas for future developments at home.

In the general euphoria following the passing of the Act some occasional discordant voices were heard. The *Quarterly Review*, for instance, delivered a comprehensive broadside at Rowland's plan, at the *Mercantile Committee*, at the Commons' *Select Committee* and its misguided witnesses, and at the government itself. The article maintained that far from benefiting the nation, Rowland's plan made sedition and subversion easier, and that the proposed prepayment of postage by adhesive stamps was inconvenient and quite unacceptable to the general public. Much to its surprise the *Quarterly* found itself completely outgunned, shot to pieces by the logic, irony and legal astuteness of a swingeing rejoinder in the next issue of the formidable *Edinburgh Review*. Its author was none other than Matthew Davenport Hill, QC who in the best Hill family manner, instantly rallied to his brother Rowland's support: the Hills were hydra-headed.

On 10 January 1840 the great moment came when a universal penny postage was declared for the whole country. On the first day 112,000 letters were posted and all but 1,400 had been pre-paid. There were tremendous crowds in the streets celebrating the occasion, and the police were called in to keep the highways open. The young Queen Victoria marked the event by publicly renouncing her privilege of franking. Rowland's old art-master at Hazelwood, Samuel Lines,[10] celebrated the occasion in his own peculiar way; he rapped on the Post Office window in Birmingham as the chimes of midnight ushered in the historic 10 January and handed the sleepy duty-clerk a letter with a penny for its postage declaring 'It's a penny today, I believe'.

Stamped stationery, letter-sheets and envelopes bearing William Mulready's famous allegorical design were on sale early in May 1840, with Rowland Hill's alternative of the adhesive stamp bearing the young Queen's portrait. Rather to his surprise Rowland found that it was the adhesive stamp that won most approval, and soon it was clear that the age of the popular postage stamp had come to stay. In the production of the stamps and letter-sheets, involving some highly skilled design and printing work, Rowland had greatly benefited from the services of his brother, Edwin, since January 1840, as Superintendent of the Stamp Office. It was through Edwin's engineering skill and tremendous drive that the stamp – the Penny Black – and the letter-sheets were ready for sale in so short a time. To make sure of this Edwin worked eighteen hours a day for weeks on end – a striking example of the Hills' loyalty and team work.

The Penny Black was the world's first adhesive postage stamp. They were printed on large sheets and had to be cut from these by hand before becoming individual stamps. Presses turned out 500,000 stamps a day but this did not satisfy demand. In two years the number of letters passing through the post rose from over seventy million to over two hundred million. As the postage charge was now so cheap, illicit franking and other illegal expedients withered away. The whole operation was an immense success as figures were later to show; between 1840 and 1855 a total of seven thousand million stamps were printed – all under the supervision of Edwin Hill.

When Melbourne's Whig administration was thrown out by Sir Robert Peel in 1841, the Tory takeover caused difficulties for Rowland. The Post officials, inspired, no doubt, by the hostility to Rowland Hill and his reforms on the part of their master, Colonel Maberly, the autocratic ex-officer of the 76th Regiment of Foot, quietly relapsed into a policy of passive resistance and non-cooperation. By these transparently obstructive tactics they held up decisions, left communications unanswered for weeks, mislaid important documents and even falsified statistical returns. A typical instance occurred when Rowland had occasion to look into the working of the Money Order department, following a request to award an increase in salary and to authorise the services of an extra clerk to the regional postmasters. It was claimed that the heavy demands made on the staff of these particular departments merited the request, which was also supported by the two District Surveyors (or Inspectors) concerned. As usual Rowland demanded some exact figures before he would make a decision. It took a whole year before his queries received an answer; in one case the postmaster had been required to issue three money orders per day, and in the other, only two per day.

Rowland flatly turned down the requests; after spending twenty-five years as a schoolmaster he was too canny a bird to be bamboozled by schoolboy tricks like this.

The non-cooperation of the Post Office officials soon became plain for all to see; it represented a strong signal to the Chancellor of the Exchequer that Rowland Hill was probably proving to be a difficult man to work with. Sensing the tension around him Rowland began to be concerned about his two year temporary appointment. During August 1841 he made repeated calls on the Chancellor, Francis Baring,[11] pressing for confirmation of his promised permanent appointment. Shortly before he had to leave the Chancellorship Baring wrote a very friendly letter to Rowland expressing his entire satisfaction with his work and extending his appointment for a third year – but still temporary. Almost immediately there was a change of government and Sir Robert Peel and his Tories assumed office once again. The new Chancellor was Henry Goulburn,[12] MP for the University of Cambridge, a staunch Tory and a man of integrity. At his first meeting Rowland found him to be cautious and resistant; he turned down Rowland's plea to be allowed to communicate with the Postmaster General direct, and not through the Treasury. Nothing daunted Rowland took his case direct to the newly appointed Postmaster General, Lord Lowther,[13] but he found him to be cold and suspicious and this very soon turned into open hostility.

Rowland could feel the ground crumbling under his feet; he knew that a number of influential people were trying to discredit and to annul his whole plan on grounds of alarming decline in revenue. But Rowland had always warned every government that initial losses were inevitable; given time, everything would come right. When in 1842 the Treasury asked him to supply accurate figures on the Post Office financial position, he found it impossible to obtain them. Incomplete records, suspected and sometimes, it seemed, deliberate falsifications and general non-cooperation made Rowland's position almost impossible; the termination of his third year appointment now seemed inevitable. Then to Robert Peel's credit in March 1842, the Prime Minister publicly stated that in spite of the loss of revenue following the introduction of penny postage, the government were not considering reverting to the old system, nor increasing the postage to twopence, as all were agreed that the penny rate was a deliberate experiment adopted by the previous government and needed time to prove itself.

Peel's Chancellor, Henry Goulburn, appeared to have endorsed the general go-slow policy, for he blankly refused to do anything to improve the rural postal service as had been agreed by his predecessor, Francis Baring, before he left office in September 1841. Try as he may

Rowland was never able to get an explanation for what he saw as a clear dereliction of duty which condemned huge areas of rural Britain to be virtually without any postal service.

Next, Rowland could see that he would soon be attacked on the rising costs of switching long-distance mails from coach to the railways which were then rapidly developing. Prudently he made a close examination of the costs involved and found that sheer inefficiency was largely responsible for the increases. To take one example, he found in one area that two railway compartments, capable of holding sixteen passengers were being reserved and extravagantly paid for simply to transport two or three mail-bags. On the strength of this and many similar discoveries he asked the Chancellor to require the Post Office to carry out a comprehensive investigation backed up by accurate returns. Nothing happened; to the end of his career he never received this information.

In the course of his probings Rowland discovered that many provincial post-masters were embezzling thousands of pounds every year, chiefly by falsifying their Money Order accounts. He was able to deal with this himself by demanding daily settlement of all Money Order transactions which were then recorded and checked by Head Office, and were subject to quarterly audits.

In 1841, the Postmaster General, Lord Lowther, insisted on implementing his own scheme for the compulsory registration of money and valuables sent by post. Rowland disapproved; he considered the postal charges to be unreasonably high. He therefore wrote a long letter to Lord Lowther outlining his own scheme and asking for an interview to explain it further. The Postmaster General agreed to this, but at the interview Rowland realised that his detailed arguments had never been carefully studied. With his bulldog persistence Rowland asked for a further interview, seeking permission to go ahead with his own plan which he undertook to implement without upsetting Post Office routine and without incurring greater expense. By this time Lord Lowther had lost patience with Rowland's relentless badgering and bluntly told him so. Smarting from this rebuff Rowland consulted the family council who urged him to consider telling the Chancellor and Lord Lowther that unless his own plan was adopted he would send in his resignation – a bold and cheeky action from one whose extension of his temporary appointment was still in jeopardy.

Things went from bad to worse; he had little support in the Post Office and he knew that Lord Lowther had now got his knife into him. Then in September 1842 the Prime Minister, Robert Peel, curtly dismissed him from his post without even a perfunctory golden handshake or expression of gratitude. Bitterly hurt and disappointed Rowland offered

to work for the implementation of his plan without salary, but his offer
was refused.

There was an immediate outcry in the Liberal newspapers and his
many supporters rallied around him; the *Mercantile Committee* joined the
fray, but resistance in Parliament was too strong. Rowland found himself
unemployed, but as if by a stroke of providence, within a few months
out of the blue came the offer of a Directorship with the *London and
Brighton Railway Company*, with the results we have recorded in another
chapter. The general disgust felt far and wide over Rowland's dismissal
was admirably summed up by a comment made by the poet Thomas
Hood[14]:

> It would never surprise me, after such an instance of folly and ingratitude,
> to hear of the railway people some day finding their trains running so well,
> proposing to discharge their engines.

But the public's reaction was more than one of disgust; they were
eager to demonstrate their gratitude and loyalty and gladly rallied to the
Mercantile Committee's nation-wide appeal for an appropriate testimonial
to the man who had already done so much for them in creating the
penny post. Within a few years the sum of £13,000 was raised and two
months after resigning from the *London and Brighton Railway* Rowland
was presented with the cheque at a grand ceremony at Blackwall on
17 June 1846, attended by old Thomas Wright Hill, then eighty-three
years of age, and by Rowland's four brothers. One of the last actions
of Peel's mean-spirited administration before its leader resigned on
29 June 1846 was to insist that Rowland paid income-tax on his £13,000
testimonial. But after an immediate appeal by Rowland, guided no
doubt by his brother Matthew, the demand was withdrawn. Perhaps
Robert Peel carried the day, for although he had always been hostile to
Rowland's plan for penny postage, it is good to record that, with some
magnanimity, he had personally subscribed to the testimonial.

On the fall of Peel's Tory government in 1846 Lord John Russell
became Prime Minister and things began to move in Rowland's favour.
Continued ill-health caused Rowland to resign from his post as Director
and Chairman of the *London and Brighton Railway* in March 1846,
a month before the amalgamation took place creating the *London,
Brighton and South Coast Railway*. In November he was summoned back
to the Post Office itself. This came about through the good offices of his
friend Henry Warburton,[15] MP who as Secretary of the *Select Committee*
in 1843 had been deeply impressed by the strength of Rowland's case
so ably presented and argued in committee and later recorded in 134
folio pages of the Report. Warburton was able to persuade the new

Postmaster General, Lord Clanricarde, and the Chancellor of the Exchequer to appoint Rowland to the newly designated post of *Secretary to the Postmaster General*. This was a gratifying come-back with enhanced status, but it still left Colonel Maberly as *Secretary to the Post Office* to whom Rowland was subordinate both in rank and salary. He was not yet out of the wood.

The Postmaster General, Lord Clanricarde, was a man of principle and very receptive to new ideas. He was well-disposed to Rowland and tried to allay his fears of difficulties with Maberly by assuring him that 'at no distant period' he would be promoted to higher authority. But Rowland still had misgivings; he had been through all this once before. Moreover he was now fifty-one years of age and had already been battling for his plan for nearly ten years; he doubted whether in his present state of health he had the resilience and determination to continue the fight indefinitely. A solution could only come about by Maberly's departure from the scene; as early as 1841 he had told his superiors that his plan could never be implemented unless Colonel Maberly were persuaded to retire or promoted to a better-paid post outside the Post Office. Over the years Rowland kept repeating this but his masters always said they could not do it.

On 5 December 1846 Lord Clanricarde accompanied Rowland to meet his future colleagues, this time as a member of the Post Office staff. He was received correctly but coolly by Colonel Maberly. When on the following Wednesday Rowland began his duties he found on his desk a personal letter from the Postmaster General, ostensibly referring to routine office matters, but informing Rowland quite clearly that he was forbidden to refer to, or ask for, any papers, memos or letters without first putting his request in writing for the prior permission of both the Postmaster General and Colonel Maberly. Dismayed and angry Rowland straightaway called on the Postmaster General to demand an explanation. Lord Clanricarde was sheepishly apologetic and tried to dismiss the incident as of no significance. Rowland had made his point and withdrew.

He next discovered that Colonel Maberly's assistant and several clerks in his office were able to obtain any papers and letters without difficulty. It began to dawn on Rowland that these and other restrictions and obstacles were deliberately put in his way as a retaliation for the embarrassment to the Post Office and its senior officials caused as far back as 1843 when he had exposed the unscrupulous 'fallacious return' made by them in a Parliamentary report to weaken Rowland's case. This refers to some deliberately misleading financial information attributing to the Post Office a loss of £10,000 per annum instead of a profit of

[77]

£600,000. This was contrived by including foreign and colonial postage revenue in the accounts for the first time, and it was here the massive losses were made. Rowland was never forgiven for this exposure.

During his investigations Rowland unearthed many systematic frauds and promptly dealt with the problem. Then in his quest for economies he issued a smaller and simpler Money Order form thereby hoping to save £700 per annum. But the Stationery Office objected to this interference and pointed out that the new forms on their own would cost £1,500 more than the existing ones. Rowland instantly challenged this and was able to prove his point through his intimate knowledge of printing processes and costs – a legacy of his Hazelwood days. Eventually through the changes he introduced he achieved a saving of £2,500 per annum – a small sum in relation to the Post Office's total budget, but nevertheless a victory on principle. His investigations revealed unbelievable carelessness and dilatoriness in the return of 'pro formas' and in answering letters. At one Yorkshire Post Office over forty unanswered letters were found languishing in a drawer, some over six months old.

In spite of these problems and shortcomings the postal service showed an astonishing growth in the first eight years of Penny Postage; the number of letters in the post rose from 76 million in 1839 to 322 million in 1847. But the constant strain of the tug-of-war arising from dual control in the Post Office was beginning to have an adverse effect on Rowland's already precarious health, so once again he reminded his masters of their promise to regularise his position 'at no distant period' – six months being understood. He saw the Chancellor personally and the latter confirmed his earlier promise that Rowland would soon succeed Colonel Maberly in the post of Secretary to the Post Office but regretted that at the moment there was no alternative post for the Colonel.

In January 1849, returning to the attack, he wrote a long letter to the Postmaster General drawing the latter's attention to the impossible difficulties he was facing through the concerted obstructionism of his colleagues. He enumerated fifteen significant improvements he had introduced in spite of these obstructions. These, he suggested, were ample proof of the administrative effectiveness that was required of him before his promotion could be implemented. Lord Clanricarde in due course sent a courteous but seemingly inevitable reply – 'I see no possibility of a change at present. . .'.

Soon real troubles were to descend upon Rowland – 'the most painful and unhappy period of my life'. Having refused salary increases to his Post Office employees in his zeal to keep expenses down, knowing that this was his Achilles' heel, he next turned his attention to Sunday working. Rowland was genuinely anxious to reduce, if not eliminate, these unpopular duties. After a few experiments he decided to close 450 Money Order offices altogether on Sundays. He also limited other Sunday working by closing all Post Offices between 10.00 am and 5.00 pm. He claimed that this would give 'some thousands needful rest and the opportunity of attending the services of the day'. Rowland went out of his way to pay tribute to Colonel Maberly for supporting him in this matter.

But these policies did not please the Press nor the *Lord's Day Society* as the latter was standing out for the complete abolition of all Sunday working, and in next to no time a venomous campaign was whipped up, completely ignoring the fact that Rowland's proposals had done much to protect the interests of the workers and the religious factions. A number of Bishops weighed in with righteous indignation, never having studied the true facts, but blindly accepting the public and Press rumpus as being based on truth. Rowland wrote a long letter to *The Times* and this gradually influenced the Press as a whole as well as the general public. Within the Post Office antagonism persisted in spite of their being aware that by January 1850 the team of Sunday workers in London had been reduced to three volunteers with ten extra being brought in either before 5.00 am or after 8.00 pm.

In this whole unhappy episode great credit is due to *The Times* for dispassionately reviewing the whole question. In its issue of 25 April 1850 it showed conclusively how Rowland had fought long and hard to protect the Sabbath and the postal workers without inflicting inconvenience to the public. With its usual trenchant irony *The Times* wrote:

> Even vaccination was never described as a device for actually perpetuating small-pox, whereas the most judicious and effective step in a series of measures expressly designed to abridge Sunday labour has been thus, in the middle of the 19th century represented, taken and accepted as a deliberate stratagem for destroying the holiness of the Sabbath day.

In January 1851 Rowland had an interview with the Chancellor once again and reminded him of his promise, but all the Chancellor could say was that he could not possibly move Colonel Maberly until a suitable vacancy became available; Rowland had to be patient. But Rowland had already lost his patience and persisted with his argument until the Chancellor in exasperation said 'We may talk like this until we are black in the face but it's no use. I can't do it yet'. To keep Rowland quiet he said he would raise Rowland's salary and give him all the additional clerical assistance he required and in addition would authorise the appointment of some members

[79]

of Rowland's own family. Concealing his astonishment at this strange turn of events Rowland drily informed the Chancellor that if he asked for the same amount of clerical help that Colonel Maberly enjoyed it would cost the Exchequer £10,000. At the time all the assistance Rowland had was a private secretary and four or five clerks whereas the Colonel had a private secretary, an assistant secretary and fifty or sixty clerks.

However Rowland took the Chancellor at his word and secured the appointment of his brother Frederic as his assistant; his own son Pearson was already in the department. But he kept up the pressure and contrived that Richard Cobden,[16] the anti Corn Law reformer, and Mr Moffatt, representing the still active *Mercantile Committee*, secured interviews with the Chancellor on his behalf. By this time the Chancellor declared he was thoroughly 'fed up' with the harassment he was being subjected to; four visitations within two days was a little excessive.

The whirligig of politics then brought a change of government in 1852 and Rowland had to begin all over again with a new Postmaster General, Lord Hardwicke, an ex-admiral who slowed up the business of the office by gratuitous red-tape. He tried to run the place like a warship, demanding ridiculous returns as for example, how many fires were lighted daily. When Rowland raised the inevitable question of the difficulties of dual control he found that his new chief was fully convinced that Maberly was superior to Rowland in status: 'there cannot be two kings in Brentford' he was wont to declare.

Rowland made sure that Lord Hardwicke was fully acquainted with the promises made to him, pointing out that he had now been fobbed off for five years. As a sop to Rowland's importunity the powers that be eventually made a recommendation that he should be put on actual parity with Colonel Maberly as a *Joint Secretary to the Post Office*. But this did not satisfy Rowland, and he made his views clear: nothing less than complete autonomy was acceptable.

This was not mere vaulting ambition; it was not a thirst for power for its own sake, but merely to be able to implement his plan unimpeded by lesser mortals. After all, his personal sacrifices proved his integrity. Even in 1851 his Post Office salary was only £1,500 per annum; back as early as 1839, no doubt on the strength of his and Edwin's patented Rotary Printing press, he had been offered a partnership with Messrs Clowes, a leading printing house, at a remuneration of at least £2,500 per annum. Again, when he left the *London and Brighton Railway Company* in 1846 he was earning over £3,000 per annum in salary and Directorships, and on leaving he was offered the well-paid post of

Chairman of the *South Western Railway Company*. In addition in the same year he was presented with a nationally raised Testimonial of £13,000. In other words he had achieved reasonable financial independence. Moreover, he had more than once offered to work without salary for the Post Office if he were given a free hand to implement his plan of postal reform. In short, such single-minded dedication to an ideal untarnished by considerations of personal gain is difficult to match.

But soon the long battle of attrition was at last to be resolved. It started in the usual manner, with Rowland yet again presenting his closely argued case to the new Postmaster General, Lord Canning, who had promised to pass his appeal to higher authority. In his long letter of 18 June 1853 Rowland painstakingly recapitulated the events of his whole career, from his temporary post for two years with the Treasury in 1839 right up to the present moment. He claimed that the records showed that he and Frederic (who had been appointed in 1851) had already saved the government at least £100,000 per annum, which he was convinced would shortly rise to £200,000. The general expansion of the service, its improved efficiency and the vast increase in the number of letters carried were already well-known; and all this had been achieved in the face of unbelievable opposition and obstruction in every quarter.

Lord Canning was duly impressed and faithfully reported Rowland's case to the Chancellor of the Exchequer and even to the Prime Minster, Lord Aberdeen. Yet again came the usual 'brush-off'; no change could take place until a suitable vacancy was found for Colonel Maberly. Rowland was near to despair, but out of the blue relief at last came. In April 1854 a high-level vacancy became vacant in the Audit Office and Colonel Maberly was happy to accept it. Then in May Rowland was notified that he was forthwith being promoted to the post of Secretary to the Post Office at a salary of £2,000 per annum. It had taken Rowland fifteen gruelling years, from the time of his first temporary appointment in 1839, to reach the top, but he did not allow his moment of triumph to deflect him from his further goals.

He first directed his attention to the use of the rapidly developing railway systems for the carrying of mail, of which he had obtained some pioneering experience with the *London and Brighton Railway Company* back in the years 1843/46. Extremely complicated legal problems had to be tackled of which the ordinary person had no conception. For example, before a letter could be sent by rail from London to John O'Groats no fewer than twenty-one separate railway contracts had to be negotiated. There was also a constant battle to prevent railway companies from demanding exorbitant fees for the carriage of mails; the prevailing 'Railway mania' made investors insatiable for large, quick profits on their investments.

To meet this situation Rowland cunningly encouraged competition between the railway companies to speed up their time-tables; he knew all about this from his Brighton days. Soon the *North Western Railway* beat their rivals the *Great Northern* by achieving an average speed of 40 mph including stoppages – a vast improvement on the prevailing 27 mph. Next he experimented with a device for improving the automatic pick-up and delivery of mail-bags at speed. He relates how it seemed as if half the population of Yorkshire turned up at Northallerton Station to witness a demonstration. The pick-up and delivery operation happened so quickly that many people doubted that anything had happened. Rowland's son, Pearson, later made some significant improvements in the device and very soon a much more effective automatic system was introduced with considerable success.

Rowland had long been anxious to improve conditions of service for his employees. As we noted on page 41, he and Frederic initiated improved salary scales and better conditions of service for all postal employees in 1852, and this in turn influenced Civil Service salaries as a whole, giving the service a truly professional status.

All the time Rowland was improving other aspects of the postal service. For instance he introduced a properly organised first-delivery in London at 9.00 am instead of the former 11.30, and this was soon further improved to 8.00 am. Apart from the introduction of house letter-boxes as already mentioned he also agitated for a reform of street names and house numbering. His annual reports illustrated some of the difficulties facing sorters and postmen. In the city itself there were 50 *King Streets*, 50 *Queen Streets*, 60 *John Streets* and so on and in some streets up to seven different houses carried the same number. One house had an elegant brass plate bearing the number 95 but the adjacent houses were numbered 14 and 16. Inquiries revealed that the householder had put up the number of his previous house as he liked the brass plate too much to throw it away.

The extensive expansion of services that Rowland was working on during the 1850s still provoked the usual opposition and even quiet sabotage from many of the Post Office staff, and this nagging battle took its toll on Rowland's health. On top of this a few active malcontents, usually employees who had missed promotion because of their incompetence and general sloth, embarked upon a bitter and unprincipled campaign against him by distributing scurrilous handbills and placards and by publishing defamatory articles in the Press. Quite in the modern manner headlines and slogans screamed their venomous message:

WHITE SLAVES OF THE POST OFFICE:
AGITATE, AGITATE!

The frenzy of some of the agitators knew no bounds and three serious threats of assassination were made in the years 1854, 1856 and 1858. In 1856 Rowland was warned by anonymous letter that he would be shot on a certain named day. With courageous contempt he threw caution to the winds and steadfastly refused to alter his daily routine and followed his usual route to the Post Office as normal – a horse-bus to Grays Inn Lane, Holborn, then a walk to his office in St Martins le Grand. He had no bodyguard and carried only his customary umbrella, declaring 'but of this I was determined to make, if necessary, good use, believing that if properly handled it would prove a very formidable, not to say deadly, weapon'. Rowland had not forgotten the fencing classes he had organised at Hazelwood over thirty years earlier, when he used to demonstrate the efficacy of the quick thrust in preference to a clumsy slash. Happily he was not called upon to put his confidence to the test.

In spite of the small handful of confirmed trouble-makers the majority of the Post Office work force were Rowland's loyal and enthusiastic supporters; they appreciated what he had done for them as regards conditions and hours of work, in salaries, career prospects and in his humane concern for their well-being. Gradually a new professional pride was being created among the Post Office employees, which contributed to the universal admiration in which the British Civil Service came to be held, and still is held, throughout the world. Rowland Hill, it was said, had 'inspired the department with a new spirit and founded a new school of officials.' The Post Office had come of age.

A striking example of such devoted loyalty and high morale, for long typical of the service, occurred when the mail-steamer, *VIOLET*, foundered in the English Channel in 1855. The Post Office employee responsible for the security of the mail, a Mr Mortleman, seeing that the ship was sinking, ordered all the boxes of mail to be brought up on deck. When the vessel eventually sank with considerable loss of life, including that of the faithful Mr Mortleman, the sealed boxes remained afloat and all but one were recovered.[17]

With his appointment as Secretary to the Post Office in April 1854 Rowland had at last reached the summit of his hopes, but he still found himself in turbulent waters. Bitter wrangles arose over complicated issues of railway charges, and over the financial arrangements covering Money Orders, bringing him into conflict with Frank Scudamore the champion of cross-subsidies. Then in 1858 a real deterioration in health set in and on the advice of two medical consultants Rowland was compelled to take a long leave and then radically reduce his hours of work – a prescription that his active mind found irksome.·He struggled on but was forced to take occasional complete breaks. Soon his medical advisers felt bound to advise him to retire, which he eventually did in March 1864. But once he was relieved of the day to day pressures he gradually regained his strength and from 1865 to 1867 he was able to play a valuable part on the *Royal Commission on Railways*. During these years he also organised his voluminous records, writing his Memoirs and compiling with the help of his brother, Arthur, his *History of Penny Postage*.

Honours had been showered upon him beginning with the Freedom of the City of Aberdeen as early as 1844. In 1857 he was elected *Fellow of the Royal Society*, and in 1860, with the support of Lord Palmerston and Lord Elgin, he was knighted with a KCB by Queen Victoria. In 1864 the *University of Oxford* honoured him with the degree of DCL – a gesture that was a matter of real pride and joy to him, the self-educated outsider. In the same year he became the first holder of the *Albert Gold Medal of the Society of Arts*. On his retirement in 1864 Parliament awarded him his full salary as a pension for life, together with a special grant of £20,000 as a token of appreciation for what he had done for the people of Britain.

The final touching scene in the drama of Rowland Hill's life occurred in 1879 when he was honoured with the Freedom of the City of London. Too feeble to make the journey to the Mansion House, Rowland was visited at his Hampstead home by a deputation of city worthies. In a simple but moving ceremony he listened to the City Chamberlain's closing words with tears streaming down his cheeks:

> May your remaining days be consoled by the thought that your name and services can never be forgotten, and may the sunset of your life be brightened by the reflection that you have been permitted to become one of the greatest benefactors of mankind.

Similar tributes from every quarter expressed the gratitude that was felt for Rowland's great work. His old Chief, Lord Clanricarde, referring to the handsome monetary gift given to Rowland by the government declared:

> Upon the whole this country had never rewarded by a grant of money any public servant who more richly deserved it. . . . Rowland Hill's name

would live in every country, for every country had derived benefit from his labours.

In September 1879 W. E. Gladstone echoed these sentiments when he declared:

> . . . his great plan ran like wildfire through the civilized world, and never, perhaps, was a local invention . . . and improvement applied in the lifetime of its author for the advantage of such a vast multitude of his fellow-creatures.

Before he died Rowland Hill had the satisfaction of seeing a spectacular worldwide expansion of his Penny Postage scheme which was soon adopted throughout the globe. Before long it had covered 107 countries, states, colonies and dependencies, beginning with Brazil in 1843 then spreading year by year throughout the New World, Australia, West Indies, Africa and the Far East.

The final word can appropriately be those of his grandson, Colonel H. W. Hill, CMG, DSO, who with proper pride says:

> His name will be recorded in letters of gold among the very foremost of those great Englishmen who have, directly or indirectly, made the greatest contribution to the development of science, literature, and commerce, whilst at the same time vastly increasing the sum of happiness of the poorest of the poor.

[VI]

Rowland Hill And Thomas Arnold

THE account given in the opening chapter of Rowland Hill's innovations at Hazelwood School revealed the tremendous gulf between the education provided by the Public Schools and that offered by the Hills. But even in the restricted area of the Public Schools a dramatic change was soon to take place when in 1828 Dr Thomas Arnold entered upon the Headmastership of Rugby School. Arnold was an unusually vivid charismatic figure, and by his sheer personal magnetism and persuasive Christian ideals he brought about a profound transformation in Rugby that gave a new image to the Public Schools. The long-established ones at least paid lip-service to his message, but, more important, a rapidly growing number of new boarding schools began to spring up throughout the country. They all, to greater or lesser degree, attempted to reflect something of the Arnold idea which made the ethical teachings of evangelical Christianity the main plank of a new educational outlook. But Arnold made an impact that went beyond the world of education; he gained early notoriety as an outspoken critic of the Established Church and as a radical reformer in social and political fields – a dangerous mixture for the Headmaster of a famous Public School.

What Thomas Arnold achieved at Rugby in a comparatively short time invested him with the aura of a guru around whom a legend was born, leading to an absurdly uncritical assessment of his work as an educationist. No one would deny his outstanding contribution to the moral side of education, nor would anyone challenge his rare gifts as a teacher of pupils of high academic potential. But as an innovator of developments in the content of education – in the curriculum – the evidence shows that he was less of a giant than his admirers tended to believe.

The originator of the Arnold legend, some would say myth, was his close friend, Dr Arthur Stanley,[1] who entered Rugby as a boy in 1829, during Arnold's second year; by 1831 Stanley had become Arnold's archetypal *Praepositor*. The two had much in common and the adolescent

[86]

Stanley frankly admits that Arnold became the 'lodestar of my life . . . I fear I have passed the limit and made him my idol'. Stanley's classic biographical study *'The Life and Correspondence of Thomas Arnold'* was first published in 1844, within two years of his master's death, when the author was still numb with grief at the loss of his idol. It seems unlikely that a truly objective study could have been produced in such circumstances. But the book made a big impression on the cosy, inbred world of the Public Schools, Oxford and the Church of England, and so the legend took root. Dr Stanley quite naturally stressed the moral and spiritual leadership Arnold gave to nineteenth-century education. In the matter of curriculum Stanley was clearly out of his depth, but he unfortunately created the myth that Arnold was also one of the greatest innovators in the field of the content of education. He completely ignored what Arnold owed to his predecessors whose interesting novel developments can be traced back at least to the 1790s.

For instance, creditable short dramatic productions were staged on Parents' evenings as early as 1791 during the headmastership of Dr Thomas James. These were kept up by his successor, Dr Henry Ingles and by Arnold's immediate predecessor, Dr J. Wool, stimulated in the latter case by the keenness and expertise of a talented young pupil, William Charles Macready, who was later to grace the English stage with his versatile talents.

Among other activities promoted by Dr James in the 1790s were Art, fencing and dancing, available as 'extras'; in the classroom lessons were given in Scripture-History, Roman and British History, some English literature as well as Speech and Declamation; French and advanced mathematics could also be taken as 'extras'.

All these interesting developments were ignored by Dr Stanley in his classic biography of Thomas Arnold. Speaking of what he deemed to be Arnold's progressive views he declares:

> He incorporated the study of modern history, modern languages and mathematics into the work of the school, which attempt, as it was the first of its kind, so it was at one time the chief topic of blame and praise in his system of instruction.

This clear misconception has been perpetuated by Mr Norman Wymer in his very readable *Dr Arnold of Rugby*, published in 1953, in which he says that Arnold's curriculum innovations were 'wider than anything yet known'. If these commentators mean that Arnold was the first person to introduce these subjects into the curriculum of schools in England, then it is just not true. If they mean that Arnold was the first to do so at Rugby, this is also not in accord with the truth. In point of fact Arnold's curriculum reforms were not very impressive; of the actual twenty hours per week of class-room lessons, classics, including some Roman and Greek history, took the lion's share of sixteen hours, leaving two for French and two for mathematics. This was not much more than Dr James had offered back in the 1790s.

Again on the material side of the school Arnold merely continued with policies initiated by his predecessors. Dr James had provided a certain number of individual studies for the older boys, for which a special fee was charged. His successors, Dr Ingles and Dr Wool, both added to these by encroaching on passage-ways and by dividing up larger rooms. In the 1830s Arnold tried to carry on this policy, but with a roll rising to 300 in 1840 he did not have much spare space for any large scale developments. He certainly cannot claim the credit for this policy. In fact the historians of education usually attribute the provision of studies for the older boys to Edward Thring[2] of *Uppingham School* around the year 1860, oblivious of the fact that Rowland Hill had done so in 1820 and that Dr James at Rugby had attempted the same thing in the 1790s.

The shrewdly penetrating eye of Lytton Strachey in his *Eminent Victorians* had no difficulty in separating the fact from the fiction when he says:

> So far as the actual machinery of education was concerned, Dr Arnold not only failed to effect a change, but deliberately adhered to the old system. . . . Under him, the public school remained in essentials a conventional establishment devoted to the teaching of Greek and Latin grammar . . . the ancient system became more firmly established than ever.

Even so, Lytton Strachey, like most of us, readily admits that on the moral and spiritual side Dr Arnold did more than anybody 'to change the face of education all through the public schools.'

We must, however, give the greatest credit to Dr Arnold for his innovations in giving his masters genuine professional status. He took them into his confidence by consulting them regularly and, most important of all, by raising their salaries to the unprecedented height of £500 per annum. But his staff had to conform to certain demanding criteria; they had to be recognisably 'gentlemen' of sound middle-class background, with a Public School education, a degree of Oxford or Cambridge, preferably in Classics, and, if possible, in Holy Orders.

Arnold's master-stroke, however, which was to have a profound influence on the growth of the new Public and Boarding schools that proliferated after his death, was to close the long-established 'Dames' Houses' in Rugby town and set up his own boarding houses each under the control of a master and his wife (where possible).

[88]

By the end of 1838 all the Dames' Houses had been closed and eight official boarding houses established in their place. The consequences were dramatic and the practice was eagerly followed in the growing number of new Public Schools then springing up. For the first time in history a schoolmaster in charge of a House could enjoy a comfortable and lucrative 'gentleman's' life with style and status, not only with a steady income as a modest hotelier in addition to his basic salary of £500 p.a., but with everything laid on – accommodation, heating, lighting, laundry, meals, garden and servants until he retired.[4] A Nabob rarely enjoyed such luxury and prestigious authority. This new conception of a schoolmaster's status undoubtedly influenced conditions and standards in the State system that was shortly to come into being.

By a curious irony it was left to his somewhat rebellious son, Matthew, to do for the State system what his father had done in some areas of the independent sector. As one of the earliest Inspectors of Schools Matthew was largely responsible for the move to systematise and humanise the field of elementary education which was his main responsibility. Then by his writing and reports based on his extensive studies of continental educational systems, which were mostly far in advance of ours, he plotted the way forward for the next big step for us to make – the establishment of a worthy State secondary system. This came into being, after Matthew Arnold's death, in the Balfour *Education Act of 1902*. It represented a very significant breakthrough; for the first time it spelt out what an enlightened secondary curriculum should contain – English language; English literature; one foreign language; geography; history; mathematics; science; physical education including organised games; craftwork; music and art. At last the curriculum was beginning to come close to what Rowland Hill had been doing at Hazelwood eighty years earlier.

When we consider the question of moral training there is a world of difference between Rowland Hill and Thomas Arnold; the former followed purely ethical principles coloured with a touch of Utilitarianism; the latter based his teachings at Rugby on an emotional Evangelicalism bounded by the New Testament and adjusted to the susceptibilities of his youthful and captive audience. The Hills had always put moral training and the shaping of character very high in their educational priorities. Old Thomas Wright Hill made this very clear in his first Prospectus of Hill Top School on its opening in 1803. He expressed the hope that his conception of education possessed 'higher excellencies than mechanical dexterity or mere intellectual acuteness' and set the greatest store by the 'virtues of the heart'. This was the basis of Rowland's philosophy too when he took over the running of the school just before it moved

[89]

to the new Hazelwood building. It found expression in the practice of self-government and self-discipline through the Jury-court and in the unique moral relationship in his 'Circles' and 'Guardians'.

Though the dogmas of Christianity were not thrust forward at Hazelwood, most of the traditional Christian virtues were sincerely practised – brotherly love, kindliness and charity, and a deep respect for truth, honesty and justice and so on. Consideration for others – compassion – particularly for the less privileged was kept in the forefront of the boys' minds and charitable causes were spontaneously supported. Poverty and hardship were visible all round them in industrial Birmingham, particularly after the Napoleonic wars, so in 1818 the boys started a *School Benevolent Fund* with which, as Rowland tells us, 'the boys have been able to relieve many poor families with bacon, potatoes or bread. . .'.

In contrast, when Arnold was still at his coaching establishment in Laleham[5] in 1824 he, too, was concerned for the poor of the district, but his response was somewhat different. He tells us 'I have now taken up the care of the Workhouse i.e. as far as going there once a week to read prayers and give a sort of lecture upon some part of the Bible'. These early incidents reveal the fundamental difference in outlook between Rowland Hill and Arnold; the former was practical and realistic, knowing full well what poverty was like; the latter, lacking as yet this sharper understanding, offered only cold, spiritual solace. But revelation came to Arnold in due course, and during the next fifteen years his eyes and heart were gradually opened to the harsher realities of life as he threw himself into radical politics and more practical forms of charity. As early as 1830 he and his wife, newcomers to Rugby, were moved by the neglect of the poor and sick in the town, so they established a Dispensary to provide medicine free of charge. To raise funds for this they held bazaars and made collections, and Arnold in his sermons enlisted the sympathies of the boys in support of the cause.

Within the school Arnold's main plank of moral training was the message of the New Testament. This was an obsession with him; he was not satisfied unless every aspect of life was irradiated with the teachings of Christ. This evangelical fervour caused him to fall out with Henry Brougham's *Society for the Diffusion of Useful Knowledge* (founded in 1826) whose general social and educational aims he warmly supported. But unless the useful knowledge it claimed to disseminate was solidly Christian, Arnold dismissed it as useless knowledge. Likewise he resigned from a Fellowship of the University of London for the very same reason – the Senate refused to make a study of the Gospels an essential part of a degree course. So omnipresent was this obsession with Christianity in its purest and most authentic form that one felt he was capable of refusing a cup of tea unless it were made with water from the Sea of Galilee.

At Rugby, however, it was different: here he was Headmaster, an autocrat whose word was law, and before him he had an impressionable captive audience which he had no hesitation in setting out to evangelise. Such was the hypnotic power of his personality and so persuasive was his eloquence that he had no difficulty in injecting his brand of rather unctuous Christianity into the minds and affairs of his schoolboy audiences. If a boy showed serious signs of rejection he was likely to be quietly superannuated as a potential cancer-cell in the school organism.

At this time the Public Schools were for the most part brutish, narrow and devoid of moral standards and were clearly ripe for reform. Parents and teachers alike clutched eagerly at the hopeful new gospel emanating from Rugby. So it was that Arnold's outlook permanently influenced the spirit of the new Public Schools that proliferated from the mid-nineteenth century onwards: Cheltenham in 1841; Marlborough 1843; Rossall 1844; Radley 1847; Epsom 1853; Wellington 1859; Clifton 1862; Haileybury 1862 and Cranleigh 1863, as well as the chain of admirable boarding schools of the Woodard Corporation from 1848 onwards, including Lancing, Ardingly, Bloxham, Denstone, Ellesmere, Worksop and a number of Girls' schools.

Ready to hand was the magical Arnold formula which very soon became immortalised as a legend; it was as catching as cholera.

The drill was clear; first appoint a Headmaster in Holy Orders; secondly build an impressive school chapel; thirdly set up your private hotels under competent housemasters; fourthly announce a generous salary scale for all members of staff. This will attract talented teachers who will produce good examination results; then the pupils will roll along. If on top of this a well publicised prefect system is established with powers of corporal punishment – to produce leaders – and if in the fullness of time a daunting programme of organised compulsory games (including Rugby of course) is laid on to dull the sexual urges of adolescence – then the prescription for success is perfect.

Following Arnold's priorities the aim of these schools was to turn out 'decent fellows' who at least paid lip-service to Christian values, who were well trained in leadership and endowed with good manners, abundant confidence and cultivated speech. In the nineteenth century, the age of imperial expansion, hosts of these young men looked outwards to jobs in the Indian Civil Service; in the Army, particularly in India and the colonies, and in various branches of the colonial services. Alternatively they took positions abroad on the tea and rubber plantations or railways, or in the big banks and commercial institutions set up by their fellow countrymen in far-flung lands. In these walks of life the majority conducted themselves courageously, cheerfully, usefully and honourably, giving Africa and India and other undeveloped countries a long period of peace, prosperity, steady development and novel standards of honesty and justice. This was a solid and worthy legacy bequeathed by Thomas Arnold to middle and upper class education in Britain; it made possible the golden age of benevolent imperialism.

For all their emphasis on character-building, the best Public Schools are, and always have been, outstanding academic institutions, Eton and Winchester being pre-eminent. Likewise at Rugby, Dr Arnold around the year 1838 swept the board with academic successes at Oxford and Cambridge. These came just in time to silence his critics who were trying to make out that Arnold's sojourn at Rugby was an unmitigated disaster. They thought and hoped that his heavy involvement with Church and political controversies had caused him to neglect the school and lead to indiscipline and abysmal academic results. They were wrong, and a striking proportion of Arnold's products were turning out to be academically brilliant, high-minded and versatile young men with vision and praiseworthy social ideals – his Christian gentlemen. No wonder the Trustees – his Governing Body – stood by the Doctor through thick and thin, and no wonder the Arnold legend was born.

When we come to look more closely into the lives of these two unusual educationists – Thomas Arnold and Rowland Hill – we find some curious similarities and differences. They were both born in 1795 and both had seven or eight brothers or sisters. Their backgrounds and education were radically different. Rowland Hill received all his formal education at his father's private school, first at Hill Top, then at Hazelwood in Birmingham. At thirteen years of age he continued his education as best he could while working as a pupil-teacher at the school. The remainder of his education he acquired through his own efforts and in the stern university of life. He always enjoyed working with his hands and was very much at home with carpentry and metalwork. As a result he developed into a very competent engineer, supported by his exceptional ability in mathematics. On the more practical side he acquired high levels of skill in fields like surveying, navigation, architecture and practical building construction. He had an immense capacity for hard work which is said to have enabled him to get through the normal work of a lifetime before he was thirty years of age. He was ambitious but never in a selfish sense; stubborn, determined and ruthless, but never for his own aggrandisement. As a father he was loving, slightly detached, very understanding and never overtly domineering, consequently he

[92]

never produced rebellious antagonisms in his children. The whole Hill family, from old Thomas Wright Hill downwards, always displayed a deep-seated unanimity of outlook; they knew it was a matter of one for all and all for one. What a difference do we find in Thomas Arnold's domestic scene!

Arnold was educated traditionally, first at Lord Weymouth's Grammar School, Warminster in Wiltshire, then at Winchester College, whence, by the natural order of things, he progressed to Oxford University as a scholar of Corpus Christi College. After achieving a First he was awarded a Fellowship at Oriel College[6] in 1815 where he proceeded to take Holy Orders. About this he had some misgivings, for by nature he was something of a rebel, by temperament a non-conformist prone to intellectual doubts, and this made it difficult for him to subscribe to the *Thirty-nine Articles* of the Church of England which ordinands were obliged to accept. He early revealed his radical views and was openly critical of the Church of England as well as of Tory values in general.

Rowland Hill, too, had a stubborn, rebellious streak in intellectual matters. Like Arnold he was a severe critic of the Tory Establishment, but as a tolerant Unitarian by family faith he never attacked other religious creeds, whereas Arnold indulged in a relentless battle even with his own Church of England. Arnold was primitively and fanatically Christian in everything he did, and the life and teachings of Jesus were the lodestone of his life. He disapproved of the episcopal hierarchy and needed no priests to lead him to Christ. This was typical of the man's character; he was always determined to 'do his own thing' and did not worry whether he appeared to others as being cussed and egotistical.

Paradoxically, however, at times Arnold showed a rare ecumenical spirit towards other faiths; it was bewildering to find him speaking out for dissenters of all kinds (except, oddly enough, the Unitarians) and for Roman Catholics and Jews. Then in the next breath he would castigate Cardinal Newman, the most influential Roman Catholic of the age, as an apostate who in course of time 'corrupted' Arnold's own son. The Cardinal, he declared, deserved hanging! Arnold's strange and rabid intolerance of Unitarians and certain Roman Catholics bespeaks a surprising lack of the Christian virtue of charity that he so vociferously championed.

Rowland Hill in contrast was completely unprejudiced in matters of religion. He was nominally a Unitarian, but he began and ended the day at Hazelwood with strictly non-sectarian prayers. Also he arranged for boys from Church of England families to attend the local church on Sundays.

A strange feature of the many biographies of Dr Arnold and Rowland

Hill is that there is no mention of any personal contact between the two, even though their schools were originally barely thirty miles from each other. Both Rowland and his elder brother, Matthew, a prominent barrister, soon to become a QC, were foundation members of the *Society for the Diffusion of Useful Knowledge*, established by Henry Brougham and Charles Knight, the publisher, in 1826. The former knew Arnold and thought so highly of him that, later as Lord Chancellor, he offered the doctor a stall in Bristol Cathedral, which he did not take up. Arnold must certainly have attended some of the committee meetings of Brougham's Society, especially when educational matters were under discussion, for he is known to have been a keen supporter of the project. When Arnold resigned from the Society because it was steadfastly non-religious he maintained contact with some of its members for whom he had a high regard. Whether the Hills were amongst these privileged individuals is not clear. Only one small piece of evidence of any personal contact has recently come to light. In a letter[7] from old Thomas Wright Hill to Rowland dated 16 October 1831 is the comment:

> Matthew tarries at Rugby to visit the Head schoolmaster, Dr Arnold, I believe, to be the more in readiness for the sessions tomorrow.

Presumably Matthew was engaged on his Bar Circuit in Warwickshire and took the opportunity to call and see the famous Dr Arnold, then in the third year of his headship. They must have had much to discuss and it is tempting to speculate on some possible topics.

At the time of their meeting Birmingham was on the boil about the imminent clash in Parliament over the Reform Bill. Both Arnold and Matthew Davenport Hill were deeply concerned over the issue. Arnold in optimistic mood was already planning a celebration dinner at the *Spread Eagle* in Rugby to greet the passing of the Bill – this in the face of intense local Tory disapproval and at the risk of his school's reputation. Matthew Davenport Hill, equally committed to this great reform, had actually purchased a rifle ready to fight at the barricades if the Duke of Wellington, recently Prime Minister, persuaded the government to use the army to thwart the passing of the Bill. Here were strange bedfellows!

They must certainly have discussed these vital political developments. They must have reminisced, too, about the famous occasion back in 1819, when as a newly admitted barrister, Matthew Hill acted as junior Counsel to defend the well-known radical, Major John Cartwright (1740–1824) in Birmingham when the latter was charged with sedition. By undertaking this Matthew was considered to have risked his whole future at the bar. The episode, by a curious coincidence, had a special significance in 1831 as Arnold's wife, Mary Penrose, was connected with

[94]

the Cartwright family by marriage; her elder brother, John Penrose, had married Major Cartwright's niece. Matthew had even named one of his sons Cartwright.

They must surely have discussed the *Society for the Diffusion of Useful Knowledge* as they both had a deep interest in its activities. Above all they must certainly have discussed education. Arnold had heard of the Hills' school, barely thirty miles away, and had read the numerous reviews of the Hill's book, *Public Education*, published in 1822 and 1825 for he himself had been a contributor to some of the leading journals which carried the reviews. As a keen continental traveller interested in European ideas, he could not have missed reading M. Jullien's article about Hazelwood School in the latter's international journal *La Revue Encyclopédique* in 1823 which launched upon the world the school and the Hills' ideas with dramatic results. It started the flood of boys from the continent and from South America and the Caribbean.

One wonders what Matthew Hill made of Arnold's authoritarian Prefect system with its power to inflict corporal punishment, when compared with the abandonment of such a form of punishment as far back as 1818 at Hazelwood and its enlightened system of 'Circles' and 'Guardians'. Again what were Matthew's thoughts on Arnold's amateur and half-hearted attempts to reform the curriculum by adding two hours of French a week and two hours of mathematics, compared with the many innovations introduced at Hazelwood long before 1820? Also Matthew must have seen how laughable was Arnold's treatment of science – poor old D. F. Walker, a peripatetic scientist, trundling his barrow of science apparatus up to the school for twelve two-hour lectures and demonstrations every three years! One would give much for a diary record of what took place in Arnold's study that Sunday in October 1831.

There is a big difference in the approach to teaching by the two men. Rowland Hill and his brothers, as they declare in the title of their book, *Public Education*, were concerned with 'the liberal education of boys in large numbers', and in the year 1826, two years before Arnold started at Rugby, Hazelwood was actually the bigger school; it had 150 pupils compared with Rugby's 125. In the year 1824 Arnold was still at his little coaching establishment at Laleham, coping with only nine pupils! These he had selected carefully, rejecting those who were dull or backward or who had a tendency to be uncooperative. With such small numbers an informal, almost parental relationship with his pupils was possible: formal rules and strict discipline were inappropriate. Even so Arnold almost expelled two of his pupils for a fairly harmless prank compounded with insolence.

[95]

In this intimate family atmosphere Arnold enjoyed the camaraderie he was able to establish with his pupils. It was something of a revelation to him; gone were the age-old battles between teachers and pupils that he had experienced as a boy at Winchester. Instead he found at Laleham that there had grown up an easy relationship in which true educational growth seemed to flourish. To Arnold this was a significant discovery and it bore fruit when he went to Rugby. He found he was able to build up this kind of relationship with his sixth form boys: to him they seemed more like a small Laleham coaching group than a formal class. It was these boys he was most interested in and he spent much of his time with them grooming them to become his new-model Prefects. The rest of the school he met in occasional lessons, though he certainly preached to the whole assembly in chapel. He kept a sharp look out for potential undesirables and knew how to deal with them. His two most effective weapons were expulsion and superannuation. Over what he deemed to be a grave moral issue he was capable of expelling six boys between breakfast and lunch and putting them aboard the afternoon coach before three o'clock. He was no less peremptory on superannuation:

> Till a man learnt that the first, second and third duty of a schoolmaster is to get rid of unpromising subjects, a great Public School will never be what it ought to be

This is the worst confession of failure that a schoolmaster could make; it is no less than a professional betrayal. But Arnold had no doubts; he knew exactly what to do with the innately vicious and nasty-minded boy that every schoolmaster has met. Once caught out in a gross misdemeanour the unfortunate boy found himself on the next coach out of Rugby. Much more difficult was the case of the duller, lazy boy, fairly harmless in himself, but who, in Arnold's phrase 'had overgrown school in his body before he had overgrown it in wit; he was therefore a sort of hero to the younger boys for his strength and his prowess'. These are the members of the Flashman tribe, well known to every schoolmaster.

For cases like this Arnold had his special remedy – superannuation. This ritual he carried out coolly and tactfully, writing candidly to the parents telling them that no question of disgrace was involved. Often he made alternative suggestions, perhaps recommending a personal tutor or a more easy-going school. On occasions, no doubt to salve his own conscience, he used to invite such superannuated boys to spend a week or two with him and his family at Fox How, his country house in the Lake District. All very civilised! Rowland Hill, on the other hand, gladly accepted boys of very poor academic ability or of troublesome character, 'boys with a character for rebellion worthy of a Wat Tyler', and met their needs by good pastoral care, by a more interesting and varied curriculum and by providing remedial teaching for those in need. It is not difficult to see which of the two was the true educator.

What Arnold actually was doing was to ensure that he played the game of education with a rigged hand; he cunningly shuffled the cards to ensure that he held only aces and court-cards. He was acting like a doctor who accepted only selected patients, treating casualties with sprained wrists or twisted ankles but turning away those with fractures and severed limbs. Naturally such a policy helped Arnold to maintain the tone of the school, as it left him with potential Christian gentlemen only. Not surprisingly the reputation of Rugby soared and its numbers soon rocketed to three hundred.

But what sort of man and father was the learned Doctor? He had always been a vehement, passionate man, moody and prone to outbursts of temper. At heart he was very much a rebel as he had shown as a boy at Winchester where he precociously exhibited his radicalism, criticising the Tory Establishment in Church and state; he even commented adversely on the morals and behaviour of the Royal family. As a young man, before his temper began to deteriorate, be abounded with physical energy, loving to romp on the lawn with his young children at Laleham – his first-born, Jane, was seven years old when he moved to Rugby – and he took equal delight in jumping hedges and ditches on his long walks with his older pupils.

From a father once capable of games on the lawn with his infant children, Thomas Arnold soon developed into the irascible school-master, intimidating and incalculable; it all depended on his mood. Stern and autocratic as he was, he never spared his own children; with his two elder boys, Matthew born in 1821 and Tom born in 1822, he was particularly firm. Both confess to being genuinely afraid of their father and awaited the inevitable retribution with dread if they had been caught in some childish misdemeanour. This latent fear and sense of insecurity produced characteristic psychological symptoms in both boys, for both of them suffered an impediment of speech that persisted for some years. This phenomenon in children is a well-authenticated consequence of having a domineering and over-demanding father. As the boys grew up a further consequence began to show in Matthew's reaction of independence and rebellion, and in Tom's spiritual doubts and confusions, clearly a reaction against his father's single-minded evangelical faith. Their younger sister Mary at an early age expressed her resistance in a quiet agnosticism.

When Matthew escaped to Oxford University in 1840 he found

[97]

ineffable delight and relief in the freedom of university life, and rather surprisingly affected a harmless dandyism in reaction to the stern parental pressures he had endured for many years. In 1843, too late for his father to enjoy his son's success, Matthew won the Newdigate Prize for poetry, but in 1844 his rather casual attitude to his studies brought him only a second class degree.

For all his superficial charm and assumed gaiety Matthew was really a reserved and melancholy person. With a touch of the prodigal son he decamped to Paris and the continent for the best part of a year, sowing his cultivated oats. He became addicted to the Parisian theatre and fell for the charms and talent of a gifted and popular actress, Rachel,[8] and even paid court to the notorious George Sand,[9] pseudonym of Mlle Amandine Aurore Dupin (1804–76) who at that time was enjoying her latest liaison with Frederick Chopin. This was not all; whilst in Switzerland later in the year, he lost his heart to an attractive girl, Marguerite,[10] with a passion that haunted him all his life, as his poems reveal. Fortunately, as far as is known, Matthew did not complicate his life by fathering a child, as did his illustrious poetic forerunner, William Wordsworth, whom the Arnold family was later to know as their eminently respectable neighbour in the Lake District. At that time there was no hint of a skeleton in the laureate cupboard. It was a touching story; poor Wordsworth, carried away after 1789 with a young man's revolutionary fervour, had found France to be a place where 'bliss it was to be alive'. In the intoxicating air of liberation he succumbed to the charms of the winsome Annette Vallon with the inevitable result. Very honourably he wished to marry the mother of his child and bring them both to England, but the whole weight of the august Wordsworth family persuaded him otherwise. As a tribe of distinguished scholars, divines and pillars of the Establishment in concert they were irresistible. The episode left Wordsworth with a broken heart and a reservoir of pent up emotions that were to generate his most moving poetry, but it also provoked a psychological breakdown which took years of the angelic ministrations of his sister, Dorothy, to put right. The sequel for Matthew Arnold, half a century later, was not dissimilar, for the memory of Marguerite seems to have enriched the elegiac strain that is characteristic of his best poems.

This, then, was the stern Doctor's legacy to his most distinguished son - a kicking over of the traces in a determination to 'do his own thing', just as his father had done. When Matthew was thus gallivanting on the continent, the bewildered Doctor, had he been alive to witness it, would have feared the worst, remembering the wild antics of his rarely mentioned uncle, William. This colourful character, when articled to a

[98]

solicitor in London, went on the tiles and ended up, we are assured, by marrying a prostitute. He was quickly shipped out to Tobago, where, shortly after, to the relief of the family, he died of fever.

As for Matthew, he returned to the fold and in 1848, thanks to his mother's influence, accepted the post of Secretary to Lord Lansdowne, President of the Council, and minister responsible for the little developed field of education. The dandy in Matthew enjoyed to the full the glitter and grandeur of the receptions held at Lansdowne House in Berkeley Square, where he hobnobbed with the leaders of Whig society. He also took great pleasure in his visits to Bowood House, the elegant Lansdowne estate in Wiltshire where, ten years earlier the rising young barrister, Matthew Davenport Hill, QC had similarly enjoyed the privilege of smart, country-house weekends. The Hill family, incidentally, used to be much amused at Matthew's practice – this former radical left-winger and potential fighter at the barricades – of sending greetings to them and his friends, written on the aristocratically headed writing paper supplied by his host.

In 1851 Matthew Arnold decided to get married, renouncing his beloved Marguerite in his mind, if not in his heart. Through Lord Lansdowne's kindness he accepted a post as Inspector of Schools, in which capacity, it is ironical to record, he did more for national education in Britain than ever his illustrious father had done.

Matthew's brother Tom, a fellow stammerer, reacted against his father's overbearing influence in a different way. Though he achieved a First at Oxford he was left psychologically in a tangle, tormented by conflicting and uncertain religious beliefs. In course of time the 'worst' happened; Tom became a convert to the Roman Catholic faith, seduced by the charm and eloquence of Cardinal Newman. There was a flaw in the Arnold magic somewhere. However, Tom eventually did good work in educational administration in Tasmania, where he worked in close association with John Philip Gell, a former prefect of Arnold's at Rugby who went out to the island to establish a colonial form of Rugby at Hobart. This, it was hoped, would proliferate and lead to a chain of such enlightened institutions throughout the Antipodes. The idea of the independent Public School caught on in Australia, New Zealand and Tasmania very strongly, many being foundations of the various churches; they play a very influential part in the social life of these countries even today.

It is strange that as early as the 1820s Rowland Hill had similar ideas for a spread of the Hazelwood system throughout England and maybe further afield too. His first practical step was to open a London branch in 1827 in the impressive premises of Bruce Castle, Tottenham.

[99]

It survived under the control of the Hill family until 1877, albeit much changed in character. At one time an edition of its Prospectus was printed in Spanish to meet the continuing interest of parents in South America and the West Indies.

In 1829 the Hazelwood system was exported lock, stock and barrel, even down to the metal tokens in place of marks, to Sweden, where it was established in Stockholm. It was ceremoniously opened by Count Frolich whose emissary Professor Sawe had earlier made a long visit to Hazelwood to study its working. The school, like Hazelwood itself, attracted pupils from all over Europe and survived until 1846, but reunions of its former pupils, then being leading figures in the country, were held as late as 1871 and 1875.

Both Arnold and Rowland Hill passed through stormy times in fighting for their respective causes. The Doctor had no enemies or disloyal factions within the school; his antagonists were in the world outside – the reactionary Tory party and its Press and the conservative hierarchy of the Anglican church. Rowland Hill, in contrast, had to fight disloyalty and obstruction with place holders within the Post Office, as well as to battle with the serried ranks of various politicians who were all the time trying to thwart his plans.

To support him in his fight Rowland soon managed to establish a few strong points within the Post Office. He secured the appointment of his very able brother, Frederic, as head of the Money Order department, and of Edwin as Superintendent of the Stamp department. He knew he could depend upon these allies until the death. Their support was vital to him, for from the day the government accepted his proposals for postal reform, he met nothing but non-cooperation, overt opposition, jealousy and disloyalty from the officials around him as well as hostility and ridicule from many politicians. When he was struck down with illness through overwork, resulting in his being in a coma for forty-eight hours, his detractors, from the Postmaster General, Lord Stanley of Alderley, downwards, meanly took advantage of his absence to frustrate his plans in every way possible. When news of this reached the ears of Gladstone he wrote to Rowland immediately expressing his deep sense of pain and disapproval of what had been going on.

Dr Arnold was similarly beset by hostile detractors, chief among whom were the Press and the Tory Establishment in general. Having failed to nail him on his alleged subversion of his older pupils by subjecting them to biased political propaganda (no doubt his incidental cross reference to contemporary history when studying ancient history), his enemies watched eagerly for any rash move on which they could arraign him. Soon, unable to believe their good fortune, they found the

[100]

opportunity they had long waited for – a *cause célèbre* over an unfortunate flogging incident in 1832. It was ironic that this should have been his Achilles' heel.

Arnold's fatal weaknesses were his hot temper and his morbid belief in the reality of Evil. Speaking of the schoolmaster's task he declared:

> Your adversary, in plain English, is the Devil. . . It is quite surprising to see the wickedness of young boys

> A school shows as undisguisedly as any place the corruption of human nature and the monstrous advantage with which evil starts in its conflict with the good

Born devils, like Caliban, he knew how to deal with – expulsion or superannuations: acquired evil, through contamination, on the other hand, might be exorcised by beating out the offending Adam; he had some scriptural authority for this. Yet deep down he hated the humiliation that flogging involved. In his first weeks at Rugby in 1828 he declared in a letter, 'Flogging will be only my *ratio ultima*; talking I shall try to the utmost'. If he was to be cast into the role of gaoler, ruling by constraint and force, he said he would resign at once. Even so, he made it plain from the start that he would retain flogging for certain gross moral offences – lying, drinking, habitual laziness, flagrant disobedience, bad language and impurity of various kinds – the traditional capital offences of schoolboy life. Also, with certain controls, he delegated authority to his Prefects to administer corporal punishment when necessary.

Arnold had provoked the hostility of his adversaries by his short-lived *Englishman's Register* (1831) and by his various journalistic forays and pamphlets, including his provocative *The Christian duty of granting the claims of the Roman Catholics* (1831) later, in 1833, to be revised and published as *The Principles of Church Reform*. When the heaven-sent moment arrived the Tory *Northampton Herald* led the pack against him by leaking the disastrous flogging episode which had started so innocently.

It was Arnold's custom to examine boys in the lower forms in construing prepared passages from their Greek texts, on this occasion Xenophon's *Anabasis*. With him in the classroom was another classics master, Dr James Prince Lee.[11] When Arnold asked a boy named Marsh to construe, the boy told the Doctor that the class had not yet reached the part of the text he was asked to construe. Arnold's face clouded; then he asked Dr Prince Lee to confirm the boy's statement with Mr Bird, the boy's class teacher. Dr Lee brought back Mr Bird's confirmation that the class had undoubtedly covered that particular section of the text. Arnold's volatile temper began to smoulder, but the boy stuck to his story and faced the wrath to come. It soon came: the Doctor lost his temper, for here in front of him was Evil personified – the boy was a barefaced liar. Shaking the wretched boy and thumping on the desk Arnold in fury shouted 'Liar! Liar! Liar!' while young Marsh continued to protest his innocence. Then going almost berserk and acting as if he were cleansing the Temple, he there and then flogged the boy with eighteen strokes. Later in the morning it was confirmed that a mistake had been made; the boy was telling the truth all the time. Within days the fat was in the fire. The parents demanded an apology, and Arnold was man enough to make it in front of the whole school. But the damage had been done.

The story leaked out and the hostile Tory *Northampton Herald* attacked Arnold with undisguised glee – the self-styled enlightened radical, the paragon of Christian virtues, had shown himself to be a reactionary flogger. Arnold's colleagues on the staff loyally rallied to their Head-master's cause, but were foolish enough in a letter published in the *Herald* to say that eighteen strokes was a perfectly fair penalty for the offence in question, if it had actually occurred. This was a fatal argument and the newspaper jubilantly drew the obvious conclusion – how many strokes would a really serious offence have earned? Twenty-five, thirty or perhaps fifty? To the *Herald* Dr Arnold was clearly no high-minded idealist, no pacific Christian, but a cruel sadistic bully, a pedagogic Bligh.

Arnold, however, survived the storm and it is greatly to the credit of the Trustees that they stood by him for they knew what in reality their Headmaster was achieving in the school. Apart from Arnold's public reputation, the only casualty was the unfortunate Mr Bird, who very soon made a quiet departure from the school.

This brief comparison between the educational practices and theories of the two outstanding Headmasters of the day, supplemented by a sidelong glance at their characters as family men and social and political reformers, should help to provide a sound basis for a re-assessment of their achievements in the age in which they lived.

[VII]

The Influence and Message of Hazelwood

THE strangest and most baffling aspect of the Rowland Hill story is that educational historians in his own country appear to have been, and still are, blissfully ignorant of the extent and nature of Rowland's remarkable innovations. Yet his name and educational achievements were known and revered throughout the world – from Egypt, Greece, Switzerland, North Africa, France, Spain, Portugal, North and South America to the West Indies and Scandinavia. In his own country he has been a prophet without honour, at least as an educationist. This may be accounted for by his all-enveloping world-wide fame as the pioneer of Penny Postage, which has apparently eclipsed everything else he did. Here his fame has endured, but now, with our deeper insight into Rowland Hill's educational achievements, we can reasonably hope that his reputation in this field may be restored to the eminence it held in the 1820s and 1830s. Likewise he should from now on be remembered and honoured for the high standards of public care and responsibility that he established in his work with the London and Brighton railway, and with the colonisation of South Australia.

The final question that inevitably arises is why did Hazelwood School and its system fail to survive as the natural pattern to follow from 1830 onwards? The reasons are not difficult to find:

First, the creation of the school and its day to day running in its early and most striking form depended wholly on the combined efforts of the family. Thomas Hill and his sons gave everything they had to bring about the success of their novel venture; it was their brain-child and one and all they were prepared to work for twelve to fourteen hours a day to make it work. Then gradually the sons, as they grew up, began to move on to other preoccupations; first Matthew left to become a barrister; Edwin took up engineering; Frederic, too, left to become a barrister and an Inspector of Prisons; finally in 1833 Rowland suffered a breakdown in health and was forced to give up schoolmastering. Clearly the Hill influence had become too diluted. Unfortunately it was impossible to find competent and enthusiastic teachers who would subject themselves to the complicated routines and queer ideas of the school and be prepared to work more than twelve hours a day for the cause.

Secondly, around the years 1828 to 1832 the Hills as a family became too closely involved with the social and political agitations of the day – championing the controversial Reform Bill and lobbying for the granting of corporate status for Birmingham. These activities led to middle-class parents looking upon the Hills as Jacobins or communists, and as such were deemed to be a dangerous influence on their schoolboy sons. Even so, many staunch Tory and Anglican parents never lost faith in the school.

Thirdly, as well-known Unitarians the Hills were outside the pale of 'respectable' religion, and again were considered a doubtful influence on young people.

Fourthly, the Hazelwood conception of education, so radically different from what had gone before, struck most ordinary parents as being decidedly 'cranky'; they were bewildered by the fantastic rigmarole of rules, rewards and penalties, which seemed to become more elaborate as time went on.

Fifthly, the Hills' insistence on science as a cultural subject for every pupil to study broke away too radically from what the ordinary parent imagined education to be.

Finally, the moral climate evolved by the system was too priggish, too artificial and above the heads of the average pupil. The natural care-free high spirits of childhood and youth were stifled.

In spite of Hazelwood's lack of progeny in its original eccentric form, the new spirit of enlightened relationships that Hazelwood engendered, as well as the necessity of a broad enriched curriculum, have left a permanent mark on our prevailing philosophy of education. Nobody today believes in a formal, rigid, authoritarian pattern of society, whether in the family, the school, or in the state at large. Choice, self-motivation and an acceptance of responsibility exercised within a community are considered to be essential ingredients of our democratic way of life; and these were the dominant features stressed in the Hazelwood system. As such they certainly contributed to that all-important climate of opinion, the ethos, which is the pre-requisite for progress of any kind.

Once we cut away the superficial trappings – the tiresome mechanics of *Aggregate rank*, the rigmarole of *penal* and *transferable marks*, the over-sophisticated routines of the *Jury-court*, the sometimes unseemly pressure of *Voluntary labour* and the ever-present tyranny of bugles and bells – we find ourselves in a caring community in which honest conscientious work of every kind was encouraged and appreciated, in which enterprise and originality were stimulated, and in which a sensible discipline was self-imposed and in which tolerance, friendship and mutual support were as natural as breathing.

This was recognised even by the anti-radical *Blackwood's Review* as is shown in the comment quoted on pages 6 and 7.

Kindness and affection were rare commodities in the Public and other schools of that time; today we cannot fully appreciate the contrast between the civilised values of Hazelwood and those of most other educational establishments. But the people who mattered were aware of this difference. By the time Rowland Hill had left Bruce Castle in 1833 the novel concepts that had inspired the Hazelwood system had become common currency among the progressive intellectual and political leaders of the country. The favourable comments published in the recognised Reviews and Journals, as we have seen, played a big part in this. But in addition a noteworthy array of these leaders had been impressed by Rowland Hill's many talents and by his achievements at Hazlewood, and many of them had actually visited the school. They seemed instantly to recognise Rowland as a man with a message for the time. Many of these have been mentioned in Chapter II (page 37) beginning as enthusiastic admirers of Rowland's achievements at Hazlewood; fifteen years later these very people, both inside and outside Parliament, were nearly all passionate supporters of his Penny Postage plan – a turn of events they could never have anticipated at that time. Amongst these active supporters were the Hon. George Anson,[1] MP; Richard Cobden, MP; Daniel O'Connell,[2] MP; Thomas Wyse,[3] MP; John Bowring, MP, FRS; Robert Wallace, MP; Francis Baring, MP; Sir Henry Cole; Charles Knight; James Mill[4] and Dr Southwood Smith.

The support of Hazelwood's own *alumni* was another factor in influencing national and local opinion; in Parliament Lord Clarendon's younger brother, the Bishop of Carlisle (later of Durham) as well as Matthew Davenport Hill, MP for Hull, and William Scholefield, MP for Birmingham, were all active in the cause of reform. In the learned societies, in influential national councils and in Birmingham civic affairs, former Hazelwood pupils played a worthy part. Amongst these were Arthur Follett Osler, FRS,[5] a leading manufacturer, philanthropist and social reformer and an early patron of the University of Birmingham; Sir William Bowman, FRS, FRCS,[6] ('the father of general anatomy'); John Dent Goodman, the first Chairman of the *Birmingham Small Arms Company* and Director of the *Midland Bank*; and William Lucas Sargant, an enterprising and scholarly manufacturer with a deep interest in progressive education. He was one of the early Governors of

[105]

Edgbaston Proprietary School which was founded in 1838 to fill the gap left by the transfer of Hazelwood to Bruce Castle, Tottenham. The new school showed the influence of Hazelwood in abandoning corporal punishment and in introducing science and mathematics as major courses of study. The school was later incorporated into the King Edward Foundation and survived as *King Edward's Grammar School, Five Ways*, until modern times.

William Sargant was a leading member of the *Birmingham Education Association* which was later to become the nucleus of the powerful *National Education League*. The latter was formed in George Dixon's[7] house in Edgbaston in 1869 and was largely responsible for the successful passing of Forster's[8] *Elementary Education Act of 1870*, the very foundation of our state system of education. William Sargant was also elected as the first Chairman of the *Birmingham School Board* which was immediately set up to implement the requirements of Forster's Act. On his committee were such influential national figures as Joseph Chamberlain, George Dixon and the Reverend R. Dale,[9] the eminent Congregational Minister. Remarkable in those days, the Board's first instruction to Head Teachers declared:

> It is the earnest wish of the Board that punishments of any kind should be used as little as possible. Teachers are reminded that when children are interested in their work and are made happy, very little punishment is needed.

This is the unmistakable voice of William Sargant who had not forgotten his experiences as a Hazelwood pupil some forty years earlier. Likewise Sargant must have been mindful of the Hazelwood air-duct heating system when his School Board introduced the 'Plenum' air-duct heating system in many of the new schools built in Birmingham during the 1870s and '80s. Many of these have continued in operation until our own times.

All the progressively-minded people we have mentioned, in Parliament and in the world at large, had been enthusiastically infected with the spirit of Hazelwood, and were destined to become some of the shapers of the future; they were an important part of the spearhead of the nineteenth century liberalism that set the mould of our modern world. Hence it is true to say that Rowland Hill's vision is still living and still valid, and if as a nation we wish to survive economically we shall even today have to take his message to heart. First, we must always be vigilant to modify our educational system to meet the changing needs of the modern world; secondly, we must give science and technology their rightful place in our educational planning; thirdly, we must yet again address ourselves to questions of discipline, moral training and human relationships in schools, colleges, universities and in the world of work. Needless to say, the starting place for all these is in the school: this is the message of Hazelwood. Somewhat belatedly this is precisely what the Minister of State, Mr Kenneth Baker, is attempting to embody in the philosophy of his new urban Science Centres as explained on page 21.

It needed, however, some official action before the Hazelwood innovations were embodied in the underlying structure of the established education system, and this eventually came about through the Balfour Education Act of 1902 which followed closely the recommendations of the Royal Commission on Secondary Education of 1895, generally referred to as the Bryce Report. So it is that Viscount Bryce proves to be the key-figure responsible for the dramatic widening of the secondary curriculum that the Balfour Act ordained. But from our point of view the strange and significant fact of this sequence of events is that Viscount Bryce's progressive views on the curriculum were largely the consequence of his close friendship with Rowland Hill's nephew, Dr George Birkbeck Hill. The latter and Bryce were fellow members of the *Old Mortality Club* at Oxford in 1857; their distinguished associates later became widely-known as Professor John Nichol, Professor A. V. Dicey, Professor T. H. Green, Professor Henry Nettleship, the poet A. C. Swinburne and the critic and writer Walter Pater. Their mutual friendship and loyalty endured for many years after their Oxford days, and in particular G. B. Hill and Bryce continued to meet quite frequently. On leaving Oxford the former took up teaching under his father, Arthur Hill, at Bruce Castle school, becoming its Headmaster in 1867. Well into the 1860s he and his friend James Bryce went on long continental tours together, and with his deep interest in education Bryce must inevitably have visited Bruce Castle and actually seen the school in action, and talked about the palmy days of Hazelwood in its innovative prime.

The second key figure in the story of curriculum reform was Sir Michael Sadler (1861–1943) who throughout his distinguished career devoted himself to the cause of education. As Vice-Chancellor of the University of Leeds and later, in 1923, as Master of University College, Oxford, his influence on educational development was immense; indeed, he was referred to as 'the greatest living authority on educational matters'. As early as 1900 he had put on record his conviction that Rowland Hill, as an educationist, was on a par with Dr Arnold of Rugby. It was an opinion he held with great tenacity throughout his life, and as late as 1923 he published a paper, *A 19th. Century Experiment in Education: the Work of Matthew and Rowland Hill,* and he spoke on the subject at a conference of the Private Schools' Association.

In 1893 Sadler persuaded Oxford University to convene a high-powered conference, with himself as its secretary, to discuss the inadequacies of the prevailing forms of secondary education and to suggest lines of development for the future. Such was the strength of the support that a formal memorial was addressed to the Prime Minister, W. E. Gladstone, beseeching him to appoint a Royal Commission to investigate the problem further. So the Bryce Commission on Secondary Education was established, on which Michael Sadler was to be a very active member.

Sadler and Viscount Bryce, as we have seen, were both very fully acquainted with the Hills' educational innovations and reforms at Hazelwood and Bruce Castle schools, and they were determined to introduce some of the most important features of the Hills' system into the new state secondary schools they hoped to create, particularly as regards the extension of the curriculum. Whatever is officially recorded in the questions and answers given in the Bryce Report of 1895, the fact remains that the ensuing Balfour Act of 1902 firmly laid down an extended curriculum that the newly created secondary schools were obliged to follow. It included English language; English literature; one foreign language; geography; history; mathematics; science; physical education and organised games; craftwork; music and art.

Seventy years earlier in 1833, the Hills' short account of their work entitled 'Sketch of the System of Education, Moral and Intellectual, in practice at the schools of Bruce Castle, Tottenham and Hazelwood, near Birmingham' – (London; Baldwin and Cradock, and Birmingham; J. Drake, 1833) recorded the curriculum being followed at that time in the two schools as follows:

English; Greek, Latin, French, German, Spanish, Italian – as options; Geography; History; Penmanship; Mathematics including Arithmetic, Algebra and Geometry; Science; Fencing; Dancing; Music and Art.

In addition we know that other non-academic subjects, for which there were special facilities, were included, namely, Drama; physical education and organised games; and Craftwork – apart from the wide range of subjects and activities followed as 'voluntary labour'.

Even today most pupils and parents will confirm that the curriculum they followed in their secondary schools, particularly in Grammar schools, almost exactly conformed to the Balfour 1902 curriculum, which in itself is a mirror-image of the Hazelwood and Bruce Castle curriculum of the 1820s and 1830s.

In view of all these striking similarities it is difficult not to recognise that the Hills' curriculum of those years directly and powerfully influenced the curriculum followed in our secondary schools right up to the present day. But yet again it must be made clear that it is not claimed that Rowland Hill was solely responsible for this new curriculum pattern, but as with the Penny Post, it was his genius, drive and leadership that drew together the various uncoordinated strands of the problem and forced the whole issue through to a seemingly revolutionary conclusion.

[VIII]

A Final Assessment

THE time has come for us to draw together the various strands of the life of Rowland Hill; in Chapter VII we dealt with the nature and impact of his work in the field of education, and now it behoves us to look carefully into his achievements in the field of postal reform. There is always a danger of misinterpretation unless we remind ourselves of the basic facts of a very tangled tale and look back at the whole matter in a grand perspective. What follows therefore, is more than a recapitulation; it is an attempt to give a balanced reassessment of Rowland Hill's career in the Post Office, relying on the eye of hindsight and a close examination of the facts to sift the gold from the dross. This is now of special importance in view of the publication in the autumn of 1985 of Dr M. J. Daunton's book, *Royal Mail: The Post Office Since 1840*. This very thorough survey of postal history is flawed by the author's denigration of Rowland Hill's part in the story – a blemish also noted by Dr A. L. Rowse who says, speaking of the Hills, 'This detailed history is more concerned to write him and his forceful brothers down'.

From the evidence provided by his achievements at Hazelwood School it should now be beyond doubt that Rowland Hill's reputation as a remarkable educational innovator, generations ahead of his contemporaries, is assured for all time. Below him in the hierarchy stand, first, Edward Thring of Uppingham, and second, Thomas Arnold of Rugby whose reputation as a reformer has been outlined in Chapter VI. But Rowland Hill's most enduring fame rests on his achievements in the field of postal reform; it eclipses everything else in his career.

There are four distinct stages in Rowland Hill's involvement with the Post Office:

1. His pre-employment period up to 1839 when he was incubating and finally published his pamphlet on Postal Reform in January/ February 1837, followed by two years of marshalling support for

[110]

its passage through parliament. (During most of his time he was working for the South Australian Emigration Commission.)
2. His three years temporary employment at the Treasury from September 1839 to September 1842.
3. His first permanent employment with the Post Office service itself as Secretary to the Postmaster General from 1846 to 1854.
4. His final promotion to the post of Secretary to the Post Office in April 1854, and as such holding supreme administrative control.

Great leaders and pioneers in the public eye are almost inevitably to some extent egotistical, overbearing and ruthless, and cannot help provoking controversy, jealousy and hostility on the part of their rivals. In our own day, in the military field, we can think of commanders like Montgomery, Patton and MacArthur; in the civilian sector we can recall figures like Lord Reith of the BBC: Lord Beeching of British Rail, Ian MacGregor of the Coal Board and in politics, Winston Churchill and Margaret Thatcher as Prime Ministers – all of whom had clear ideas of what they wanted and a ruthless determination to see them implemented.

It must be frankly admitted that Rowland Hill was one of this breed; he was by nature brimming with self-confidence, very determined to have his own way, and perhaps lacking in tact when dealing with people who were ultra-cautious and incapable of accepting new ideas. He certainly resented glib criticism by ill-informed and perhaps interested parties of the plan he had worked on for years, but he was not really bluntly stubborn and inflexible as is sometimes alleged. Indeed there is abundant evidence that he was always willing to listen to informed suggestions, and quite prepared to modify his ideas when he had been convinced of the soundness of the views put forward.

The minister who was most closely associated with Rowland in the latter's early years in the Treasury was Sir Francis Baring, Chancellor of the Exchequer from August 1839 to September 1841. Baring's testimony[1] in the Commons in 1843 gives the lie once and for all to extravagant stories of Rowland's stubbornness and intransigence, as the following quotation from Hansard shows, referring to his appointment to the Treasury to implement his plan of postal reform:

> . . . at this period when it was determined to carry out this plan he had not the slightest personal knowledge of Mr Rowland Hill. . . . He had expected that a person who had been long engaged in the preparation of an extensive system of this kind would not carry out the change with that coolness and judgment that was requisite; and he had expected that he should have great difficulties to contend with in inducing Mr Hill to adopt

any alterations in his plan that might appear requisite. He found quite the contrary to this. . . .

Hansard records many other tributes to Rowland Hill's readiness to accept practicable suggestions. For example, at Rowland's retirement Lord Clanricarde, a former Postmaster General, bore testimony in the House of Lords 'to the extraordinary zeal for the public service, the judgment, the discretion, the temper and unvarying urbanity to which he met all the difficulties he had to encounter . . . he always found that Mr Hill laboured zealously and efficiently and always to his satisfaction. When objections to his plans were raised, Mr Hill always received them in a fair and temperate manner, and never complained of being overruled when fair grounds for so doing had been shown'.

Similar tributes were paid by two other Postmasters General – Lord Stanley (who had not always seen eye to eye with Rowland) – and the Duke of Argyle. Time and again his natural courtesy and respect for good manners showed how his impatience and annoyance in the face of criticism and obstruction is tempered into a mild civility.

Though it is clear that Rowland regarded Colonel Maberly as the chief obstacle to the implementation of his plan, his attitude to Maberly and other senior officials in the Post Office was not always resentful and hostile. There were many occasions when he went out of his way to pay a generous tribute to the Colonel and his colleagues for the support they had given him on particular issues. On looking back on his career in the Post Office Rowland showed a balanced magnanimity in declaring:

> . . . without forgetting the struggles, delays, disappointments or mortifi-
> cations . . . I cannot but acknowledge that when I compare my experience
> with that of other reformers or inventors, I ought to regard myself as
> supremely fortunate.

There is no rancour or bitterness here, only a heartfelt admission of his good fortune.

Dr Daunton belabours Rowland for his 'peremptory and high-handed manner' and for being 'incapable of working with anyone outside his own family'; but this is a wild generalisation contradicted at the top by Sir Francis Baring as we have seen. Rowland Hill, we know could be blunt and abrasive on occasions, but he was far from being blindly dictatorial and intransigent. It is true that he frequently speaks of 'my plan' and looks warily on any attempts to interfere with it, but the evidence shows that he by no means considered it to be sacrosanct and unalterable; quite the contrary. For example, in the first edition of his pamphlet in January 1837 he suggested a penny postage on the first ounce, but the Chancellor suggested changing this to half an ounce, and

Rowland duly incorporated this in his second edition in February of the same year. Again, responsive to discussion and to the declared wishes of the public he adopted the adhesive stamp in preference to the stamped envelope though the latter was his own original choice. Further, when the penny black stamp and the Mulready cover were both found to be not entirely suitable, Rowland on his own initiative replaced them with the penny red-brown and an embossed stamp in 1841. It needed no 'battle' to make Rowland change his mind on these points; they were adopted coolly and rationally on the evidence before him. Again, he yielded to persuasion over the question of making the pre-payment of postage compulsory. He had always wished to introduce such a regulation, and actually tried to enforce it in 1859, but opposing· voices were so insistent that he almost immediately withdrew the order. To this day a letter may be posted unstamped, but the recipient has to pay a double 'postage-due' penalty. Where, pray, is Rowland's peremptory, high-handed, intransigent manner?

Rowland Hill is further demeaned by Dr Daunton for being an 'amateur propagandist' of his own views, a distorter of truth for his own self-glorification, 'a man who considered himself to be misunderstood and unappreciated, facing malicious attacks from all quarters'. All these allegations are themselves distortions or exaggerations of the facts, as we shall proceed to demonstrate in considerable detail.

But first we should consider Rowland's relations with Maberly. The Colonel had been Secretary to the Post Office – the senior administrative post – since 1836, and had been grappling with the day to day problems of a rapidly growing service. He knew at first hand the extreme complexity and delicate balance of the organisation for which he was responsible, and quite understandably he was reluctant to accept with open arms the unsettling and unproved innovations of an outsider who, he believed, was ignorant of the realities of the situation. Maberly was pretty sure of this, for during the years 1835–37 when Rowland was writing his pamphlet Maberly and his colleagues had seen to it that this interfering busybody had been prevented from catching a glimpse of the internal workings of the postal service. To the Colonel it was clear that Rowland was little more than an unpractical theoriser.

Rowland could not be expected to appreciate Colonel Maberly's feelings; all he knew for certain, looking at the matter from the outside, was that the whole atmosphere had been soured from the moment he had published his challenging pamphlet in January 1837. This impression was not a figment of his imagination for there was plenty of evidence that the immediate reaction of the Post Office hierarchy and of many government officials was one of ridicule and hostility. This is vouched for by Robert Wallace, MP for Greenock, who had long been an advocate of postal reform and who had eagerly teamed up with this energetic and brilliant newcomer as soon as Rowland's pamphlet hit the headlines. In his own words Wallace declared that 'the whole of the high postal officials were against us'.

This was further corroborated by Colonel Maberly's evidence to the Select Committee in 1838 when he roundly dismissed Rowland's plan as 'most preposterous and utterly unsupported by facts and resting entirely on assumptions'. Such an extravagant and largely unfounded allegation must have stung Rowland as a personal attack on his judgment and integrity. This was not all, for the Postmaster General of the day, Lord Lichfield, added salt to the wound by declaring Rowland's plan 'as the most wild and visionary scheme he had ever heard of'. With those in authority holding such downright views Rowland realised that his hopes of a sympathetic and fair hearing of his case were virtually nil.

In spite of all these doubts and criticisms the Penny Postage Act was passed in August 1839, influenced very materially by the public support given far and wide to the measure. In September of the same year Rowland was given a two-year temporary appointment in the Treasury (later extended to a third year) in order to help in the implementation of his plan, but from the start his position was made as difficult as possible. He was told to communicate his views to the Treasury who would then issue appropriate instructions to the Post Office. He was expressly prohibited from issuing any orders himself to officers in the Post Office, and made to understand that he had no executive authority of any kind.

It would be impossible to find anyone less likely than Rowland Hill to accept the role of a neutered kitten; some tension and discord was inevitable from the start. Colonel Maberly was as apprehensive as was Rowland, and he could see all sorts of difficulties ahead; prudently he took special pains to warn his subordinates not to lay themselves open to charges of obstruction and non-cooperation that he feared would be forthcoming from Rowland on the slightest pretext. How sincere was the Colonel's concern for impartiality is impossible to tell, but he was shrewd enough to cover himself by putting this instruction on record.

In his recent book Dr M. J. Daunton has recorded something of the battles Rowland Hill had with the sitting tenants in the Post Office, but in his account he perhaps tends to rely too much on the testimony of the two officials who, more than others, were brought into professional conflict with him. These were his immediate superior Colonel Maberly, Secretary to the Post Office, and his subordinate colleague Anthony

Trollope, the famous novelist, who was one of the more active and colourful Surveyors or Inspectors.

In essence the mutual antagonism between the two camps was a confrontation between the blunt, confident Midlander and two smooth, rather easy-going Southerners, one of whom – Maberly – was neatly summed up by a later Postmaster General, Lord Clanricarde, as having more than a touch of Irish blarney; in that day and age they were completely different animals. In Rowland's eyes Colonel Maberly and Trollope were little more than 'upper-class' playboys; they both belonged to the traditional huntin', fishin' and shootin' fraternity whose very existence was anathema to the hard-working, strait-laced Unitarian Rowland Hill.

Colonel William Leader Maberly had been a full-time professional soldier until he was thirty-two years of age, and it is a measure of his general competence that he was apparently able to combine his Army career with his work as a Member of Parliament from 1819 to 1834. For a few years he was Surveyor of the Ordnance and also Commissioner of Customs. This rather meagre background of nominal administrative experience could hardly compare with Rowland Hill's highly demanding work in organising the logistics of the colonisation of South Australia from 1835 to 1839, during which time he had chartered thirty-eight ships and conveyed over 5,000 emigrants to their destination near modern-day Adelaide under model conditions and without loss or serious accident to any of them. Then from 1843 to 1846, as Managing Director he had rescued the London and Brighton Railway from impending bankruptcy to astonishing profitability and exemplary service. Add to this his twenty-five years of unremitting toil in creating his educational breakthrough at Hazelwood School which surely represents the most striking example of original and intricate administration to be found in our educational history. In evolving his wide curriculum, experimenting with new teaching methods and working out his novel system of self-discipline and pupil participation (without the sanction of corporal punishment) Rowland Hill had to use his imagination and acute brain to handle new ideas, lively pupils, critical parents and a sceptical Establishment.

At all events Colonel Maberly had been appointed to the very senior post of Secretary to the Post Office in 1836. Of course he was well-connected and had the right background; his elegant novelist wife belonged to a titled family, and together they enjoyed the smart social life among London's élite. According to reliable contemporary reports (which Dr Daunton quotes) the Colonel was wont to turn up at his office around eleven o'clock, and then summon his orderly to bring him his breakfast, after which he went through the motions of dealing with his correspondence. In contrast, back at the Treasury from September 1839 onwards, his new colleague, Rowland Hill, the dedicated 'workaholic', had been at his desk soon after 7.00 am, much to the irritation of his office colleagues. It is hardly surprising that he and the Colonel were, on the personal level, mutually antagonistic from the start. Such a strained relationship hardly contributed to the cool, dispassionate discussion of controversial matters.

Anthony Trollope, like his master Colonel Maberly, was also an 'upper-class' dilettante with the cachet of Winchester and Harrow stamped upon him, but without doubt he performed his professional task with some pride and sincerity. He had the happy knack of combining work and pleasure, and much of the time he spent in the West Country and in Ireland inspecting the working of the postal service gave him the opportunity to enjoy the hospitality of the local squires, riding to hounds with them, fishing in their rivers and shooting on their estates. At the same time he never forgot his true calling as a writer of novels; this he carried on religiously, on his portable knee-table in railway carriages, in hotel bedrooms and in the libraries of the landed gentry he was visiting. He was a gifted writer who saw life through the novelist's eyes, dramatising casual incidents, relishing a touch of satire and sharpening his characters to the edge of caricature. It is therefore quite typical of him, speaking of Rowland Hill, to declare, 'I was always an anti-Hillite; it was a pleasure to me to differ from him on all occasions. . . . I never came across anyone who so little understood the ways of men – unless it was his brother, Frederic.' This is pure Barchester backbiting, and it explains why it has been frequently said that the best piece of fiction Trollope ever wrote was his own auto-biography.

If we need further evidence of Trollope's unreliability as a serious commentator on Rowland Hill's performance in the Post Office, it is not difficult to find it. He himself lets the cat out of the bag when he says in the Barchester Chronicles, 'It is so easy to condemn, and so pleasant too; for eulogy charms no listeners and detraction does.' Even more to the point is the comment of Trollope's own friend and literary companion, George Augustus Sala, who was one of the most distinguished journalists of the day as well as being a travel-writer and novelist. He sums up his friend in these words: 'crusty, quarrelsome, wrong-headed, prejudiced, obstinate – and thoroughly honest Tony Trollope.' Likewise a colleague tells of the occasion at a meeting of fellow-surveyors (the Post Office Inspectors) when Trollope delighted the company as he roared, 'I differ from you entirely . . . What was it you said?' It is clear that here Dr Daunton has backed the wrong horse.

Trollope, however, had been bred and brought up as a gentleman, and even his horrendous experiences as a boy at Winchester and Harrow did not pollute his native decency or eradicate his acquired conviction that 'manners makyth man'. So when Rowland finally retired in March 1864 Trollope did not hesitate to drop the mask and reveal his true feelings in a memorable letter he wrote as soon as he heard the news:

> My dear Sir Rowland,
>   . . . As there is no longer any official connexion between us, I may perhaps say a few words which I could not have said while you were our secretary. I cannot but have felt for the last year or two since I was called upon to make one of a committee of inquiry during your illness, that you have regarded me as being in some sort unfriendly to your plans of postal reform. I am not going to trouble you with any discussion on that matter, but I cannot let your resignation from office pass without assuring you of my thorough admiration for the great work of your life. I have regarded you for many years as one of the essential benefactors, not only of your own country, but of all the civilized world. I think that the thing you have done has had in it more of general utility than any other measure which has been achieved in my time. And there has been a completeness about it which must, I should think, make you thoroughly contented with your career, as far as it has gone. There are national services for which a man can receive no adequate reward, either in rank or money, and it has been your lot to render such a service to the world at large. I hope that you may live long to enjoy the recognition of your own success.
>   Believe me, my dear Sir Rowland,
> Very faithfully yours,
Anthony Trollope.

This letter, many would agree, has a ring of touching sincerity about it, and it reveals Trollope as a nobler character than he usually represents himself to be. It is 'thoroughly honest Tony Trollope' in the end. Also it shows how, in spite of his unsympathetic exterior, Rowland Hill could win the admiration and concealed affection of his less sympathetic staff.

Dr Daunton is right, up to a point, in claiming that our evaluation of Rowland Hill's achievements in the Post Office is partly based on his own and his family's account of his work. But to attach prime importance to these sources is not acceptable, for there are masses of documents in the late 1830s and in the 1840s that provide us with an objective and reliable picture – from the reams of evidence put before the Wallace Select Committee on Postage in 1843; the information contained in the Post Circular, started in 1839 (admittedly partly propagandist); the various other Reports and Commissions that came thick and fast in that period; and the accounts given by subsequent historians of postal developments in that period.

[117]

Quite naturally Rowland speaks very confidently about the economics of his plan, having based his case on the best evidence available to him and it is inconsistent with his character to suggest that he was deliberately and habitually distorting the facts. Indeed there were precious few facts on which he could have based his forecasts. We should also remember, as Maberly did, that at the time of writing his pamphlet in 1837 Rowland had never had the opportunity of crossing the threshold of the Post Office administrative centre, consequently he was writing with very little firm information and with no first hand experience of the complexities of the organisation. The government statistics that Rowland was able to consult could never tell him the whole story. Being aware of all these handicaps Colonel Maberly had every reason to be somewhat sceptical about Rowland's plan, but the latter, perhaps somewhat unreasonably, tended to interpret Maberly's doubts as blatant hostility.

One must admit that in the short term Rowland's economic forecasts for his plan were over-optimistic, but in taking such a big step into unknown territory his calculations and extrapolations could not be expected to be a hundred per cent correct. Today, even with a battery of sophisticated computers occupying the area of half a football pitch our mandarins in the Treasury do not always get their sums right. Looking at the matter broadly one can see that Rowland's basic claim was sound enough. He maintained that the cost of the Postal service was inflated by unfair and unnecessary charges and expenses, and he suggested some easily-applied remedies to eliminate them. His prime principles were simplification and rationalisation. To this end he diagnosed the chief sources of waste and loss of revenue to be: the inhibiting cost of unnecessarily high postal rates; the many blatant and illegal abuses of the existing postal service; and plain inefficiency combined with the survival of too many outdated practices.

Rowland's reasoning in tackling the underlying weaknesses of the existing system can be summarised under five headings:

1. He saw quite clearly that it was a sensible economy and a step towards greater efficiency if he simplified and co-ordinated the workings in London of the General and Foreign Posts with that of the London Twopenny Post, and bringing under one head the Inland Office which served the country as a whole, and the Foreign Office which had been handling only the overseas mail. In its evidence to the Select Committee in 1843 the Post Office opposed these seemingly sensible proposals. This reflects the extreme caution that Colonel Maberly and those he advised

almost automatically exercised. Rowland Hill had always been a generator of new ideas and naturally looked upon such a negative and ultra-conservative attitude with dismay and incomprehension.

2. Like his experienced supporter Robert Wallace he firmly believed that by reducing postal charges the Post Office in the long run would derive great financial benefit. He knew that, back in 1823, a reduction of tax and excise duties on tea, coffee, soap and silks had brought astonishing increases in revenue. His general assumptions concerning future postal revenue proved in principle to be correct, for with the reduced postal rate the number of chargeable letters carried between 1839 and 1850 increased by 357 per cent, and despite possible temporary set-backs, he had no doubt that the Penny Post had come to stay and in the long run the revenue from the cheaper postage would continue to rise. What actually happened was quite remarkable, for not only did his Penny rate for ordinary inland letters survive until 1918, but by the mid 1890s, according to the official statistics on postal rates, the whole of the Post Office revenue surplus was derived solely from the Penny Post, and the profit was so large that it cancelled out the losses made on the Telegraph service, the newspaper and open post and the Foreign and Colonial post. What more convincing proof is needed to show that Rowland Hill's Penny Post plan was triumphantly successful and uncannily accurate in economic terms in the long run, even if his time scale was originally a little conjectural and over-optimistic?

3. Rowland Hill could see quite clearly that the high cost of postage coupled with the absurdity of the single-sheet regulation and the practice of charging by distance instead of by weight had driven business people and large companies to devise ways and means of avoiding such prohibitive charges. It had led to a vast proliferation of smugglers, fixers and 'spivs' who, between them, deprived the Post Office of immense sums in revenue, as explained in Chapter V. The classic case, we may recollect, was that of the mails carried by the first steamship to be used for postal traffic between Liverpool and New York, when there were precisely five letters in the official bag and over ten thousand in unofficial contraband bags. Colonel Maberly's confident assertion that not more than 25 per cent to 50 per cent of the mail was illegally carried is clearly grossly inaccurate in this instance.

4. To cut down the vast waste of time and money involved in the collecting of postage when letters were delivered, he introduced his scheme for pre-payment which led to the pre-eminence of

the adhesive stamp as the most popular and convenient way of achieving it.

5. Rowland Hill was convinced that a modest postage charge by weight rather than by distance would simplify and accelerate the work of the sorters and counter-clerks, reducing the forty possible operations involved, when distance was the criterion, to about two when weight alone was considered. This, of course, was the corner-stone of his whole plan – a uniform postal rate irrespective of distance – and it was by his own observations and calculations that he made this important discovery.

These were some of the more obvious simplifications introduced by Rowland Hill in the earlier stages of his reforms. This is not to claim that he was the first person to point out the need for such action. Many of these problems had been talked about for years, but it is the measure of Rowland Hill's greatness that not only did he demonstrate the justice and economic viability of the proposed uniform rate of postage, but he had the drive, determination and administrative skill to draw all these factors together and rationalise their shortcomings once and for all. Moreover, he had to do this in the face of what he saw as inertia, obstruction and bitter resentment, and of the frank disbelief on the part of the postal officials in the wisdom and practicality of his plan.

In his study of Rowland Hill's career Dr Daunton observes with astonishment that the whole of the Post Office story is dominated by one man, and that the development of the Post Office 'is now viewed almost entirely by the distortions of Hill's own voluminous writings, works of self-justification which do not provide an objective view of the reforms introduced before 1840.' This is demonstrably an overstatement. Granted that Hill was egotistical and desperately ambitious for the success of his plan, the facts show that most of the alleged distortions are pretty close to the truth, as we shall shortly make clear. Also, there is no doubt whatsoever that Rowland was fully aware of the slow but steady progress made by the Post Office up to 1840, and in particular he never stinted his praise for Robert Wallace as one of the great pioneers of postal reform. But Wallace's quite modest reforms had not made much progress, and he had reached the point when he had almost lost heart.

Colonel Maberly and his supporters, including Dr Daunton, have tried to make out that the ideas of Robert Wallace and other early would-be reformers were already well advanced before Rowland Hill appeared on the scene, and would in due course have brought about the Penny Postage and the rest of Rowland's plans without any dramatic upheaval. This is sheer wishful thinking and the experience of history shows unmistakably that all great surges of progress have always depended on the vision and drive of certain individuals.

All great causes need a dynamic leader to tie loose ends together and force events to a successful conclusion. Robert Wallace, MP, after a lifetime of frustrating struggle in fighting for postal reform, had reached the end of the road as a lone combatant by the time Rowland's pamphlets on postal reform appeared in 1837. It was with relief that he welcomed the dynamic newcomer, feeling that at last a doughty champion had appeared to whom he could confidently pass the torch. He knew only too well that Colonel Maberly and his gang were incapable of providing the necessary drive to bring about the urgent postal reforms that were demanding attention and to which various uncoordinated and fumbling moves were beginning to be made.

In our country's history we can see how often vigorous leadership has emerged to serve us well in moments of need. In the 1914/18 war it needed the dynamic leadership of David Lloyd George to resolve the disastrous shell shortage that could easily have led to defeat in the early years of the conflict. Again, in 1940 we called in the relentless drive of Lord Beaverbrook to produce the bombers and fighter planes we so desperately needed to win the war. In both cases production programmes were already in being, but it required a charismatic figurehead to galvanise the sluggish flow of production into the torrent that our perilous position demanded.

One can quote case after case to prove the point; in the mid-nineteenth century it was Richard Cobden who reformed the Corn Laws; William Wilberforce who abolished slavery, and in more recent times Sir William Beveridge created the modern Welfare state in 1942, and R. A. Butler completely refashioned secondary education in 1944. In every case it was a gifted and single-minded individual who brought about the reforms. So it was with Rowland Hill.

We know that the world has to pay a price for its outstanding leaders, however difficult they may be to work with. In the global adoption of Hill's general ideas that immediately followed his success in Britain, it shows that the world at large unhesitatingly recognised a great achievement, and never stinted its admiration because of the petty personality-squabbles that were rumoured in the United Kingdom. Against the background of Rowland Hill's immense triumph, the bickerings of his critics – officials and politicians alike – seemed to the world to be pitifully childish and trivial.

If we study the evidence, as we shall in a moment, it seems indisputable that Rowland Hill did in truth suffer from more unfair detraction, obstruction and malicious hostility than almost any other contemporary

figure. It is not surprising that after years of such treatment, in addition
to the strains of the job itself, his mind lost something of its edge and
his final years were made a misery. He gave voice to his feelings in
his introduction to his own definitive account of his career in the Post
Office, written towards the end of his life. It sums up the darker side of
his treatment by some of the senior postal officials and politicians, but
to keep it in perspective it should be read alongside his magnanimous
comment quoted on page 112.

> . . . If the reader finds too much of self-assertion – if he thinks I have too
> often quoted what is complimentary to myself – I ask him to consider how
> much I have suffered from detraction and injustice; how my conclusions
> were ridiculed, my success denied; and how, when success was incon-
> testable, the origination of my plan was claimed by others. . . . Let him
> see me dismissed from office without recompense by a man of Sir Robert
> Peel's high character . . . let him observe how long and pertinaciously the
> progress of Postal Reform was troubled, thwarted and how loudly and
> confidently I was charged with proceedings for which I of all men was
> farthest from being responsible. He will readily be aware that claims and
> accusations may revive when I am no more. . . .

We can see how prophetic were his final words when today we read Dr
Daunton's comment: 'Hill created twenty years of acrimony and tension
within the Post Office which probably hindered rather than helped the
successful development of the Penny Post'. If the reader will study the
evidence submitted in the remainder of this chapter, he will probably
consider this judgment to be somewhat wide of the truth; in any case it
takes two to create a tension.

By nature Rowland fought instinctively against the creeping paralysis
of bureaucracy; he was a doer, and individualist who had had his own
way for over thirty years as the director and headmaster of Hazelwood
School, as the organiser of the colonisation of South Australia and the
Managing Director of the London and Brighton Railway. When he
left these positions of authority for the anonymity of a minor post in a
government department, he found himself in a different world in which
fools, knaves, political careerists and place-holders had to be listened to.
He soon came face to face with the harsher facts of the outside world.

His first shattering experience that brought him up against the
inertia, lack of vision and enterprise of officialdom had occurred in
1835 when Rowland and his engineer brother, Edwin, tried to persuade
the Treasury to adopt their recently patented rotary printing press for
registering the statutory revenue stamp on newspapers. Their response
was a blunt 'No' without even a courteous explanation or chance of
discussion, let alone the opportunity of giving a demonstration of the

potentialities of their invention. The story of this early rebuff has been told on page 65.

Let us now look more closely into Rowland's *cri de coeur* to see to what extent his alleged grievances were subjective distortions of the facts, or whether they were in fact true. In doing this we readily admit that Rowland was liable to interpret other peoples' honest doubts and scepticism as being an indication of vindictive hostility. But there was no imaginary grievance in one of the most memorable of his unhappy experiences which revealed to Rowland the deliberate duplicity and distortion of the truth that was perpetrated by what can only be described as the dirty-tricks department of the Treasury.

This deplorable episode, thereafter referred to by Rowland as the 'fallacious return', was aimed at wrecking the implementation of Rowland's plan by exposing its financial inaccuracy. Rowland was well aware that this was his Achilles' heel. In case it might be thought that this falsification could have occurred through the unwitting error of some unsuspecting junior clerk, the whole story reveals something very different.

It all happened in November 1842 just after Rowland's three year appointment with the Treasury had been terminated. Fearing that this might mean the abandoning of Rowland's plan, the officers of the *Mercantile Committee* sent a deputation to call on the Prime Minister, Sir Robert Peel and the Chancellor of the Exchequer, Henry Goulburn, to plead for the continued implementation of the plan. To the deputation's surprise the Prime Minister assured them that there was no question of the plan being abandoned as there was no longer any hostility to Rowland on behalf of the postal officials. This at least let the cat out of the bag in admitting that there had been hostility on the part of the officials.

Then, catching the deputation unawares, the Prime Minister reminded them that there was the problem of recent revenue returns that had shown that since the penny post had been adopted in 1839 revenue losses on the postal service had mounted up to around £10,000 per annum. This was news to the deputation as they had seen no figures to substantiate it; indeed they had all been firmly convinced that the penny post had been producing a healthy annual surplus. They took their leave somewhat bewildered and puzzled, and it was not until May 1843 that the explanation came to light in the pages of a report on postal finances then being submitted to the House of Commons. Rowland saw at once that the Treasury had not played fair and promptly went into action to nail the downright lie. The explanation was simple; in that particular revenue statement the substantial revenue losses that had long been sustained by the Packet-service handling foreign and colonial mails had, for the first time, been included in with the ordinary postal revenue, making it appear that there was an overall loss of £10,000 per annum instead of a profit of £600,000.

Rowland at once gave wide publicity to the error in the national Press and sent copies of his statement to the Prime Minister and Postmaster General for their edification. This, incidentally, was the sort of personal comment that Rowland occasionally made over the heads of his Post Office colleagues and superiors without obtaining the prior authority of the Postmaster General or anyone else. It did not contribute to his popularity in those quarters. In this particular case, having had his Treasury appointment terminated in September 1842, he was technically free to say what he wished. Not doing things by halves Rowland wrote a full explanation of the circumstances in a short pamphlet, *The State and Prospects of Penny Postage* which was published by his old friend and ally Charles Knight.

But there is another strange twist to the story. It was extremely odd that the usually fair-minded Sir Robert Peel, the Prime Minister, should have countenanced this 'framing' of Rowland Hill, for Sir Robert on 12 March 1842 had himself declared that 'a strong disposition existed somewhere to make the loss resulting from the penny post as large as possible.' In addition, to give the devil his due – and all honour to him – Colonel Maberly himself had done his utmost to prevent the publication of what he knew to be false figures. In his evidence to the Select Committee he declared with some passion:

> As I have said over and over again, looking at it as regards the Post Office revenue as compared with what the Post Office revenue was before the penny post, the surplus of income over expenditure is somewhere about £600,000.

Even Lord Palmerston, never a very ardent supporter of Rowland, felt morally obliged to repudiate 'the wild and malicious allegations that the introduction of the penny post had resulted in massive losses of revenue; these anticipations have been falsified and the calculations of Rowland Hill have turned out to be correct.'

As we have shown elsewhere, Post Office figures corroborate this, for by 1851 a clear profit had been established, and, taking Rowland's long view to the extreme, by 1890 the surplus from the penny post more than covered all the substantial losses made by other branches of the postal service. In short is it possible to find a grosser example of detraction and injustice than this?

Rowland's next complaint is that 'his conclusions were ridiculed' and 'his success denied.' Colonel Maberly's comments to the Select Committee in 1838 – 'preposterous and unsupported by facts. . . .' and Lord Lichfield's denunciation of Rowland's 'most wild and visionary scheme' are sufficient evidence of this at highest level – as recounted earlier in this chapter. And we have seen how the story of the 'fallacious return' is a clear example of the denial of an actual success.

Following this Rowland turns to the allegation that the origination of his plan was claimed by others. No doubt certain malicious detractors were trying to belittle the originality of Rowland's plan by pointing to the valuable pioneer work on postal reform carried on by Robert Wallace, MP for many years in the 1830s, and to Colonel Maberly's insistence that steady progress in reforms was taking place long before Hill made his appearance. Rowland was fully aware of this and frequently paid generous tribute to Wallace's efforts. The latter had long shown himself to be a warm-hearted and generous friend to Rowland and they co-operated with and trusted each other implicitly. Wallace never attempted to take credit for originating the idea of the uniform, pre-paid penny post, but he worked harder than anyone to secure the adoption of Rowland's plan. He can testify this in his own words, for the *Aberdeen Herald* of 2 October 1841 recorded his statement:

> And here let me say once and for all that to Mr Hill alone is the country indebted for that scheme, for he is the real inventor and its only discoverer.

Moreover, as soon as Rowland's Penny Postage plan had been published in 1837 Robert Wallace unhesitatingly volunteered his services under Rowland's banner, recognising that this younger dynamic figure had a closely co-ordinated plan at his finger-tips and the drive and determination to see the matter through.

Examples of how persistently Rowland was 'troubled and thwarted' are legion; they occurred both at high level and low level. A particularly blatant case of deliberate 'stalling' at high level began on 14 November 1841 when Rowland, supported by the *Mercantile Committee*, sent a letter to the Chancellor of the Exchequer asking for his suggestions for an improved system of registering letters to be given early attention, as the matter was of serious concern to the business community in particular. Receiving no reply Rowland wrote again more than a fortnight later, following this up with further letters on 27 January 1842 and on 7 March. On this last occasion he received a bare acknowledgement, but no action followed or was promised. Almost in despair Rowland wrote yet again on 23 March and 31 May, but no reply ever came. In September Rowland's temporary appointment was terminated. His indignation at such official indifference, incompetence and sheer bad manners cannot be dismissed as an unreasonable reaction or a figment of his imagination; the facts speak for themselves.

A typical example of low-level obstruction occurred on 12 April 1847 – even after he had been promoted to the new post of Secretary to the Postmaster General – when an internal letter addressed to Rowland in reply to an urgent query on a problem he was currently dealing with, required only a two minute walk along a corridor by the clerk concerned. Instead, Colonel Maberly being away in Ireland, the letter was sent to him there for his signature of authorisation. This stupid or malicious action delayed an important letter by more than a week; certainly Rowland was justified in having his suspicions aroused. Such delays were so frequent that he was forced to make a formal complaint to the Postmaster General who merely told the office to do better in future. Sometimes he was deliberately snubbed by having his recommendations ignored; for instance on occasions inaccurate documents were sent forward to the House of Commons ignoring the careful corrections he had made to them. This was an easy way of discrediting his efficiency.

Rowland suffered from this kind of guerilla warfare for years, with every possible variation of tactics. His letters and pro formas, both internal and external, were often ignored or put aside, virtually forgotten for months. For example it has already been told how on a visit to Yorkshire he found a whole packet of correspondence, covering a period of six months, gathering the dust in a postmaster's desk. The galling thing was that he had no doubts that if he had been given sole charge of the Post Office administration such unacceptable practices would have been stopped at once; but being subordinate to Colonel Maberly he knew he was powerless to lay down the law. But when in 1854 Rowland was eventually promoted to the highest office of Secretary to the Post Office he soon brought the whole service to a level of professional efficiency never seen before. We have Rowland's successor, John Tilley's testimony for this when he expressed his satisfaction 'at the general state of the service, so different from what he had once known . . . now everyone seemed to do his duty as a matter of course.' So much for Dr Daunton's claim that Rowland Hill was primarily a propagandist of his own ideas, without a real talent for administration.

Rowland's final complaint that he was 'loudly and confidently charged with proceedings for which I had no part whatsoever' clearly refers to the exceptionally virulent campaign whipped up against him over the question of Sunday working which we have described earlier on page 79. A hostile national Press and even the Bishops weighed in against him; yet it was proved beyond doubt that the only moves he

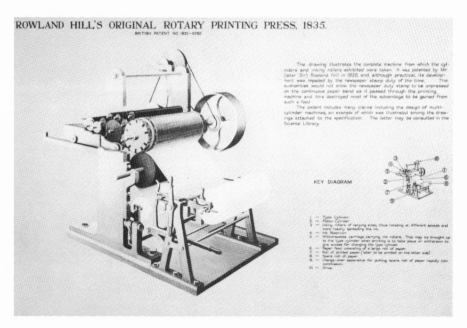

ROWLAND HILL'S ORIGINAL ROTARY PRINTING PRESS, 1835.
BRITISH PATENT NO. 1835 - 6762

KEY DIAGRAM

20. Hills' Rotary Printing Press, 1835.

POST-MAN

21. Bellmen, showing the peripatetic mail-bag, *c.* 1820.

22. London's first Letter Box at the corner of Fleet Street and Farringdon Street.

23. The Penny Black, 1 May 1840.

24. Rowland Hill (1795–1879).

25. Dr Thomas Arnold (1795–1842), Headmaster of Rugby School, by T. Phillips, 1839.

26. Big Schoolroom, Rugby (about 1816).

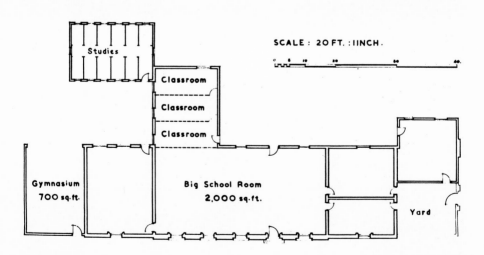

27. Ground-floor plan of Hazelwood School in 1827, based on the model made by J. D. Goodman and William Bowman. Goodman refers to the 'gymnasium on the left front . . . and studies behind'. The unnamed rooms are further classrooms or practical rooms. Three upper floors contained science laboratory, craftrooms, library and boarding, family and domestic accommodation.

had made were actually to protect his postal workers from such Sunday duties. Only *The Times* told the truth about this.

The examples quoted are really only the tip of the iceberg, but they have surely provided enough evidence to justify the validity of Rowland's complaints. If any reader still has doubts let him turn back to Chapter V where he will find yet more specific examples of obstruction and blatant non-cooperation – all based on solid fact. To dismiss Rowland as a victim of imaginary grievances and as an 'amateur propagandist' with a notable incapacity for 'systematic thought' simply does not stand up to examination. Every great cause from Magna Carta onwards through the Reform Bill to the modern Beveridge Report can be belittled down to the machinations of a few amateur propagandists whose ideas, because they are new and radical and do not follow the traditional conservative style of argument, can be deemed to lack systematic thought.

Having studied some samples of evidence, many fair-minded readers may accept the fact that Rowland did indeed suffer from extensive injustice, misrepresentation and hostility from the Post Office and government departments, but more was to come for in the 1850s a novel form of attack appeared when he was singled out for street demonstrations, mostly by malcontents who had been dismissed or passed over for promotion because of their laziness or incompetence. They depicted themselves on their posters and placards as victims of a white slave system ruthlessly exploited by a hard taskmaster. In point of fact the whole country knew that competition was unbelievably fierce to win the privilege of working for Rowland Hill's successful and expanding Post Office where opportunity for promotion was open for all, and where their Chief's concern for the workers' welfare was shown by the support he had always given to the establishment of savings schemes, health cover, insurance opportunities and pensions. This hostility shown by a handful of embittered troublemakers reached its climax in the three serious threats of assassination that were made in 1854, 1856 and 1858, as narrated earlier in Chapter V.

We need to remember that most of the efforts of Rowland Hill's critics, inside and outside the Post Office, were directed to discrediting his plan on the grounds of its alleged financial flaws; if this were proved beyond doubt, then his plan was in serious danger of dying a natural death. It has been admitted that Rowland was over-optimistic in some of his financial forecasts, but the general circumstances were very exceptional; through no fault of his own he had to try and build on shifting sand. Growth, changing conditions and unexpected new factors in the running of the Post Office were unsettling the ground under his feet even as he was attempting to build on it. For example, between 1838 and 1840 the cost of transporting letters by rail (an unavoidable new factor) had risen from £10,000 to £51,000 per annum, and the cost of running the surviving mail coaches had also increased.

Here was an unstable situation where the railways were trying to cash in on their almost monopolistic opportunity and possibly taking advantage of the prevailing uncertainties by driving very hard bargains in their contracts with the Post Office. This had been taking place even before Colonel Maberly was appointed Secretary to the Post Office in 1836, and long before Rowland Hill came on the scene. These railway costs continued to rise when the Colonel took over command, and around 1838 malicious rumours were to be heard hinting that Maberly was doing nothing about it as it was generally known that he was secretly hoping that rising costs would kill off Rowland's plan without further action on his part. Even if this were idle gossip it gives a good indication of the accepted impression that Maberly was positively hostile towards Rowland's plan.

Rowland could see only too clearly that rising rail costs could jeopardise the economics of his plan; to him the advent of the railways was an 'untoward coincidence' that had to be overcome. He was able to derive some consolation from the comment made by Edward Page, the Inspector General of Mails, that 'not only would penny postage without railways have been more practicable and remunerative, but it would have been even more profitable . . . than it is now.' At least this was further vindication of the validity of his original revenue forecasts if the railways had not become involved.

Colonel Maberly, of course, was himself fully aware of these constantly changing circumstances, the shifting sand on which the Post Office was being built; he had been grappling with such rising costs ever since he took command in 1836. It is only fair, therefore, to recognise that the Colonel was only being sensibly prudent in not accepting Rowland's theoretically based plan without some reservations. On his part Rowland was not unreasonable in insisting that it was unfair to judge it until all his main reforms of simplification had been implemented, for his scheme was based on this assumption. So, in a sense, there was a deadlock, a precarious tension between Rowland's impatient innovative thrust and the Colonel's slow-moving, conservative caution.

By a curious irony there had always been an underlying conflict in Rowland Hill's outlook on the Post Office. He knew that his first priority was to prove that his plan was financially sound. This meant being extremely careful with development costs, keeping down overheads and pegging wages to a minimum as far as possible. But this latter consideration cut right across his deep concern to improve wages and provide better conditions of work for his workforce; it was a dilemma that wore him down throughout his career, for he always remained a man of the people. The climax came in the 1860s, in the punishing years that brought on his final breakdown in health, when even his closest colleagues – his highly esteemed friend and Assistant Secretary, John Tilley, and the extremely able and energetic Frank Scudamore – openly disagreed with Rowland's policy of ruthless overall economy. They were inclined to look upon the Post Office as an essential public service in which efficiency was paramount and costs secondary. They believed there was a danger in seeking the lowest tender for a contract, and a great risk of early trouble if only the lowest possible wages were paid. To Rowland and Frederic such views were heresy; they were still haunted by the imperative of making the Penny Post profitable at all costs. But times were clearly changing, and it seemed that Rowland's basic philosophy of economics and labour was beginning to be challenged by a new generation of officials whose views were perhaps more in tune with the spirit of the age. In 1864 it was John Tilley who succeeded to Rowland's post when ill-health finally forced his retirement.

The final showdown had occurred in 1860 onwards over the question of the letter-carriers' wages. It was unfortunate that Rowland happened to be on sick leave at the time, and as the matter was urgent, John Tilley, standing in for Rowland, recommended to the Chancellor of the Exchequer that a commission of enquiry should be set up to deal with the pressing problem. Frederic Hill, rallying at once to his brother's support, raised a strong objection, and went so far as to instruct the committee not to make any decision without his and John Tilley's express approval. This was a fatal blunder, an unheard of infringement of protocol, for here was Frederic in effect trying to control the decisions of a committee properly set up by the Postmaster General and the Deputy acting for Rowland. The recently appointed Postmaster General, Lord Stanley, no friend to Rowland, and the Prime Minister himself, Lord Palmerston, bluntly and quite understandably turned down the Hills' plea.

The incident shows how far Rowland and Frederic had strayed from the democratic principles they had fought for all through their lives, and reveals Rowland's settled conviction that the only way a huge, expanding business like the Post Office could be run was by cutting it off from political influence and placing it under a strong autocratic leader – like himself.

The special and unique conditions that made Rowland Hill's years in the Post Office so difficult are still not fully recognised. With the passing of the Reform Act of 1832 a few years earlier – a triumph very dear to Rowland's heart – the whole structure and ethos of society had been radically changed. The social and political consequences of the sudden growth of the franchise and of democratic rights cast an entirely new light on labour relations and man management, at a time when the Post Office was carrying the largest single work-force in the country. On top of all these problems he faced up to the nagging issue concerning the relationship between private enterprise and public service. Was it the duty of a large public service like the Post Office to aim at maximum profit like any ordinary commercial venture, or to give priority to social considerations?

All through his life Rowland Hill's thinking had always been more than fifty years ahead of his time, as his record in the field of education had spectacularly shown. With uncanny prescience he seemed to foresee many of the problems looming in the future. It did not take him long to realise that the structure and management of such a large concern as the Post Office was inappropriate and inefficient. As early as 1835 a Royal Commission examining this very question had made a tentative recommendation that the control of the Post Office might in future be put in the hands of a Board rather than in the Postmaster General. Rowland had long held similar views, and was soon to learn by experience the disadvantages of being under the direction of a political nominee, rather than under a Civil Service administrative head. Ironically and quite characteristically he realised that from his own point of view, even this solution had its disadvantages if the administrative head were a person like Colonel Maberly and not himself.

This issue proved to be a dilemma that was to dog the Post Office until 1969 when at last the post of Postmaster General was abolished and the Post Office became an autonomous corporation. In our own day, in a similar issue, the satirical television series, *Yes, Minister* shows only too revealingly the precarious tensions existing between ill-informed Ministers of the Crown and top-level Civil Servants who have handled the very special problems of their departments for years.

Under these trying circumstances Rowland Hill occasionally showed his impatience by working with the Treasury against his own superiors in the Post Office; sometimes he went even further and made decisions as if he were holding the powers of a supreme controller. He was unquestionably made in the mould of a modern industrial supremo.

Rowland Hill's career, as we have indicated, spanned some of the most momentous years of our country's social and economic history. In the short space of sixty years or so we had crossed the threshold into the modern world in which the individualism and *laissez-faire* of earlier times were being superseded more and more by state influence and even state intervention. In this mighty movement Rowland Hill was one of the most effective catalysts. In the Post Office, as earlier in the sphere of education, he had at the beginning inherited somewhat tangled and confused organisations, some of whose elements had either ossified into irrelevance or had grown up too quickly and too piecemeal. By his clear thinking, his vision and his immense administrative drive he reduced these confused elements, as in a kaleidoscope, to some sort of order. This was more noticeable in his early days at the Post Office, but during his final ten years between 1854 and 1864, when he was in full control, the stress and complications of the huge administrative task gradually appeared to be too much for his failing constitution.

Looking back on Rowland Hill's whole varied career we can now come to some firm conclusions on what he actually achieved in his life; momentous though they be, they can be summed up in a few sentences.

In his first major field of activity – education – he pioneered a reformed secondary curriculum, new methods of teaching and a humane conception of discipline that were a landmark, a watershed, in the history of education. In his second and greatest field of endeavour – his postal reforms – he gave a new dimension, a fresh impetus and vitality to one of the finest institutions our country has known – the Post Office and the Royal Mail.

As Dr Daunton claims, Rowland Hill's presence still haunts St Martin's le Grand. But can anyone with justification now challenge his right to be revered through the generations – despite all his shortcomings – as the *genius loci* and true begetter of the great institution that he has bequeathed to us and to the world?

Appendix A

The American Connection

THE events described in this chapter mark an important stage in the development of education for problem children of various categories, and it is surprising to find that it was to a considerable degree inspired by what had been achieved at Hazelwood.

Two memorable figures in America were largely responsible for this special aspect of education. The first was William George who had notable success at his *Junior Republic* at Freeville, New York, in the 1890s; the other was Homer Lane whose similar work at his *Little Commonwealth* (originally called the Ford Republic) in Detroit around the year 1906 was soon to be translated to England to be a permanent influence on special education thereafter. Both of these practitioners were aided, abetted and encouraged by the timely appearance of a high-minded and generous sponsor, Thomas Mott Osborne, whose significant contribution is related below.

Both these institutions relied on self-government as their basis of discipline, and both delegated rule-making to the children themselves who set up their own jury-courts with their self-imposed penalties, even issuing their coinage in lieu of marks. This conception of discipline and much more had been set down in the Hills' book *Public Education*, which in its editions of 1822, 1825, 1833 and 1894 seems to have been freely available in America.

It is a fact, already mentioned, that even Thomas Jefferson himself, one of America's greatest reformers and a distinguished President from 1801 to 1809, had acquired a personal copy early in 1825, sent to him by the Hills. The reason for Jefferson's interest is pretty obvious. He himself was a great reformer and a man of wide talents and versatility, and for years he had been planning a new education system for his young country. He states that 'he had lost no occasion to make himself acquainted with the best seminaries in other countries and with the opinions of the most enlightened individuals on the subject of the sciences'.

[132]

One leading thinker with whom he exchanged ideas on educational reform was Dr Joseph Priestley, FRS, the discoverer of Oxygen and an eminent philosopher, formerly of Birmingham and well known to Thomas Wright Hill, who had actually taught at Priestley's Unitarian Sunday school. Priestley had emigrated to America in 1794, not long after the Birmingham riots when his chapel and house were burnt down and his books and scientific apparatus largely destroyed. Jefferson expressed a special interest in the science programme introduced at Hazelwood and in the working of the jury-court set up by the boys. This is why he was anxious to receive a copy of the Hills' book even though as early as 1814 he had already laid down his provisional pattern for secondary education in America. His proposed curriculum in particular included modern languages, mathematics and general science, covering chemistry, zoology, botany, mineralogy and astronomy. This seems to show the influence of the Dissenting Academies in which Dr Priestley had helped to develop the teaching of science.

It was at this moment in 1825 that Jefferson opened his new university, built to his own attractive design, at Charlottesville, Virginia, set out as a lovely campus not far from his own home, Montecello, in the hills a few miles away. Alas, Jefferson's lofty ideals of self-government and freedom, no doubt boosted by the last minute testimony of the Hills, proved to be too intoxicating for the raw young students who provided the first intake. Disorder and rioting broke out and many of the new buildings were burnt down. This was a sickening blow to the aged Jefferson and it undoubtedly contributed to his death in the following year. But his vision did not perish, for like a phoenix, the university rose from its ashes to become one of the most attractive and prestigious universities in America. Jefferson's idealism survived too in the development at Charlottesville of the 'honour system', a voluntary moral compact entered into by the students that has been copied in universities throughout America.

One of the ideas that most attracted Jefferson – that of the jury-court and the principle of self-government – was not entirely forgotten in America. After lying dormant for nearly half a century it suddenly re-appears in a striking form, helped, by the strangest coincidence, by the publication of a book on penal reform by Rowland Hill's brother, Frederic (1803–96).

He was eight years younger than Rowland, and after teaching for some fifteen years at Hazelwood (as we have related), he read for the Bar and eventually became Inspector of Prisons for Scotland. Like all the Hills, he was a radical reformer and did great work in improving the prison system. His book, *Crime; its Amount, Causes and Remedies*, published in 1853 was long regarded as a classic of 'penalogical science' and had considerable influence in Great Britain as well as in America.

It caught the attention of Thomas Mott Osborne during the 1880s, as a result of which Osborne proved to be the important catalyst in our immediate story. Like the Hills, Thomas Osborne was a staunch Unitarian and an active, practical idealist and reformer. He was a magistrate in New York and, as such, was well acquainted with the seamy side of life. It is part of American social history how in 1913 Osborne voluntarily and incognito subjected himself to a spell of unprivileged imprisonment at Auburn Penitentiary, New York, in order to see for himself the kind of experience he was sentencing law-breakers to, and to what extent the prison system was achieving anything of value. As a result Osborne set about reforming and humanising the American penal system by his philosophy of turning prison 'from a scrap heap to a repair shop', which was precisely Frederic Hill's message in his book on crime. During his career Thomas Osborne became Governor of the Naval Prison at Portsmouth, New Hampshire, as well as of the infamous Sing-Sing Penitentiary, and at each of these, we may remember, it was a point of honour for him to hang on the wall of his Governor's Office a portrait of Frederic Hill as an inspiration to himself and to all who worked with him.

Earlier in his career, worried by the increase of juvenile delinquency, Thomas Osborne became interested in William R. George who was doing unusually enterprising work in New York with deprived and delinquent children. At his 'Fresh Air' colony William George provided these city children with a long summer holiday in the country, and soon discovered that the only way to run the camp successfully was by making it a self-governing, benignly disciplined and industrious community. His motto was '*Nothing without labour*', and soon he substituted trial and penalties imposed by a jury in place of the traditional corporal punishment. Gradually he made his little community a microcosm of the world outside; it was a democracy ruling itself.

Thomas Osborne was so impressed by this work that in 1895 he helped William George to establish a better-provided location at Freeville, New York and encouraged him to write his book *The Junior Republic at Freeville*, published by Appleton, New York in 1909 in which he gave a detailed account of his methods. Thomas Osborne wrote a striking foreword:

What Mr George had really discovered was a new application of a very old principle – nothing less than *Democracy* itself. . . . I called it a 'laboratory experiment in democracy'. . . . For we have as yet only begun the possibilities of Democracy: it remains to educate citizens by applying the democratic principle to our school system (still dominated by aristocratic and paternalistic ideals – the ideals of an outworn system); to apply the democratic principle to our factories and solve the labour problem; to apply the democratic principle to our prisons and reform our ignorant brethren who have failed to adapt themselves to society. . . . I hope I may live to see the day when in every school and college in the land, alongside the standard of scholarship may be raised the standard of citizenship. . . . Social responsibility, which is citizenship, should be part of every school and college curriculum. . . . Gladstone said: 'It is liberty alone that fits a man for liberty'.

There is no doubt that Thomas Osborne is here reflecting the pure doctrine of the Hills exactly as set forth in *Public Education*. Authentic testimony of this has come to light as a result of a visit paid to William George at Freeville in 1907 by the Reverend Frederick Hankinson, later well-known as the doyen of the Unitarian community in Great Britain. In a letter to the present author dated 8 January 1954 Mr Hankinson states that at Freeville that day he also met Thomas Osborne and adds:

I found him (Thomas Osborne) full of enthusiasm for the Hills' book *Public Education* which clearly had inspired and interested him for some time. In fact, so impressed was he with this book that he had instructed the bookseller, Southern, in the Strand, to buy up any copies he could lay his hands on and despatch them to him in America.

Let us now examine exactly what William George was attempting. At Freeville he strove to make the community life real, an epitome of life itself – the authentic Hill principle. Like Fellenberg's *Hofwyl*, the regime was based on country pursuits, and his campers had to work for their clothes and their food – boys and girls alike. For currency he introduced, first cardboard, then metal tokens with denominations 1, 5, 10, 25, 50, 100. The boys and girls, mostly fourteen years of age and over, made their own rules and held a jury-court to enforce them. This led to the nomination of appropriate law-enforcement officers; prosecuting counsel, constables, record-keepers and the like. Soon a complete written constitution was built up defining the functions of the Executive, Judicial and Legislative branches. From this the young people could see how all the other impedimenta of the State evolved – taxation, health-care, community budgets, indictments, law and order, search-warrants and so on. In this way they learnt about rights and duties, and the whole art of citizenship, for they were living in a miniature real world which they themselves had created.

The significant point about this is that it reflects so closely the practice of Hazelwood that it is difficult to believe that it has not been copied direct from *Public Education*. The circumstantial evidence is overwhelming on this point, as the following seven features are common to both establishments:

1. Citizenship must be achieved by *work*. Compare the Hills' motto '*All is the gift of industry*' with that of William George '*Nothing without labour*'.
2. No corporal punishment.
3. Laws made by elected committee.
4. Pupils' jury-court for the trial of offenders.
5. Use of token coinage:
   Hazelwood: 1, 3, 5, 10, 50, 100, 500, 1,000.
   George Republic: 1, 5, 10, 25, 50, 100.
6. Monthly school Magazines written and printed by the pupils themselves.
7. Jury-court officials similarly named.

It has been mentioned earlier that there must have been plenty of copies of the Hills' book circulating in America. Not only were the two editions of 1822 and 1825 available, but in 1833 a further exposition of the system was published under the title *Sketch of the System of Education, Moral and Intellectual, in practice at the schools of Bruce Castle, Tottenham and Hazelwood near Birmingham*; Baldwin and Cradock, London 1838. Then in 1894 a reprint of the second edition of *Public Education* of 1825 was published under the title *The Organisation of Hazelwood School*, by Biggs and Co. London, 1894.

Thomas Osborne and his protégés, William George and Homer Lane, honourably took advantage of the free trade in ideas that has always been traditional in the academic world to translate the Hills' ideas for the benefit of American children, but, regrettably, other teachers in America resorted to deliberate plagiarism for their own pecuniary ends. A blatant example of this (which again proves that in 1835 the Hills' book was readily available) occurs in a text-book on *Penmanship* by B. F. Foster, a commercial school proprietor, published in Boston in 1835. In it are to be found page after page copied almost word for word from the Hills' chapter on the subject in *Public Education*.

The *George Junior Republic* made a notable impact on education in America – always years ahead of Great Britain in enterprise and innovation. In 1908 a *National Association of Junior Republics* was founded to press for the establishment of similar institutions throughout the States. Then the *School Citizen Committee* was established, pledged 'to advocate pupil self-government or participation in self-government as an essential of practical training in citizenship'. In the big cities, particularly where the schools had very mixed nationalities, the idea was eagerly accepted. In next to no time six States had established very close approximations to the *Junior Republic*, and by 1913 over a hundred schools were known to be organised on a self-governing basis, thirty being in New York alone. Since then, in America and in Great Britain, the idea of pupil-participation has been widely accepted: school councils representing the whole school are a commonplace, showing how the Hills' ideas at Hazelwood have been adopted for normal schools as well as for special schools.

Though it was William George's *Junior Republic* that triggered off these developments in America, the work of Homer Lane, which was more positively remedial and included some much younger children to make up family groups, also had a major influence in this field. It is his contribution we must now consider.

Homer Lane was born in New Hampshire where he started his working life as a railway clerk and later became a grocery delivery-boy. A friendly doctor, noticing Lane's interest in young people, paid for him to train as a teacher of woodwork. After some experience teaching in a prison, he moved to Detroit, a fast-growing industrial complex, to work as Superintendent of Playgrounds where he learnt a good deal more about young people. In 1907 a wealthy philanthropic businessman in Detroit invited Lane to take on the post of Warden and Director of a country-based community for delinquent young people. It was called the *Ford Republic* after its sponsor's name, but the name was changed later to the *Boys' Republic* to avoid suggesting any connection with the Ford Motor company.

As the name implies, the community, similar to William George's prototype ten years earlier, was run as a model republic, a little commonwealth, controlled by a written constitution which echoed the Constitution of the USA. It had three branches – Legislative, Executive and Judicial; the latter comprised a Citizens' Court with Homer Lane as Chief Justice. Self-government was the ideal and Lane planned to hand over responsibility for discipline to the boys and girls themselves. At first corporal punishment was used, administered by Homer Lane and also by the older boys. Citizenship was earned by working for the community; the boys and girls had to work for their board and lodgings and even for their clothes.

In 1912 a minor scandal and various disagreements caused Lane to hand in his resignation, but at this moment he had a visit from a distinguished Englishman who was deeply interested in the pioneering work of Lane and of William George at Freeville. This was the Hon. George Montagu, soon to become the ninth Earl of Sandwich, who was destined to play a crucial part in this story of the American connection. He had shown an early interest in penal reform and when he heard about the *George Junior Republic* he decided to visit America to investigate for himself. He inspected many State prisons and reformatories and met William George and Thomas Osborne at the *George Junior Republic* in Freeville and went on to see the *Ford Republic* where Homer Lane had established his little commonwealth.

On returning to England George Montagu resolved to establish a similar community for disturbed and delinquent children. To this end he convened a most impressive committee of knowledgeable and interested people, with himself as Chairman of the Executive Committee, and his uncle, Lord Sandwich, as Chairman of the General Committee (until his death in 1916). Other eminent members included Lord Lytton (later Viceroy of India), Sir Otto Beit, financier and philanthropist, Sir William Nathan, the Duchess of Marlborough, Lady Evelyn Jones, Sir William Mather, Dr A. A. David, Headmaster of Rugby School, Sir Bernard Hawker, representing the Montessori Society (who wished to be associated with the experiment) and last but by no means least our friend Thomas Mott Osborne who had already shown a deep, enduring interest in the work of William George and Homer Lane in America.

The committee invited Homer Lane to England to discuss the project and forthwith asked him to be its Superintendent; so in June 1914 the *Little Commonwealth*, as it was called, was opened in Dorset with sixteen boys and eleven girls aged sixteen and under, together with eleven younger children between two and five years of age sponsored by the Montessori Society; these helped to complete the family units which were an essential part of the community. The basic premises and surrounding land, all part of Flowers Farm, were provided by the Earl of Sandwich, in a pleasant position near Yeovil. The premises consisted of the farmhouse, some barns and three cottages, which were named Bramble, Bracken and Heather, and over the years additional buildings were constructed by the boys themselves – workshops, schoolrooms, an assembly hall and more cottages. The latter formed the 'cottage homes' which housed the various family units of boys and girls of mixed ages, under a house-master or mistress, on the lines of M. D. Hill's and Mary Carpenter's pioneer efforts in Bristol over seventy years earlier. The numbers of the community never exceeded forty, although there was ample accommodation for more.

Homer Lane organised the community on less formal lines than he had at the *Ford Republic*, as he was now concerned with smaller units and younger children in his family groups. In 1917 the Home Office said it was prepared to recognise the *Little Commonwealth* as an accepted reformatory under its regulations, to take up to twenty girls and twenty-five boys. ·

Turning more and more to religious inspiration and basing his creed on the gospel of 'love and affection', Lane declared that his overriding aim was 'to make citizens'. To this end he insisted that his young people, except the babes, earned their living by working in the various departments of the community – on the farm, in the garden, in the laundry, in the kitchen, in the workshops or as housekeeper, cook, painter and carpenter. A boy engineer and a stoker looked after the steam boiler which powered the various pieces of machinery. At first wages were paid in cardboard currency, but soon metal tokens were struck as at Hazelwood ninety years earlier.

As at *Hazelwood* and the *George Junior Republic*, a citizens' court was established in which offenders against the community were tried and sentenced by their peers. There was no 'lock-up' as there had been at the *George Junior Republic*, but those convicted of serious misdemeanours could be put in detention; this meant that the defendant was confined to the grounds and 'sent to Coventry' for a period. Fines or hard labour were imposed for the scores of lesser crimes. The citizens' court and the general administration had a series of officers similar to those at the *George Junior Republic*, repeating once again the general practices at Hazelwood.

In E. T. Bazeley's book *Homer Lane and the Little Commonwealth* (Allen and Unwin, London 1928) the following are mentioned:

> Judge
> Chairman of Legislative Committee
> Chairman of Judicial Committee
> Commissioner for the Boys' Court (to supervise the sentences imposed)
> Commissioner for the Girls' Court (to supervise the sentences imposed)
> Clerk of the Court
> Clerk of the Public Works
> Treasurer

There is plenty of evidence that Homer Lane achieved a large measure of success in turning out reformed characters from the unruly, anti-social young people who came under his care. He attributed his success entirely to his gospel of 'love and affection' and to the system of self-government and freedom from authoritarian rules.

> It is in the Citizens' Court that one may get into closer touch with the spirit of the Commonwealth than in any other community function, and it is here that I look for the true spiritual expression of our boys and girls.

So wrote Homer Lane in his *Talks to Parents and Teachers* published posthumously in 1928.

Homer Lane had unusual gifts; this is universally conceded by all who knew and worked with him. By his obvious sincerity and personal charisma he won complete trust from most of his charges, and indeed, from most adults with whom he had dealings. In many ways he was a difficult and elusive man to deal with, quite unbusinesslike, rash, incalculable and at times extremely foolish. But most noteworthy was his remarkable intuitive understanding of the children in his care.

He was not the first teacher of neurotic and delinquent children to pay the price for risking his neck in this dangerous occupation. But he was extraordinarily naive and foolish to allow some of his girls of fifteen to bring him his morning tea in bed. This led, eventually, to some unfortunate allegations which were thoroughly investigated without actual charges being brought against him. Greatly to their credit his committee stood by him one and all, but the distressing situation eventually forced them to close the school in October 1918. One member of the committee, Dr A. A. David, then Headmaster of Rugby School and later to become Bishop of Liverpool, even offered Lane an appointment at his school – an offer which the Earl of Sandwich urged him to accept, but Lane turned it down as he felt he would be an embarrassment to the school.

Thereafter Homer Lane practised in London as a Psychotherapist with considerable success, treating many distinguished patients – as well as humble ones – and lecturing and giving talks to Training Colleges and conferences. Then in the Spring of 1925, the Home Office and the Police, animated by an unbecoming vindictiveness, had him deported as an undesirable alien and for failing to make the necessary Income Tax returns. He died in Paris in September 1925.

Homer Lane's influence in the treatment of disturbed and delinquent children has been enduring, yet in his lifetime he was called every possible name – a seducer and lecher; a mountebank and impostor; a confidence trickster and embezzler; a saint and a second Christ (in the words of Lord Lytton when he was Viceroy of India). Professionally speaking Lane was an 'outsider', lacking any recognised qualifications; hence most of the medical profession, the psychologists – especially the Freudians led by Dr Ernest Jones – and the Whitehall civil servants were determined to make life difficult for him and to show him up as a plausible rogue. Only those who knew his work at first hand saw that he was a healer with genius.

Homer Lane's *Little Commonwealth* in Dorset was the outstanding prototype of special-school education in England, and it is no exaggeration to claim that every memorable development in this field stems from this gifted pioneer. Leading teachers and writers who have worked successfully with disturbed, deprived or problem children of any kind, men such as J. H. Simpson, A. S. Neill and above all W. David Wills, have all declared their immeasurable debt to Homer Lane. Their books have put it on record for all to see, and in so doing, have brought to full circle the part played by the Hills in initiating this strange but productive American connection.

Appendix B

Hillska Skola: The Swedish Hazelwood

IN considering the general influence of Hazelwood school on education, at home and abroad, we must inevitably give a short account of the Swedish version of the school established in Stockholm in 1830. Usually England has taken over ideas from the continent, as the names of Rousseau, Pestalozzi, Froebel and Montessori remind us, but until the English Public School was imitated in various corners of the Empire, in the latter half of the nineteenth century, there was little traffic in the other direction. For this reason Hazelwood and the Hills stand out as unique in the early part of the century.

In the 1820s the wind of reform was blowing across Sweden, as it was elsewhere in Europe, and reforms in the education system naturally formed a part of this change. In 1828 a distinguished nobleman and progressive thinker, Count Frolich, published a translation into Swedish of the Hills' book *Public Education*, following no doubt the world-wide publicity given to it by M. Jullien's *Revue Encyclopédique* in 1823. So impressed was Count Frolich with the Hills' ideas that he sent two experienced educationists to England in 1829 to study the methods being used by the Hills at Hazelwood and at Bruce castle. They stayed for a month, fascinated and not a little bewildered. The result of this was that in June 1830 a boarding school very closely following the Hazelwood pattern was established in Barnängen, then a pleasant suburb of Stockholm. To help it in its initial stages, a former Hazelwood boy, Edward Lewin (who with his brother had been removed from Eton to attend the Hills' school) obtained leave of absence from Cambridge to spend a few months in Sweden for this purpose. Some years later he returned to the school as joint headmaster.

At the grand opening ceremony in 1830, after the royal toast, Count Frolich raised his glass to the very special toast of 'Mr Hill and his six sons', although Howard had then been dead for ten years. In his address the Count told the assembled parents the aims of the school – a breakaway from the traditional dusty pedantry of a narrowly intellectual curriculum by giving due emphasis to practical subjects; an emphasis on moral values and character training; a relationship between pupil and teacher rooted in justice, affection and mutual respect. Corporal punishment was abolished in favour of self-discipline, and a Hazelwood-type jury-court partly run by the boys was established to this end.

Alas, the national climate of opinion did not take kindly to these new ideas: the teaching staff were completely bewildered and worked secretly to wreck the experiment. A degree of devotion to the job was demanded that transcended good sense: teachers often started their day at 5.00 am and did not finish until 9.00 pm – so great were the calls of out-of-school activities. It is not surprising that there were frequent changes of staff. After opening with 60 boarders in 1830, numbers dropped to 46 in 1837, but in 1838 the tide seemed to turn and numbers rose to 99, going up to 114 in 1839, with a waiting list of 35. By this time the school was attracting pupils from Norway, France, Finland, Germany and England.

Hillska Skola was a fee-paying, middle and upper class school, with a strenuous open-air curriculum, rather like our own Gordonstoun today, but tending more towards a military academy. Through financial troubles and staff discord the school was forced to close in 1846, but it made an impression on Swedish education, especially for its relative success as a self-governing community and for its development of practical skills and of all aspects of physical education. It certainly turned out a proportionately large number of boys who were later to serve their country in responsible posts in the public service and in the Forces. Old students thought highly enough of the school to organise two reunions in its honour, one at Gothenburg in 1871 and the other at Norrköping in 1876. This latter reunion was attended by over fifty former pupils, many of whom were national figures in Sweden. To commemorate the occasion special medallions were struck.

Self-government was never developed to the degree practised at Hazelwood, but as time went on the boys took on more responsibility. The jury-court survived for some five years. As at Hazelwood an internal coinage system was introduced, used as 'transferable marks' in the Hazelwood manner, having the values 1 : 5 : 10 : 50 : 100. But before long the coins were abolished as the system broke down when the boys were allowed to use the coinage to buy extra food. A prefect system was employed and, as at Hazelwood, guardians were appointed for groups of ten boys, as advisers and leaders. Every four weeks 'aggregate rank' was established, again on the Hazelwood pattern, covering classroom work, voluntary work and general behaviour. As at Hazelwood the boys had various officers who gained marks for their services as prefect, guardian, recorder, bell-ringer, lost property officer and so on.

In the curriculum modern languages had an important place – French, German and English – as well as Latin and Greek as options. Art, Music and Gymnastics were also cultivated, and woodwork was well provided as a hobby interest. The school had more drum-beats, bugle-calls, parades and marching than at Hazelwood, for many of the parents were in the Services and approved of a slight military emphasis. Nature study and challenging outdoor activities were particularly popular in which the older boys were given a large measure of freedom and scope for enterprise. Rowing and sailing were especially popular, and on Saturday evenings in summer parties of senior boys used to set sail for twenty-four hours, returning on Sunday evening. The school issued rations of bread, butter and cheese, together with a bottle of water, but apart from this the boys had to fend for themselves by catching and cooking fish and sea-birds.

The governing body followed the Hills' ideas quite closely by providing ample and varied accommodation in the Hazelwood fashion. Though the school was not custom-built, a large house at Barnängen, then in open country, was carefully adapted to provide a whole range of facilities – spacious dormitories, work-rooms, refectory, numerous classrooms, craftrooms, games and hobbies' rooms, library, gymnasium, music and dance studios and isolation rooms for sickness. Academic work was confined to morning sessions, great emphasis being placed on individual work rather than class lessons; in the afternoon recreational subjects and various forms of physical education were pursued.

It is generally recognised in Sweden that the Hillska Skola introduced an improved system of education which aimed at all-round development, coupling intellectual discipline with a high degree of moral and character training in which physical activities played a major part. Though the school never reached the standard of Hazelwood in matters of discipline and self-government, the Hillska Skola by its novelty and prestige is considered to have influenced subsequent educational theory and practice in the field of secondary education. Perhaps it is not too fanciful to believe that the tolerant, peace-loving, democratic spirit of modern Sweden may contain more than a trace-element of the vision and values that the Hills of Hazelwood gave to it through the Hillska Skola.

Appendix C

The Adhesive Stamp and the Penny Black

THE story of Rowland Hill's career in the Post Office is not complete without a brief account of the introduction of the adhesive stamp, and of the evolution of the world's most historic stamp – the famous Penny Black.

The term 'stamp' goes back at least to 1694 when, under the Stamp Act of that date six heavily embossed or 'stamped' official impressions registered on thick paper or vellum, were issued in various values for excise or revenue purposes, or as a legal authentication of important documents. They were extensively used from 1711 onwards, and sometimes to facilitate quick recognition a small piece of white or blue paper, similarly embossed, was attached to the document, either stapled or stuck with an adhesive of some kind. With the growth of papers and articles carrying excise and revenue duties, these smaller embossed 'labels' or 'wafers' as they were called, were even more widely used from 1800 onwards.

It was in the second edition of Rowland Hill's pamphlet on Postal Reform, dated 22 February 1837, that the idea of a 'stamp' was used in the sense we employ it today. He described his idea in the famous words 'a bit of paper just large enough to bear the stamp and covered at the back with a glutinous wash which the bringer might, by applying a little moisture, attach to the back of the letter'.

The essence of Rowland's postal reform was the imposition of a uniform, much cheaper, postal rate, depending on weight, coupled with pre-payment of postage by means of a stamp either affixed to, or ready printed on, the envelope or letter. He demonstrated that the use of a pre-paid stamp would save an immense amount of labour costs and time when the letter was actually delivered, yielding a profit of 200 per cent on the necessary cost of primary distribution. The ready-stamped sheets, envelopes or wrappers, like the adhesive stamps, could be purchased at post-offices for the various weights of letters. The idea, Rowland tells us, was first proposed for newspaper-wrappers in 1834 by Charles Knight, the publisher and an old friend, who had been an enthusiastic supporter of Hazelwood back in the early 1820s.

Right up to the present day, however, there has been some confusion over the terms stamp and stamped-cover, but a recent letter from Dr I. D. Hill in the British Philatelic Bulletin of April 1985 does much to clarify the matter:

> There is difficulty in interpreting some of the writings of the 1830s concerning this, because the phrase 'stamped-covers' was sometimes used *specifically* to mean ready-stamped envelopes, but sometimes *generically* to mean all forms of stamped mail.

Rowland Hill clearly considered the ready-stamped envelope or cover and the adhesive stamp as alternatives, but expected the ready-stamped envelope to be preferred by the public. This is confirmed by Jean Farrugia in her recent booklet *The Life and Work of Sir Rowland Hill, 1795–1879*, published by the *National Postal Museum* in 1979, on the centenary of the famous reformer's death:

> To Rowland Hill's own great surprise, the Penny Black (which he had envisaged as an expedient for use only when a supply of stamped stationery was not on hand) quickly proved to be the most popular method of prepaying postage.

Just as the idea of a national postal service evolved gradually from early, uncoordinated beginnings, as mentioned in Chapter V, so, as we showed, Hazelwood School itself had absorbed the ideas of many earlier innovators. In the same way the concept of the adhesive, pre-paid postage stamp emerged from various earlier practices. But it needed the vision, drive and creative touch of a genius like Rowland Hill to conjure out of these earlier elements a new and wider application appropriate to the changing demands of a different situation. On a grander scale, we may recollect, Shakespeare's genius effected a similar transformation in creating his masterpieces out of a rag-bag of ideas and characters culled from the histories of Holinshed and Plutarch and from various Italian and French story-tellers.

Rowland Hill originally had no thought of publicly claiming that the adhesive stamp was his own 'invention', but unfortunately the Hill family were forced to assert this distinction for him when in 1879, just after Rowland's death in the same year, Patrick Chalmers, the son of the deceased James Chalmers, vociferously proclaimed that his father was the real inventor of the adhesive stamp.

James Chalmers had died in 1853, twenty-six years before this. Long before his death he had written in a friendly spirit to Rowland Hill in

May 1840 renouncing his admittedly mistaken claim to priority, and it is said that he never again raised the issue. He did, however, say that he had started experimenting with the idea of an adhesive stamp in November 1837, but it was then a known fact that Rowland Hill had clearly described his idea of such a stamp in the second edition of his historic pamphlet *Post Office Reform; its Importance and Practicability* in February 1837.

In rejecting Patrick Chalmers' claim, the Hills, largely through the intervention of Rowland's son, Pearson Hill, referred to the evidence in Rowland's pamphlet and to the statements Rowland made to the *Commission of Post Office Inquiry*, also in February 1837. In 1837, too, a *Select Committee on Postage* was set up by Parliament under the chairmanship of Robert Wallace, MP for Greenock, who was extremely well-informed and active on all matters of postal reform. The Committee published a very comprehensive report in 1839, which included the evidence of a large number of witnesses, amongst whom was Rowland Hill. In answer to Question 129 he once again quoted his definition of the adhesive stamp.

But in 1879 Patrick Chalmers apparently ignored all this evidence and charged in with his uncompromising allegations. The Hill lobby was quick to respond, and though Chalmers was publicly accused of falsifying dates and documents in making his claim he refused to take legal action for defamation. To many interested observers this seemed to indicate that Chalmers had little confidence in the validity of his case.

Patrick Chalmers persisted in his claim right up to his death in 1891, but after intensive investigations by Pearson Hill and by the *London Philatelic Society* under its chairman Mr F. A. Philbrick, QC, the Chalmers' claim was officially repudiated. Unfortunately erroneous support for Chalmers had been given by the *Encyclopedia Britannica* and by the *Dictionary of National Biography*, but this was corrected in subsequent editions. But in spite of all this, renewed counter-claims still emerge from time to time; the matter still appears in some quarters to be an issue of acute controversy.

It is ironic that in their own contacts Rowland Hill and James Chalmers conducted themselves with courtesy and exemplary decorum; it just happened that they were both men of the utmost probity and integrity. Rowland was well aware that Chalmers had long concerned himself with matters of postal reform and in no way looked upon him as an antagonist. It would have deeply saddened Rowland to see the bitterness and rancour that was later to develop over a simple confusion concerning the origin of the adhesive stamp.

Amongst the most important counter-claims were those made by

Dr John E. Gray; Charles Babbage; Francis Worrell Stevens, Lovrenc Kosir, and the Reverend Samuel Roberts, all of which, according to expert opinion, have been shown to be invalid. Another interesting point of similar significance is that the Treasury minute referring to Rowland's retirement incorrectly mentioned 'those who, before the development of the plans of Sir Rowland Hill, urged the adoption of the uniform penny postage'.

Rowland challenged this later and had the comment withdrawn, but he regarded it as no more than an unfortunate mistake on someone's part, not a malicious piece of last-ditch hostility.

Notes and Comments

I   *The Hazelwood Breakthrough* (pp. 1–21)

1. The South Australian Commission: See Chapter III.
2. The London and Brighton Railway: See Chapter IV.
3. A comparison of Rowland Hill's and Thomas Arnold's personal and educational achievements is given in Chapter VI. They were exact coevals, both born in 1795. Arnold began his work at Rugby School in 1828.
4. *A. J. Balfour's Education Act* of 1902 owes much to the experience and guidance of Viscount Bryce who had been one of the most active Assistant Commissioners involved in the *Schools' Enquiry Commission* of 1868, known as the *Taunton Report*. This report made recommendations for a radical reform of the curriculum and for government and local responsibility for a secondary education system. These suggestions were further examined and developed in Viscount Bryce's own Report – *The Royal Commission on Secondary Education* of 1895. This was a very important landmark as it led to the setting up of the *Board of Education* in 1899 and to the first attempt to co-ordinate the various branches of education into a coherent whole, and, as Professor H. C. Barnard has pointed out, it contains the germs of much of the educational progress that has been made in this country since the beginning of the twentieth century.

   It is significant that Viscount Bryce was a close friend of Dr George Birkbeck Hill, Rowland's nephew, who took over the Headmastership of Bruce Castle school from his father, Arthur Hill in 1867. At Bruce Castle the wide and liberal curriculum of Hazelwood had been followed ever since it opened in Tottenham in 1827, except for the strange back-pedalling on science in the later years (p. 44) and there is little doubt that Viscount Bryce was fully acquainted with the nature of the radically reformed curriculum that was followed there. At all events, the wide curriculum outlined in the Balfour Act of 1902 very closely reflects the Hazelwood and Bruce Castle pattern. Further details on pages 107–9, Chapter VII.
5. Dr Joseph Priestley (1733–1804) was a leading Unitarian and eminent as a theologian, philosopher and scientist. Thomas Wright Hill was one of his Sunday school teachers and was responsible for rescuing some of Priestley's books and scientific apparatus when, in 1791/2 the mob during the 'Church and King' riots set fire to Priestley's house and Meeting Place in Birmingham. Priestley emigrated to America in 1794 where he corresponded with Thomas Jefferson, the former President, on matters of educational reform.

[149]

6. Details of the lives and works of the six sons are given in Chapter II.

7. Dissenting Academies played an important part in the development of new educational ideas. Under the *Act of Uniformity* of 1662 non-conformists were forbidden to teach in, or attend, church schools and grammar schools, so they established their own elementary schools, Sunday schools and charity schools. In addition, because they were debarred from Oxford and Cambridge universities they set up their own forms of secondary and higher education in their famous Dissenting Academies. These highly efficient and progressive institutions were mostly situated in the midlands and the north of the country, the most famous being the Warrington Academy where Joseph Priestley was a tutor. Here he developed the teaching of science as part of a broad and enlightened curriculum, and this influenced other educational experiments including those at Hazelwood school. Like Priestley, the Hill family were practising Unitarians, and Thomas Wright Hill was closely associated with Dr Priestley in the Birmingham of the 1790s.

Joseph Priestley's progressive ideas on education attracted the attention of Thomas Jefferson in America when Jefferson was fashioning America's national system of education. Priestley had emigrated to America in 1794 and had many contacts with the former President.

8. 'Dotheboys Hall' was immortalised by Charles Dickens in his novel *Nicholas Nickleby* as a classic example of an appalling private boarding school.

9. The fourth Earl of Clarendon (G. W. F. Villiers: 1800–70) later became Chairman of the Royal Commission set up to examine the education provided by the nine original Public Schools. In its report – the *Clarendon Report* of 1864 – it exposed the narrowness of the almost exclusive classical curriculum of these schools, but while accepting the classics as a valuable intellectual and cultural discipline, the Report recommended a radical widening of the curriculum in which every boy should be taught mathematics, one modern language, geography, history (including modern history), some natural science and either art or music. This was the first official hint of a move to widen the secondary curriculum.

It seems more than probable that the Chairman, having had some acquaintance of the broad, enlightened curriculum followed at Hazelwood (for one of his younger brothers had been a pupil), was able to influence his committee to give this radical lead. It proved to be the seed that was later nurtured by the *Taunton Report* of 1868, and again by the *Bryce Report* of 1895. It finally came to full flower, as already noted, in the *Balfour Act* of 1902, which established the liberal secondary curriculum that has been generally followed right up to the present day.

The Earl of Clarendon had been a leading politician and served in the governments formed by Lord John Russell, Lord Aberdeen and Lord Palmerston; he twice held the office of foreign minister.

10. . . . 'his own architect'. Rowland was no doubt inspired and advised by his Birmingham friend, Thomas Steed Whitwell, a talented practising architect who had studied under Sir John Soane. Following Rowland's

experiment with his Hazelwood air-duct heating system, Whitwell introduced a similar air-duct system in his design of the Anatomical Museum
and Chemistry lecture-room in Cambridge in 1834, as well as in the
fever-ward of Addenbrooke's Hospital, Cambridge.

11. James Silk Buckingham (1786–1855) was a distinguished traveller and
author, and the founder of the *Oriental Herald and Colonial Review* in 1824. In
1832 he entered the new Parliament as a radical member for Sheffield, and
worked hard for social and humanitarian reforms, including the abolition
of flogging in the armed services, and for the Temperance movement. He
was a kind and generous man, always a strong supporter of Hazelwood
school and later of Rowland Hill's Penny Postage plan.

12. ... 'Jerry Bentham and company'. Jeremy Bentham (1748–1832) was a
leading radical and constitutional lawyer of the day, and the founder of
the Utilitarian school of philosophy which was further developed by J. S.
Mill. With Dr Southwood-Smith (1788–1861), a Unitarian friend of the
Hills, and John Bowring, Bentham founded the radical *Westminster Review*.
Bentham was called to the bar at Lincoln's Inn, but with little success, as
his interests were mostly concerned with jurisprudence and constitutional
law, and with all manner of social, political and legal reforms. His writings
were voluminous and wide ranging. Crime and punishment interested
him, prompting him to put forward a plan for a novel form of prison, the
Panopticon, in which every prisoner was under constant observation from
a central tower – a blue print for the concentration camps of later years.
A proposed experiment at Millbank in London came to nothing; the idea
was little more than a flight of Benthamite fancy. In 1822 Bentham read
the Hills' book *Public Education*, and was much impressed with the school's
system of democratic self-government, based on the boys' own rules and
their jury-courts. He invited Matthew Hill to dinner (a rare privilege from a
hermit-like recluse) to discuss the Hazelwood ideas, and thereafter proved
to be a warm supporter of the school, even sending amusing letters to the
editor of the school magazine for publication.

Just as the Hills in 1825/6 were planning the opening of a London branch
of Hazelwood, they heard that Bentham with Henry Brougham and James
Mill were thinking of establishing a *Chrestomathic* school (that is a school
following a modern, practical and largely utilitarian curriculum) on the
site of Milton's house in Queen's Square Place, London (where Bentham
himself was living), much to the disgust and indignation of William Hazlitt
– 'a paltry Chrestomathic school in the garden where Milton breathed the
air of Truth and Heaven.'

The Hills, however, had only contempt for this threat: as Matthew Hill
declared, 'They don't know what they are about, but we can teach them'.
The Hills knew that Bentham, brilliant though he might be, was merely
a dreamer of dreams, a word-spinner; like so many educational pundits
from his day to this, he had never stood in front of a class actually to teach
real boys.

When Bentham and his colleagues heard of the establishment of Bruce

[151]

Castle school in 1827, they threw their hands in and generously complimented the Hills on their 'beautiful offset taken from Hazelwood and planted at Bruce Castle'. Though some Utilitarian ideas are to be found in the Hazelwood system, Bentham was in no way its inspiration; rather did Bentham jump on to the Hazelwood band-wagon once he saw that he had been beaten to the post by real educationists. Some years later, in 1830, University College School, London, was founded incorporating some of Bentham's Chrestomathic ideas, and it proved to be one of the few successful progressive schools of the period.

Besides being something of a recluse in his later days, Bentham always manifested a zany, eccentric sense of humour; he called his walking-stick Dapple and treated it as a ceremonial sword; his teapot he called Dickey and he had a cat called Langhorne which he first elevated to a Knighthood as Sir John, then inducted him into the Church as the Reverend Sir John Langhorne. At Bentham's death in 1832, his body was dissected by his friend Dr Southwood Smith in the presence of Henry Brougham, James Mill and George Grote during a spectacular thunder storm, when the faces of the onlookers were as white as that of the corpse. Bentham's skeleton, dressed in his familiar clothes, but adorned with a waxen head, still guards the portals of University College, Gower Street, London – utilitarian to the end.

13. Dr Thomas Southwood Smith, MD (1788–1861), was originally an influential Unitarian minister, but later, with William Blake's encouragement, he qualified as a doctor. In 1824, he helped Bentham form the *Westminster Review*.

    In 1826 he became an active member of the *Society for the Diffusion of Useful Knowledge*, founded by Henry Brougham and Charles Knight: he also wrote extensively for the latter's *Penny Encyclopedia* on medical and public health matters. In this latter field he was a brilliant pioneer and soon won world renown.

14. Captain Basil Hall, FRS, FRAS (1788–1844) was a man of wide talents. He had a very distinguished career in the Royal Navy and had written extensively on his world-wide travels. He was well informed and deeply interested in scientific matters as well as in education, and for this reason the *Edinburgh Review* asked him to visit Hazelwood school and write a report on his findings.

15. Sir John Bowring, FRS (1792–1872), was a very influential figure in the nineteenth century. He was a gifted linguist and a great traveller. He helped Bentham found the *Westminster Review* and became Vice-President of the group known as the *Philosophic Radicals*. He was an MP for many years, championing radical causes associated with commerce, education and science. He was particularly active with the affairs of the *British Association for the Advancement of Science* and with the activities of the *Social Science Association*.

16. Johann Heinrich Pestalozzi (1746–1827) was a gifted Swiss teacher and educationist who particularly influenced the education of young children. His fame travelled to America where a Pestalozzi school was opened

in Philadelphia in 1806. He stressed the religious and moral values in education, which, he said, should be a matter of 'head, hand and heart'. His curriculum was made as practical and real as possible, and he stressed the importance of a happy relationship between pupils and teachers. This was precisely the philosophy of Thomas Wright Hill when he opened Hill Top school in Birmingham in 1803, where all the Hill brothers were pupils and later teachers.

17. Philipp Emanuel Von Fellenberg (1771–1844), was also a Swiss teacher and educationist, well known for his school at Hofwyl from 1807 onwards. Here he developed Pestalozzi's liberal ideas, associating practical work at Hofwyl with agriculture and husbandry linked with handicrafts, science and music. He also aimed at creating a self-governing community. Henry Brougham visited Hofwyl in 1816 and presented a report on the school to a committee of the House of Commons. He also publicised the work of the school in two articles in the *Educational Review*.

18. Sanderson Miller (1717–80), a man of letters, antiquarian, architect and friend of the nobility, lived at The Grange, Radway, Warwickshire. The house is situated at the foot of the Edgehill ridge on which he built his well-known Gothic tower (mentioned in Richard Jago's poem *Edgehill*) to mark the spot where Charles I raised his Royal Standard on the fateful Sunday morning of the battle of Edgehill in 1642. The tower overlooks the whole battlefield and stands a little west of the point where Prince Rupert mounted his flank attack with his cavalry.

One of Miller's notable buildings was Hagley Hall in Worcestershire, completed in 1760, the house of the Lyttelton family, where generations of Lyttelton boys learnt their cricket in the Long Gallery during the winter months. He also designed the handsome County Hall in Warwick, as well as the Great Hall of Lacock Abbey, Wiltshire. The tower he built for his neighbouring Wroxton Church, Oxfordshire, in 1748, unfortunately collapsed during its first winter, but his octagonal tower and its associate buildings and gardens at Radway still stand to provide a welcome hostelry for the hot and thirsty wayfarer.

19. William Shenstone (1714–63) was a minor nature poet steeped in the sentiment of the period and a man of exquisite and fastidious taste. He was perhaps best known for the excellence of his small landscaped garden, his 'ferme ornée', called the *Leasowes*, near Halesowen, which attracted many admiring visitors from far and wide. Its charm has been beautifully recorded by Robert Dodsley the well-known contemporary publisher. Shenstone's association with William Somerville (1675–1742), Lady Luxborough, Richard Graves and Richard Jago (a fellow pupil at Solihull School) stimulated a flow of elegant letter-writing and poetry that won them the name of the *Warwickshire Coterie*.

Shenstone and Graves as fellow students at Pembroke College, Oxford, were among a group of talented versifiers whom Dr Samuel Johnson, himself an alumnus of the same College, had in mind when he declared, 'Sir, we are a nest of singing birds'.

20. Maria Edgeworth (1767–1849) with her father, Richard Lovell Edgeworth, were lively innovators in the field of education. Maria was unusually short in stature and indulged in alarming exercises to remedy this defect, even hanging herself by the neck. She began writing stories for children and this led to her interest in education. At her home town in Ireland she conducted a small progressive school for children living near the estate and farm. In 1798, with her father's help, she published a two-volume work called *Practical Education*, clearly influenced by Rousseau's *Emile*. She later turned to writing adult novels with some success. She and her father became quite well-known in London and Paris. In August 1821 Rowland Hill and his brother, Arthur, visited the Edgeworths at their home in Ireland and looked over their curious school. They were interested to hear Maria's first-hand account of her visit to Switzerland to study the day to day working of Pestalozzi's school and of Fellenberg's establishment at Hofwyl. It happened that Rowland had with him the final proofs of his book, *Public Education*, which Maria read with great interest and warm approval.

On one occasion Maria had the temerity to call on Jeremy Bentham at his home in London, but as the aged philosopher told Matthew Hill – 'the jade came to my door, but I would not let her in. . . .' Maria's play *Eton Montem* was presented at Hill Top in 1816, and again at Hazelwood in 1820.

21. William Bowman (1816–92) was a pupil at Hazelwood around 1828, when, with his young friend John Dent Goodman, he made an accurate scale model in cardboard of the Hazelwood building, as an exercise of *Voluntary Labour*. It still survives in the Birmingham City Museum, but on temporary loan to Birmingham University School of Education. On leaving school Bowman studied medicine, well equipped by the manual skills and science background provided by the Hazelwood curriculum. He qualified as MRCS in 1839 and soon became the leading Ophthalmic surgeon in England. His brilliant research work on the eye, the liver and the kidney brought him a Fellowship of the Royal Society at the early age of twenty-five. Medical students today are still familiar with *Bowman's Capsule* in the kidney and *Bowman's membrane* in the eye. During the Crimean war he did much to organise the training and despatch of nurses to help Florence Nightingale behind the battle lines. In 1884 he was Knighted for his outstanding services to medicine and his country.

22. John Dent Goodman (1816–1900) joined Hazelwood in 1828, an exact contemporary of William Bowman, and like the latter enjoyed the opportunities for craftwork and science that the curriculum provided. He later became the leading authority on the gun-trade, and in 1861 was made the first Chairman of the newly founded Birmingham Small Arms Company whose guns, motor-cycles and other engineering products have long enjoyed world wide reputation under the famous BSA trade-name. Throughout his life John Goodman entered fully into the social and educational life of the town. He was a Governor of King Edward VI School for

forty years, and was the founder of Edgbaston Church of England College for Girls in 1885 which still flourishes today.

23. Lord Brougham, MP, FRS (1778–1868) began life as plain Henry Brougham and soon made his mark on society. He was called to the Bar at Lincoln's Inn and became an MP in 1810. In 1802 he helped to found the influential *Edinburgh Review* and wrote for it extensively on scientific, economic and political subjects. He did much for the cause of education, for the anti-slavery movement, for the freedom of the Press and for the reform of the laws of libel. In 1826 he was the effective founder of the *Society for the Diffusion of Useful Knowledge*, which brought him into close association with Rowland and Matthew Hill and with Thomas Arnold, just as the latter was about to move to Rugby School. Brougham's interest in educational reform led him to visit Pestalozzi's school at Hofwyl in 1816 and to report on it to the House of Commons. It is not surprising that he also took a great interest in the developments going on at the Hills' school in Birmingham. Recognising the unusual genius of Rowland Hill he later became a leading supporter of Rowland's Penny Postage plan and played a major part in forcing the Penny Postage Act through parliament in 1839. As Chancellor of the Exchequer in 1830 he helped to simplify legal processes and procedures. He was an ardent supporter of the new *Mechanics' Institutes* and campaigned for the introduction of science in the education of the upper classes, warmly reinforcing Rowland Hill's pioneer efforts in this field. As a strong supporter of the founding of the University of London through its secular based University College in Gower Street, he hoped to promote the study of science. In 1837 he initiated a Bill for the establishment of a national system of education, but the idea was ahead of its time: it did not come about until *Forster's Act* of 1870. In 1857 he was the founder and first President of the *Association of Social Science*. All in all he was one of the leading figures in the Whig hierarchy for much of the nineteenth century, and always an inspiring reformer.

24. Friedrich Wilhelm Froebel (1782–1852) was an enlightened German educationist, well known as the founder of the Kindergarten system in 1837. The first Kindergarten school established in England in 1854 was enthusiastically supported by Rowland's younger brother, Frederic. A happy atmosphere, freedom from unnecessary restraint, lively play activities and facilities for inner self-development were the basis of the system, whose benign influence still permeates the better Infant schools even today.

25. Maria Montessori (1870–1952) was a very gifted Italian doctor who developed her special system for teaching children from three to six years of age, especially those who were sub-normal in some respect. She stressed the importance of freedom of choice and action, and by exercises, games and special simple apparatus she aimed at developing the child's co-ordination and perceptual skills. The best Infant schools today embody the influence of both Froebel and Montessori.

26. Dr W. H. D. Rouse. A lively account of his work in teaching Latin and

Greek by direct method is given in the Board of Education Pamphlets, No. 20 and Nos. 28, 1910 and 1914.

27. Dr Lant Carpenter (1780–1840) was a well-known Unitarian Minister and writer on theological issues. He was born in Kidderminster, as was his close friend Rowland Hill. He was highly respected as a successful and imaginative teacher, and his book *The Principles of Education* (1820) was much commended. His daughter, Mary Carpenter, was closely associated with Matthew Davenport Hill in Bristol in connection with the care and education of destitute and delinquent children.

28. Rugby football was certainly played at Hazelwood in 1828, if not before; a couplet in a mock-heroic poem in the school magazine of that year seems to confirm this:

> A daring hero stoops beneath the blows,
> Exerts his hands, and back impels the ball. . . .

Rugby football is said to have been started at Rugby School in 1823 when young William Ellis picked up the football and ran for the goal line. Hazelwood school attracted boys from many Public Schools from Eton downwards, so it is likely that some pupils left Rugby (barely 30 miles distant) to attend the internationally famous Hazelwood. These boys may have introduced the handling code.

29. Cricket must have been enthusiastically played at Hazelwood, and some of its overseas pupils must have taken the game back to their homelands when they left. The game certainly thrived in the Argentine where it was exceptionally popular and clearly reached a high standard. No doubt the brothers Rivadavia, sons of the President, and young Rodriguez, the son of an earlier President, made a contribution in this field. Travellers also record having seen the game played in Mexico, introduced by ex-Hazelwood pupils. Possibly some ex-Hazelwood pupils also took the game to the West Indies, with the astonishing results we have discovered to our cost.

30. Thomas Jefferson (1743–1826) was one of America's greatest statesmen; he held the Presidency from 1801 to 1809. He drafted much of the *Declaration of Independence* and laid the well-planned foundations of the American education system. He was remarkably versatile and widely travelled, and in particular he built up close links with France. He was an accomplished architect as his design of the beautiful campus of the University of Virginia in Charlottesville, and his own remarkable country house, Montecello, amply prove. He had progressive and liberal views on education, and took great pains to inform himself of the latest developments in Europe. When Dr Joseph Priestley settled in America in 1794 a lively correspondence was started with Jefferson. The latter was particularly interested in the part Priestley played in developing the teaching of science in the Dissenting Academies. This led to Jefferson's requesting from the Hills a copy of *Public Education*, as he was keen to hear more about the Hazelwood system of self-government and the pupils' jury-courts. Matthew Davenport Hill

duly sent Jefferson a copy of the book in 1825, accompanied by a long letter, which is still in the archives of the Library of Congress in Washington, as is a record of the book having been sold as Lot No. 231 in the catalogue of sale of Jefferson's effects after his death in 1826.

Further details of the wide circulation of *Public Education* from then onwards, and its influence on educational developments in America are given in Appendix A – *The American Connection*.

31. C. P. Snow (1905–80), later Lord Snow, FRS, won a reputation as a leading Physical Chemist at Cambridge, then blossomed out as a very talented novelist and playwright. Coming from quite humble stock in Leicester, he displayed a versatility ranging from top-level science, to administration, politics, education and creative literature. He is specially remembered for his timely warning about the 'two culture' society into which our education had led us. On his elevation to the House of Lords he became the official Labour spokesman on education at a time when the issue of Comprehensive schools came to the fore. At first he was a doughty champion for this cause, but later recanted and seemingly repudiated his former enthusiasm. At all events, he chose a leading Public School for the education of his own son. At the time this episode provoked the present author to produce a *jeu d'esprit* suggested by Dryden's *Absalom and Achitophel* (with apologies to Zimri):

> A man so various that he seemed to be,
> Not one, but all mankind's epitome;
> A prole by birth, he had his betters beaten,
> Then cut his kind and sent his son to Eton.

32. This younger Matthew Davenport Hill was the grandson of the original Matthew, the distinguished lawyer, and was born in 1872, the year in which his grandfather died. As a very young boy he remembers sitting on the bed of his uncle Rowland then in his final years, and being vastly impressed by Rowland's orange-coloured dressing-gown which he invariably wore. He also remembers weeping during Rowland's funeral in Westminster Abbey in 1879 when he was a lad of seven. In 1886 he entered Eton as a Colleger and declares he enjoyed school life far more than his years at Oxford in the years 1890–94 where he duly achieved a First Class degree in Natural Science. At New College one of his tutors was the celebrated Dr Spooner, but the only Spoonerism Hill actually heard was when his tutor, speaking of St Paul's conversion, declared that Paul after his conversion believed himself to be a 'Gervant of Sod'. Hill enjoyed his years as Housemaster at Eton, but retired a few years early and bought himself a farm near Ledbury, believing that elderly schoolmasters could be more of a liability than an asset. He remained a devoted OE to the end of his days.

II   *The Hill Family* (pp. 22–43)

1. Major John Cartwright (1740–1824) had a successful career in the Royal Navy, and after leaving the service he was appointed in 1775 to the rank of major in the Nottinghamshire militia. His interests then turned to politics, and he campaigned vigorously for the reform of parliament, for universal suffrage and for the democratic use of the ballot.

   He was soon referred to as 'the father of reform', but he several times failed to win a seat in the House of Commons. The cause of Greek independence won his support in the 1820s, and he was a committed campaigner against slavery. His outspoken speeches and writings eventually led to his arrest in 1819 on a charge of sedition, but thanks to his own integrity and the skill of his counsel (who included Matthew Davenport Hill, recently called to the Bar) he suffered nothing worse than a fine of a hundred pounds. In spite of his outspoken political activities, he was recognised as a true gentleman even by his bitterest opponents. It is a curious coincidence that Dr Arnold's wife, née Mary Penrose, was connected with the Cartwright family, as is explained in Chapter VI. By general consent Major Cartwright was a truly noble character.

   He is fittingly remembered by his statue in Cartwright Gardens in front of Commonwealth Hall, a University student hostel which is built on the site of the house, 2 Burton Crescent, just south of Euston Road, where Rowland Hill lived in 1836. It was here he completed his famous pamphlet, *Post Office Reform* in 1837. In October 1985 Dr I. D. Hill was invited by the Post Office to unveil a plaque commemorating this historic event.

2. William Scholefield (1809–67) was a pupil at Hazelwood until 1824 when he left to join his father's export firm. As the first Charter Mayor of Birmingham in 1839 he did much to establish the fine liberal tradition of Birmingham local government.

3. The two Greek refugees rejoiced in the names Eustrathioş Rallis and Stamos Nakos. When they joined the school in 1825 they presented themselves in full national costume. Another Greek boy, G. Tombasis, became Head Boy in 1829.

4. Charles Knight (1791–1873) was the son of an author and publisher in Windsor and he inherited his father's interests. He had strong liberal principles and took a special interest in promoting the education of the masses, writing and publishing many papers and magazines to this end. In 1823/24, with the support of Matthew Davenport Hill and De Quincey he published *Knight's Quarterly Magazine*. In 1826 with Henry Brougham, in association with Matthew and Rowland Hill, he founded the *Society for the Diffusion of Useful Knowledge,* which flourished until 1846. Under its auspices Knight published the *Quarterly Journal of Education* from 1831 to 1836; the famous *Penny Magazine* from 1832 to 1845 and the *Penny Encyclopedia* in 1833, as well as many other magazines, some illustrated, all of which made a big contribution to the spread of knowledge and literacy.

In 1833 he edited and published an excellent *Pictorial Shakespeare* in instalments, as well as a biography of the bard and various essays and commentaries. A similar *History of England* achieved wide popularity. He maintained a close friendship with the Hill family who admired Knight's drive, enterprise and inventive skills, particularly his original experiments in colour printing. In 1834 Rowland noted with interest Knight's suggestion for the use of stamped covers for newspapers, and this led to the train of thought in Rowland's mind which resulted in the development of Mulready's stamped sheet or envelope and to the alternative adhesive stamp.

There is no doubt that Charles Knight played a very significant part in the story of social and educational reforms in the nineteenth century.

5. Mary Carpenter (1807–77) was the eldest daughter of Dr Lant Carpenter whom we have mentioned earlier. His daughter had tremendous zeal and energy for good works. In 1829 she opened a school for girls in Bristol, then, with the co-operation of Matthew Davenport Hill (the Commissioner for Bankruptcy in Bristol), she established her first Ragged School in a slum area of the city. Her work at *Red Lodge*, in an old Elizabethan mansion in Bristol, attracted much attention and admiration: here she worked indefatigably for the cause of homeless and rejected children – 'doing the work of three people on the food of half a one'. Her effort led to pressure being brought on the government to provide funds for such schools and reformatories. She also worked tirelessly for educational causes in India, besides visiting America and Canada in 1873 to lecture on prison reform. With the active support of Matthew Hill a policy of cottage-homes in place of barrack-like reformatories was put into action: this had a considerable influence on future developments in this field. It bore fruit later in Homer Lane's work in America and in his *Little Commonwealth* in Dorset around the year 1914. This is fully recorded in Appendix A.

6. Samuel Tertius Galton was a wealthy Birmingham banker and the father of the better known Sir Francis Galton, FRS, scientist and explorer and a cousin of Charles Darwin. Francis had wide scientific interests and won fame for his study of heredity and eugenics – selective breeding – and of new statistical methods to validate his researches. He founded the first Chair of Eugenics at London University.

7. William Leader Maberly (1798–1885) joined the 7th Foot Regiment as Lieutenant in 1815, rising in course of time to be Lieut. Colonel of the 96th Foot and finally the 7th Foot.

For some years from 1819 he was an MP. He was appointed to the top administrative post of Secretary to the Post Office in 1836, and from the first he resisted all ideas of reform as proposed by Rowland Hill in his famous pamphlet of 1837. When Rowland was given his temporary appointment at the Treasury in 1839 to help implement his reforms as embodied in the Penny Postage Act of August 1839, Colonel Maberly and his officials obstructed Rowland in every way possible, and continued to do this after Rowland had been appointed Secretary to the Postmaster General in 1846.

It is estimated that the Colonel's intransigence cost the country millions of pounds. It was not until 1854 that Colonel Maberly was transferred to a higher paid post in the Audit Office and Rowland was at last able to take full control as Secretary to the Post Office. The whole story is briefly recounted in Chapter V.

8. William Lucas Sargant (1809–89) was a member of a well-known family of gun makers in Birmingham. He was a pupil at Hazelwood from the 1820s onwards along with his two younger brothers. On leaving school he entered the family business, but always took a lively interest in civic and social affairs. He was a Governor of the Edgbaston Proprietary School that was founded, largely by Unitarians, in 1838 to fill the gap left by the closure of Hazelwood. The school carried on many of the Hazelwood traditions, particularly in the emphasis given to mathematics and science. For many years he was also a Governor of King Edward VI School. With his former school friend, J. D. Goodman, he became an active member of the *Birmingham Education Association* which later expanded to become the *National Education League*. This body was the driving force behind Forster's *Education Act* of 1870, which laid the foundation of our national education system.

Though, like his friend Goodman, he was a manufacturing engineer specialising in the gun trade, William Sargant published a whole range of books and pamphlets on topics ranging from Social Science, Taxation, Economics and modern Political Economy to a substantial biographical study, *The Life and Philosophy of Robert Owen*.

William Sargant was a typical product of the Hazelwood system, with the practical skills, the scientific knowledge and the social conscience that the Hills aimed at developing.

9. Jeremy Bentham, Lord John Russell, Thomas Campbell and the others mentioned here represented a modest roll-call of some of the best known reformers of the nineteenth century. They were all men of great distinction and influence in their various spheres of activity, whose talents and special interests speak for themselves. They seem to have been drawn to Hazelwood as by a magnet, for they instantly recognised that it provided the sort of educational experience and established the wholesome relationships that were needed to create their ideal world of the future; it was their good society in miniature before their very eyes. Against the dark background of prevailing educational and social values Hazelwood stood out as a bright new guiding light. No wonder they looked upon Rowland Hill as a hope for the future, for they all realised that their brave new world had to begin with the enlightened experience of the child.

Years later these same influential leaders of opinion, confident in the genius of this rare educationist that they had discovered, recognised that Rowland Hill's Penny Postage Plan was but another stage in the creation of a new society. By providing vastly improved communications between families, between societies and institutions, between the government and the governed, it facilitated commerce for the benefit of all. Hence it is not unfair to claim that it was the Hazelwood phenomenon, by bringing together such disparate elements, that triggered off much of the radical upsurge in the nineteenth century which once and for all changed the face of British social and economic history.

10. George Grote (1794–1871) is of special interest; he was a talented classical scholar, historian and philosopher, and a close friend and associate of James Mill and his son J. S. Mill, as well as of Jeremy Bentham. Grote's well-known History of Greece in eight volumes is a monument to his industry and scholarship. He was deeply interested in progressive ideas, particularly those connected with education. He was immediately drawn to the novel ideas and practices to be found at Hazelwood School, and promptly showed his faith in the Hills by withdrawing his two nephews, the Lewin brothers, from Eton in order to send them to Hazelwood. He was also a leading figure in the moves taken to promote the colonisation of South Australia, again showing the confidence he had in the directing hand of Rowland Hill in the venture.

George Grote was an active MP for London between 1832 and 1841, and played a big part in the founding of the University of London. He was also an energetic supporter of the Reform Bill in 1832. Gladstone offered him a peerage in 1869 but Grote declined it; he felt himself to be essentially a man of the people. Without doubt he was a very eminent figure among the elite of the great Victorians.

11. Anthony Trollope (1815–82) in his autobiography gives us an horrific account of his experiences as a boy at Harrow and Winchester which makes a dramatic contrast with the school life of boys at Hazelwood at the very same time, between 1827 and 1833. Savagely beaten, regularly humiliated and consistently ill-taught, he claims he left school ignorant and almost illiterate. Yet by his natural talent and incredible industry he became one of our most memorable novelists.

For most of his life Trollope worked as a surveyor or inspector of postal services, first in Ireland and then in the West Country of England. Occasionally he undertook interesting overseas assignments. He found it a 'jolly life', mixing with the gentry, riding to hounds and travelling through delightful countryside. In his early days he did much of his novel-writing on his knees in railway carriages or in hotel rooms; it became an addictive passion with him and it accounts for his vast literary output. He was always a most conscientious employee and a dedicated professional. Within the Post Office he was not in sympathy with the personalities or politics of Rowland Hill and his brother, Frederic, but he wrote a generous and warm-hearted tribute on Rowland's retirement (p. 117).

12. Dr George Birkbeck Hill (1835–1903) was born at Bruce Castle, Tottenham, the second son of Arthur Hill, Rowland's youngest surviving brother. He was educated at Bruce Castle and proceeded to Pembroke College, Oxford, where he was a close friend of the Pre-Raphaelites, Burne-Jones, William Morris and Gabriel Rossetti. As a member of the Old Mortality Club he associated with Swinburne, Professors Dicey and Nichol, James

Bryce, T. H. Green, Henry Nettleship and Walter Pater – all men of eminence in their professions and public service.

His friendship with James Bryce (later Viscount Bryce) undoubtedly coloured Bryce's understanding of education. This bore fruit, as has been mentioned earlier, first in the *Taunton Report* of 1868, on which Bryce was an Assistant Commissioner, and more strikingly in Viscount Bryce's own *Bryce Report* of 1895 which clearly outlined the broad and liberal secondary curriculum later to be embodied in *Balfour's Education Act* of 1902. This proved to be the curriculum pattern of secondary education that has been followed to the present day.

In 1855 Birkbeck Hill began teaching at Bruce Castle and assumed its Headship in 1868 on his father's retirement – on grounds of ill health. In 1887, after twelve years' intermittent work, he published his six volume edition of the life and work of Samuel Johnson, and thereafter published other works on this great eighteenth-century figure on whom Birkbeck Hill is regarded as one of the leading authorities.

13. Mr Serjeant Wilde was Thomas Wilde (1782–1855) (later to become Lord Truro), who was called to the Bar in 1817 (two years before Matthew Hill) and elevated to King's Serjeant in 1827. In 1831 he became an MP and worked for liberal causes such as anti-slavery legislation and for the jealous preservation of the privileges of the House of Commons. He formed a personal and professional friendship with Matthew Davenport Hill whose reforming zeal he admired. In 1839 he rose to the office of Solicitor-General and in the same year he introduced and commended Rowland Hill's plan for postal reform to the House of Commons. In August of that year the Penny Postage Act reached the Statute Book. There is no doubt that his friendship with Matthew Hill and his admiration of Rowland's genius led to the appointment of Frederic Hill as his Parliamentary Secretary.

III *The Colonisation of South Australia* (pp. 44–52)

1. Edward Gibbon Wakefield (1796–1862) worked as an assistant in legations in Turin and Paris. He had considerable natural ability, but a certain roguishness led him into two matrimonial misadventures that resulted in a three year prison sentence. After this he thought it wiser to live abroad again, and this induced him to make a study of colonisation. He advocated careful land surveys and an accurate assessment of trade possibilities before a policy of colonisation was embarked upon. His views were published in his *Letter from Sydney* in 1830, which, incidentally, he had never visited. But his views were sound and led to the formation of the *National Colonisation Society*. The government, however, showed no interest, so with Australia in mind a powerful *South Australia Association* was formed, with influential people like Colonel Robert Torrens and George Grote, the famous historian

and later MP, on the committee. This in turn resulted in the setting up of the official South Australian Commission in 1835, and the appointment of Rowland Hill as its secretary. The authorising legislation for this was drafted by Matthew Davenport Hill, QC – always at his brother's side. This led to the very successful colonisation of South Australia in the years that followed.

Edward Wakefield remained officially in the background, but devoted his energies to the colonisation of Canada and New Zealand, where, after some difficult years, he finally died. Wakefield's general ideas were sound and sincere, but certain flaws in his character seemed to vitiate the successful implementation of his impressive plans.

2. Thomas Arnold was approached by Lord John Russell in 1839 to consider taking up the Headship of a new educational institution – high school or university – that the government was contemplating establishing in Hobart, Van Dieman's Land (Tasmania today). It was to reflect the best of the Rugby traditions and set the pattern for other schools of the same type. Arnold hesitated, and meanwhile an old Rugbeian, John Philip Gell, took on the responsibility. Arnold had often seriously considered emigrating with his family to Australia and in due course actually bought land in New Zealand and in Western Australia – some 200 acres in each. His motives were undoubtedly mixed. First of all he was convinced that Britain was over-populated; secondly he had a sincere belief in his country's 'imperial destiny' and felt it a duty to send some of its best young people to help to colonise new territories. He also felt it was just the place to send any rather wild or work-shy youngsters. Strange to say, he classed his two eldest boys, Matthew and Thomas, as such. Writing to an Australian friend he said:

> My two sons, Matthew and Thomas, do not yet work as they should do, and I often think that nothing would raise their energies as sending them out to you, where they must work or starve.

(Could he really imagine the sensitive and fastidious Matthew working as a lumberjack, digging wells, shearing sheep and grilling kangaroo steaks over a camp fire?)

Thirdly, in spite of his passionate support for the Reform Bill of 1832, he continued to have uneasy feelings that the reforms had been too rash and hasty. The floodgates had been opened and he feared the results would be either a 'wild democracy' or some form of military dictatorship. He kept looking over his shoulder for a safe bolt-hole. As an insurance he bought land, as we have seen, in Australia and New Zealand, and he took care to salt away quite substantial investments in America. In a letter to a nephew in July 1832 he said:

> I hope we may both manage to live in peace with our families in the land of our fathers, without crossing the Atlantic.

To another friend, speaking of the consequences of the Reform Act and the upsurge of the masses, he declared:

> ... The game is yet in our hands if we would play it; but I suppose we shall not play it, and in five or ten years' hence it will not be ours to play. 120,000 copies of the Penny Magazine circulate weekly! ... Would that we might ever meet, before we meet perhaps in America or at sea after the Revolution.

Again, in a letter to the Rev. F. C. Blackstone in February 1839 he sadly confessed:

> 'Too late', however, are the words which I should be inclined to affix to every plan for reforming society in England; we are engulfed, I believe, inevitably, and must go down the cataract.

Finally, shortly before his death, in a lecture at Oxford, Arnold spoke as a prophet of doom in words that might chill the hearts of today's politicians:

> Woe to that generation that is living in England when the coal mines are exhausted and the national debt not paid off.

In his heart of hearts Arnold must have been hard pressed to reconcile these gloomy and defeatist views with the optimistic 'good news' of the New Testament that he so fervently proclaimed to all and sundry around him.

IV *The London and Brighton Railway* (pp. 53–63)

1. Queen Victoria's tacit displeasure on the occasion of Rowland's investiture in 1860 is vouched for by the younger Matthew Davenport Hill, the Eton science master, who related the episode to the present author in 1954; it was certainly the impression Rowland Hill and his family had at the time.
2. Fashionable Brighton is inevitably associated with its famous Pavilion, built in 1815 on lines suggested by the Prince Regent, who, it is said, derived his inspiration from a visit to Sezincote House, near Moreton-in-Marsh in 1807. Sezincote was built in a unique Indian style, complete with elegant onion-domes, in a garden-setting landscaped by Humphry Repton, overlooking the delightful Evenlode valley.
3. Parliamentary trains: we have all laughed at Gilbert's witty ripostes poking fun at 'the silly old duffers, who ride on the buffers of Parliamentary trains'.

V   *Rowland Hill's Postal Reforms* (pp. 64–85)

1. Lord Monteagle (1790–1866), originally Thomas Spring-Rice, was elected Whig MP for Limerick in 1820 and in 1832 for Cambridge, a seat which he held until his elevation to the peerage in 1839. He was an influential authority on Irish affairs. In April 1835 he became Chancellor of the Exchequer in Melbourne's second administration. He was impressed with and well-disposed towards Rowland's Penny Postage plan and vigorously introduced and supported the Penny Postage Bill in July 1839.

2. Jean Jacques Rousseau (1712–88) was the famous philosopher whose ideas and seductive theories helped to provide the philosophic basis of the French Revolution of 1789 and of nineteenth-century Romanticism in general. His *Social Contract* (1762) had a profound effect upon political theory, as did his *Emile* (1762) on education. As with so many accredited experts in education, Rousseau had never taught a class of real pupils in his life; the most he achieved in the practice of teaching was possibly the tutoring of a few individual pupils from time to time – chiefly young girls to study music. In contrast Rowland Hill and his brothers had been teaching full classes of boys as soon as they reached the age of thirteen. However, in the field of special education for rejected and deprived children Rousseau could be deemed to be something of an expert, for he had packed off his own batch of five illegitimate children (by his mistress, Thérèse) to a foundling hospital to be cared for by strangers. It is not surprising, therefore, that his famous *Emile* is little more than a fairy tale quite remote from reality, but a plausible effusion of a gifted intellectual word-spinner. Though most informed people would dismiss him, socially and morally, as a hypocritical scoundrel, his influence has been remarkable.

   Most educationists of the nineteenth century were inevitably influenced by the radical thinking of Rousseau and his successors Pestalozzi and Fellenberg, and Rowland Hill and his brothers freely acknowledge this. But the Hills were different in so far as they were major pioneers in the reform of education for older pupils, and we have shown how dramatically they shattered the long-established and exclusive mould of classical education which had for generations dominated the world of Public Schools and ancient Grammar schools of our country.

3. William Dockwra (1650?-1716) was an enterprising London merchant who initiated a private penny post service in London in 1681, covering the City, Southwark and Westminster. He established six large offices in various districts with many sub-offices in the main streets to provide from six to eight deliveries of letters per day. The charge was one penny for the central areas and twopence for the suburbs. In 1697 his enterprise was officially recognised by his being appointed *Comptroller of the Penny Post*, but because of various difficulties he was dismissed in 1700. Similar penny posts were soon set up in Dublin, Edinburgh and Manchester. The service expanded, and by the time Rowland Hill published his pamphlet

[165]

in 1837 nearly 2,000 villages were being served from more than 700 post towns.

4. Ralph Allen (1694–1767) was a distinguished resident of Bath where he lived in gentlemanly style in his elegant Prior Park as a man of taste and original ideas. He is buried in a very handsome tomb in the churchyard of Claverton church near Prior Park. In 1729 Ralph Allen officially organised 'Cross-posts' to carry mail to towns and villages along the principal post-roads out of London. The mail was mostly carried by Post-boys on horseback and rarely exceeded a speed of five miles per hour.

5. John Palmer (1742–1818), also of Bath, carried on his father's well-established theatres in London and Bath. He had long experiences of the slow, uncomfortable journeys between these towns, so he set out to design really well-built stage coaches that would carry mail as well as passengers. In the early 1780s he was planning services on the main post-roads out of London, and in 1784, having been appointed Comptroller General of the Post Office, he initiated the first official armed Mail Coach between London and Bristol: it averaged 12 miles per hour. This represented a major advance in regularity, speed and security.

6. Thomas Telford (1757–1834) was a Scots engineer and a versifier of some talent. In 1793 he was appointed engineer and architect of the Ellesmere canal project to connect the rivers Mersey, Dee and Severn. His impressive aqueducts over the Dee and the Ceiriog valley near Chirk gained him a national reputation. In 1801 he was given a major contract for the building of nearly a thousand miles of road and 120 bridges in Scotland which provided much needed work for thousands of men, and in consequence advanced a rather desolate area of the country by at least half a century. Between 1804 and 1822 he completed the famous Caledonian canal, and then undertook a vast road-building scheme in England, particularly the Shrewsbury – Holyhead road with its spectacular Menai Bridge between Caernarvonshire and Anglesey which was opened in 1825, followed by the attractive Conway Bridge in 1826. He always retained his love of literature and became the friend of many literary figures, including Thomas Campbell and Southey.

   He remained unmarried and was indifferent to money; indeed he was altruistic to a fault, preferring to work for the benefit of his fellow men rather than for reputation and wealth.

7. John Louden McAdam (1756–1836) was also a Scot. When he was orphaned at fourteen years of age his uncle took him to America where he lived for many years. In 1790 he was back in England and interested himself in methods of building better roads. In 1815 he was Surveyor–General of Bristol Roads and began publishing articles and books on the science of road-building. He used small granite stones, hard compacted, slightly raised for drainage to the side of the roadway. The surface became pounded smooth by the constant wear of traffic and easily shed rain-water into the side gullies, retaining its firmness over a long period of use. The term 'macadamised road' soon became common parlance, and the McAdam

system had an enormous influence on road communications. McAdam declined to accept a Knighthood.

8. Robert Wallace (1773–1855) is a major figure in the history of postal reform and Rowland Hill repeatedly expresses his gratitude for Wallace's generous and well-informed support. Wallace was a devoted Whig and a vigorous campaigner for the Reform Bill of 1832. He entered the first reformed parliament as MP for Greenock in Scotland and held the seat until 1846. He was particularly active in promoting reforms in the legal system and in the nation's postal service. By sheer perseverance he succeeded in securing the setting up of a *Royal Commission* in 1836 to report on the state of the postal service, and he was the chairman of the committee appointed in 1837 to examine Rowland Hill's pamphlet, *Post Office Reform: its Importance and Practicability* that had just been published. By his casting vote the plan was recommended to parliament, and this eventually led to the passing of the Penny Postage Act in August 1839. Wallace thereafter magnanimously handed over his case for penny postage into the hands of Rowland Hill and continued to support him superbly throughout the difficult years that followed. It was Wallace, incidentally, who sent a cab-load of Blue Books to Rowland under his MP's franking privilege to help him with his investigations into the running of the Post Office.

9. Henry Cole (1808–82). Along with Robert Wallace, Henry Cole is outstanding for the contribution he made to bring about the passing of the Penny Postage Act. He was born in Bath, studied Art under David Cox and developed into an accomplished water-colourist, engraver and etcher. He even used his skill as a witty cartoonist in support of Rowland Hill's postal reforms. His main career was passed as an Assistant-Keeper in the newly formed Record Office, and his competence and enterprise so impressed Richard Cobden that he appointed Cole as Secretary of the Anti-Corn Law League. At this time he became a close friend of George Grote and J. S. Mill, two leading figures of the age. His greatest contribution to Rowland's cause was his work with the *Mercantile Committee* of the City of London. Cole was the leading figure behind this organisation: he acted as its Public Relations Officer, and as such he produced and distributed on an unprecedented scale a powerful pamphlet in support of Rowland's penny postage plan. In further support he also launched the influential *Post Circular* in March 1838. With his considerable artistic skill he entered the competition for a suitable design for the proposed new stamps and stamped-covers, sharing the prize with three other contestants. His exceptional drive and vision caught the eye of the Prince Consort who enlisted him as a key member of his Commission set up under his chairmanship to plan the Great Exhibition of 1851. The Record Office gave Cole leave of absence to undertake the work, and the immense success of the venture is to a great extent credited to Cole's artistic and administrative skill.

In 1846 he became a member of the *Society of Arts*, soon becoming its chairman, and in 1853 he took a leading part in the establishment of the *Department of Science and Art, South Kensington* which co-ordinated and set the standards of ninety-one provincial schools and colleges of Art. In 1871, still indefatigably active, he played a major part in the building of the *Albert Hall*. He also took the first steps in establishing the *Royal College of Music*, founded in 1882, just before Cole's death.

His contribution to the cause of postal reform was so impressive that he was called in for consultations by the Treasury as soon as the Penny Postage Act was passed in August 1839, and in September he was appointed personal assistant to Rowland Hill who had just taken up his temporary position at the Treasury to help implement the Act. He remained in this post until 1842 when both he and Rowland had their appointments cancelled on a change of government. For his outstanding service to the nation in so many fields Henry Cole was honoured with a CB and KCB. Though perhaps not widely known today he was another very eminent Victorian to whom the country owes an immense debt of gratitude.

10. Samuel Lines (1778–1863) was for some years Art teacher at Hill Top and Hazelwood; he found Rowland to be a gifted young pupil and later a sympathetic colleague on the staff. He certainly helped to form Rowland's tastes and skills in this field. When Rowland and Edwin were creating the first of their stamps, Rowland took infinite pains to produce a first-class product, utilising the most talented artists, engravers and printers to this end. Characteristically he referred some of his final designs for the approval of Samuel Lines in Birmingham, expressing the hope that he had not let his old teacher down. Lines produced many sketches and watercolours of the Birmingham of those days, and his sketches of the Hazelwood building after the fire in August 1820 are of particular value to us today.

11. Sir Francis Thornhill Baring, MP (1796–1866), was a member of the eminent banking family of Baring Brothers. He was elected Whig MP for Portsmouth in 1826 and held the seat until 1865. He was an influential politician and held the office of Chancellor of the Exchequer from 1839 until September 1841, during the critical period of Rowland Hill's fight for Penny Postage, and throughout proved to be a good friend and supporter of the cause. It was Baring who, as Chancellor, offered Rowland a temporary post at the Treasury on the passing of the Penny Postage Act in 1839. The full story is related in the present chapter. In 1843 it was Baring who presented Rowland's petition to the House of Commons requesting the setting up of an *Enquiry into the State of the Post Office*. Rowland's evidence to the committee in question occupied 134 folio pages of detailed comment and statistics, and this undoubtedly helped to secure him his permanent appointment at the Post Office in 1846, as Secretary to the Post Master General. It was still to take him eight years before he finally took over Colonel Maberly's post as Secretary to the Post Office.

12. Henry Goulburn, MP (1784–1856), was active in Irish affairs, then in 1826 he was appointed Chancellor of the Exchequer in the Duke of Wellington's administration. In 1826 he became MP for Cambridge, a seat he held until his death. Under Peel's second administration he again held the office of

Chancellor of the Exchequer. He was liked and respected by both parties as a man and as a politician.

13. Lord Lowther (1787–1872), second Earl of Lonsdale, was a somewhat reactionary Tory who voiced his opposition to the Reform Bill. He was Postmaster General in Peel's short administration in 1834/5. As a very wealthy man he carried some influence in the Tory ranks, but he was a good, progressive landlord and a generous patron of John McAdam, the pioneer of modern road-making.

14. Thomas Hood (1795–1845) was a friend and associate of Lamb, Hazlitt and De Quincey. He became sub-editor of the London Magazine and later Editor of the New Monthly Magazine, and was an accomplished versifier. His verses had a social compassion, for example, his *Song of the Shirt*, but he was more popular as a wit and humorist. Throughout his life he was plagued by ill-health and poverty.

15. Henry Warburton (1784?–1858) was educated at Eton and Cambridge and was looked upon as a 'scholar and a man of science'. He associated himself with the philosophical radicals, supporting Brougham in founding London University in 1827, and was a member of its first council. He won a parliamentary seat as a radical in 1826 and worked closely with George Grote and Joseph Hume. Few people gave Rowland more active support for his penny postage plan than did Warburton and it was through his efforts that Rowland was appointed Secretary to the PMG in 1846.

16. Richard Cobden (1804–65). A self-educated and self-made businessman. His main political interests were education and commerce. In 1838 he was a leading light in founding the Manchester Anti Corn-Law League which became a powerful force in parliament and the country. In 1841 he became MP for Stockport. He travelled widely and developed a liberal, international outlook which made him a great advocate for peace, free-trade and financial retrenchment. He and George Moffatt (the founder of the *Mercantile Committee*) were amongst the most active supporters of Rowland Hill in the country.

17. There are many records of loyalty and courage on the part of mounted post-boys fighting off robbers even from quite early times. Likewise at the end of the eighteenth century the armed guards attached to John Palmer's mail-coaches frequently routed groups of highwaymen after a brisk engagement. In more recent times there is the stirring story of the five Sea Post Office sorters who did everything possible to save the 200 sacks of mail on board the Titanic when it met disaster in 1912. They failed and went down with the ship.

VI *Rowland Hill and Thomas Arnold* (pp. 86–102)

1. Dr Arthur Stanley (1815–81) entered Rugby School in 1829 and soon proved himself to be a brilliant scholar and a fine example to the school.

He was immensely impressed by Dr Arnold who became an object of pure hero-worship to him – 'I have made him my idol' he admits. Stanley's personality and influence at Rugby is immortalised in the character of Arthur in *Tom Brown's Schooldays*. He proceeded to Balliol College, Oxford, where he achieved a first-class in Classics and won numerous university prizes. In 1839 he was ordained into the Church of England in spite of some inner doubts which account for some of the doctrinal controversies he became involved in throughout his life. He was always an enthusiastic traveller in Europe and Asia, and his writings on his experiences were outstandingly colourful and vivid. Dr Arnold's early death in 1842 was the greatest catastrophe in Stanley's life, but it led to his best and most memorable literary work, *The Life and Correspondence of Dr Thomas Arnold* (1844), which became the source of the subsequent Arnold legend. As a tutor and Professor of Ecclesiastical History, as well as Canon of Christ Church, he exerted an inspiring influence on the young men who looked up to him. This was continued when he became Dean of Westminster in 1864. He died in 1881 having been Arnold's foremost and most influential disciple throughout his life.

2. Edward Thring (1821–87) was educated at Eton and Cambridge in the traditional classical mould. He was ordained into the Church of England in 1846 and as a curate in Gloucester he became very interested in the work of the parochial schools and in education generally. He was appointed Headmaster of Uppingham in 1853, then a small, insignificant grammar school of twenty-five boys and two masters. In the space of thirty-four years he had developed it into one of the most progressive and successful Public Schools in the country, with more than 300 boys and thirty masters. He built admirable premises, a fine chapel, excellently equipped facilities of all kinds, eleven boarding houses, housing not more than thirty boys each under a housemaster. The ideas and influence of Arnold are clear for all to see; it is a perfect example of the Arnold formula in action (see pp. 88, 89). But in the 1850s Thring went far beyond Arnold in the development of the curriculum; his emphasis on English, modern languages, mathematics, science, craftwork of all kinds, physical education, music and art closely follow what the Hills were doing at Hazelwood from the early 1820s onwards. He was following the general Arnold recipe with its evangelical emphasis, but adopted the curriculum techniques and educational philosophy of the Hills. As a widely read seeker after educational enlightenment Thring had obviously studied the Hazelwood system as expressed in *Public Education* and elsewhere, and his well-known cry for 'machinery, machinery' closely echoes the plea Matthew Davenport Hill makes in his letter to Thomas Jefferson quoted on pp. 16 and 17. It is not surprising that most perceptive critics rate Edward Thring as being far ahead of Thomas Arnold as a genuine educational innovator. His views and philosophy of education are admirably recorded in his writings – *Education and School* (1864); *The Theory and Practice of Teaching* (1883) in particular. He looked beyond his school and formed the very influential *Head Masters'*

Conference in 1869 and spoke up for the education of girls. Like Arnold and the Hills he stressed the primacy of the moral element in education.

3. Arnold's munificent basic salary scale of £500 p.a. is an outstanding example of how the independent schools have always exposed the comparative penury of the state system. The Rugby salaries were princely in their day as is shown by the fact that as recently as 1930 (a hundred years later) the Burnham Scale for graduate teachers in Grammar schools began at a basic £234 p.a., and even this paltry figure was subjected in 1931 to an across-the-board cut of 10 per cent, imposed willy-nilly by the Treasury. Left-wing extremists in our day would do well to think again before clamouring for the abolition of independent schools after what they have done and are still doing for educational standards in our country.

4. In some boarding schools a modest charge is made for the enjoyment of these facilities.

5. Laleham, a small village near Staines in Surrey, was the venue of Arnold's first venture into schoolmastering. Here, with his brother-in-law, John Buckland (both in Holy Orders) he set up a small school or coaching establishment, and they both undertook duties at the parish church. In 1824 the partnership split up, each running his own school. By this time Arnold had nine pupils and in the ensuing years the number grew steadily until he took up his appointment at Rugby in 1828.

6. It was largely through the interest and support of Dr Richard Whately, a senior Fellow of Oriel, that Arnold was appointed tutor and Fellow of the college in 1815, and was later persuaded to apply for the Headmastership of Rugby School.

   In 1831 Whately was appointed Archbishop of Dublin and continued to support and influence Arnold in his many political and ecclesiastical activities. In his Oxford days Whately had been a powerful force in the university; he was an unorthodox character, careless in dress, boorish in manners, gruff and outspoken in utterance, but he carried undeniable authority. Even his best friends could not dissuade him from his habit of spitting on the commonroom floor.

7. The letter came to light among a collection of papers in the possession of Dr I. D. Hill of Chorleywood, Herts.

8. Rachel – née Elisa Felix – was born in Switzerland in 1820 – just a year older than Matthew Arnold. She died in France in 1858. When she was eighteen she began her distinguished career in classical plays and captivated the Parisian audiences with her tragic roles in particular. She had beauty, grace, elegance and a striking contralto voice with which she expressed a wide range of emotions. Probably the susceptible Matthew merely worshipped from afar – just intellectual and aesthetic calf-love.

9. George Sand (1804–76) is the pseudonym of Amandine Lucile Aurore Dupin, Baronne de Dudevant, who was internationally known as an original and provocative novelist. At an early age she left her husband, Baron de Dudevant, a retired army officer, and lived a Bohemian life in Paris. She was an emancipated feminist, notorious for her liberated life-style and for

her philosophy of life which advocated free love. She was no mere theorist for she openly formed liaisons with various artistic celebrities amongst whom were Frederick Chopin and Alfred de Musset, the romantic French lyric poet and playwright. She wrote two types of novel, first, those that depicted the struggle of progressive women against obstructive social conventions, especially those against sexual freedom, such as *Indiana* (1832); *Lelia* (1833) and *Jacques* (1834). The second type of novel was artfully composed around idyllic and not so idyllic rustic life. Amongst the less idyllic was *A Winter in Majorca* (1841) which relates an episode in her long relationship with Frederick Chopin. During their short sojourn in Majorca, Chopin was suffering from a rapidly developing consumption and George Sand was more of a nurse than a mistress. For many winter months, unusually bleak, she coped with shortages of food and fuel, with her two children, a French maid and the debilitated Chopin – all this in the face of the overt hostility of the natives who regarded her as nothing more than an immoral adventuress.

Her other well-known novel in this style is *Elle et Lui* (1859) which is based upon her liaison in Venice with Alfred de Musset.

When Matthew Arnold paid court to her during the year 1844/5 she was forty years of age compared with his twenty-two years. He could only have been motivated by curiosity to meet this famous free-thinking amorous intellectual, the *femme fatale* who was the talk of every country in Europe. She was a too-experienced and hot a property for a callow, impressionable student to make any headway with. But it must have been a strange experience for a young man with Rugby Chapel sermons and his father's stern admonitions on the reality of sin and evil still ringing in his ears.

10. Marguerite, the attractive young girl he met in Switzerland, remains rather a mysterious, shadowy but persistent presence throughout Matthew Arnold's life. Unlike his association with the afore-mentioned intellectual and artistic acquaintances, his relationship with Marguerite seems to have been the real thing – his first experience of disturbing romantic love. It is not surprising that, given his background, he is extremely reticent about this chapter of his life, though the underlying emotion oozes out in many of his poems.

11. Dr James Prince Lee (1804–69) was reported to have been one of the most brilliant classical scholars ever to have passed through Cambridge. He was ordained in 1830, and in the same year he started his teaching career at Rugby, just two years after Arnold's advent. Arnold considered him to be one of his outstanding teachers and he certainly contributed to Rugby's phenomenal academic successes when the school swept the board in 1838. In that year Prince Lee was appointed Headmaster of King Edward VI School, Birmingham where his administrative ability and stern methods, backed up by a ready use of the birch, brought good academic results. One of his victims, R. W. Dixon, who no doubt displeased the Headmaster from the start by being a Methodist, relates the daily floggings he received,

sometimes in front of the whole school, from the learned Doctor, for being unable to recite the (to him) meaningless and pointless jingles from the Eton Grammar that constituted his very first lesson and homework in the Latin language. He did not suffer alone, for generations of schoolboys all over England were likewise being flogged through rigmaroles like the following, dealing with the gender of nouns:

Propria quae maribus tribuunter mascula dicas;
Ut sunt Divorum, Mars, Bacchus, Apollo: Virorum;
Ut Cato, Virgilius; Fluviorum: ut Tibris, Orontes;
Mensium; ut, October; Ventorum; ut Libs, Notus,
                                        Auster. . . .

As the young Dixon later commented, 'If Lee was a reformer, what must others be!'

Dr Prince Lee had few democratic sympathies and he resented the policy of his Governors in widening the admissions to the school to include the clever but often socially disadvantaged boys emerging from the commercial and industrial families of Birmingham at that time. He was used to Arnold's young Christian gentlemen, with proper manners and cultivated speech. Prince Lee found it difficult to accept the sometimes boorish boys with unattractive flat Midlands accents. Like his Master at Rugby Prince Lee wanted to accept boys with the right background and values, and looked back with envy at Arnold's powers of rejection, suspension and expulsion. This was a direct legacy of Arnold's lack of professionalism as an educator (see p. 96).

To the relief of many, Dr Prince Lee was elevated in 1847 to the Bishopric of the newly instituted see of industrial Manchester. From the first he was unpopular and distrusted by many of his colleagues and the public; he was too autocratic and pedagogic in his relationships. In spite of his skill as an able administrator and his recognised brilliance as a speaker and preacher, he failed to win the hearts of his flock. The despot of the classroom did not cut much ice in the rougher, real world of the industrialised north – for such it was to him. At the time of Dr Lee's appointment as Bishop of Manchester a nine days' wonder was created by a libellous attack on him by a Mr Gutteridge, a Birmingham surgeon. It was an almost unheard of situation as dramatic and shattering as a public challenge of banns of marriage when read in open church. The libel consisted of a letter that Mr Gutteridge had sent round to the Archbishop, Bishops and members of the Government, and otherwise extensively circulated, including a communication to the editor of the *John Bull* newspaper. Dr Prince Lee was charged with being morally disqualified for the office of a Bishop on account of his 'lying, drunkenness and malignity'. Affidavits in defence, containing an absolute denial of the charge, were submitted by the Bishop of Worcester, various clergymen, private friends and a medical man. They asserted that the appearances on which the charges were made were founded on 'nervousness arising from indisposition'.

[173]

Mr Gutteridge appeared in court, making no affidavit, but strongly reiterating his allegations and asserting that the charge of intoxication was clearly borne out by the evidence. On his judgment on the full circumstances of the libel Lord Chief Justice Denman declared that the omission of an affidavit on the part of Mr Gutteridge convinced him that the charges were utterly false, emphasising that, as a result, Dr Lee's reputation 'so far from being tarnished, his character shines the brighter for the charges that have been made against him'. Accordingly the rule against Mr Gutteridge was made absolute.

In spite of this complete legal vindication, it was an unhappy beginning to Dr Lee's episcopacy, and it must have nurtured hidden doubts and suspicions in his new diocese and contributed to the mixed feelings with which he was accepted. Regrettably in this imperfect world some of the mud sticks even when the victim of a libel has been exonerated by the highest court in the land.

As an interesting footnote it is worth mentioning that Dr Prince Lee's favourite whipping-boy, R. W. Dixon, eventually got to Oxford, took a degree in Classics (*mirabile dictu!*) and was ordained into the Anglican church. He is remembered as a distinguished Church historian, poet and divine, as well as a dedicated parish priest in Cumberland and Northumberland. Somewhat ironically he won the *Arnold Historical Prize* in 1858 for an essay on *Christianity in the Tenth Century*.

While he was at Oxford he was an intimate friend of Burne-Jones (a former King Edward's boy) and of William Morris; he also became acquainted with D. G. Rossetti and helped all three with the famous frescoes they painted for the Oxford Union. This association really marked the beginning of the *Pre-Raphaelite Brotherhood*. He officiated at the wedding of William Morris to Jane Burden in 1859.

VII *The Influence and Message of Hazelwood* (pp. 103–9)

1. George Anson, MP (1797–1857), was a brother of the first Earl of Lichfield and he served with the Guards at the battle of Waterloo. He was elected MP in 1818, and conscious of the handicap of his stammer he went to Thomas Wright Hill for a course of treatment. (See p. 23). His army career culminated in his being appointed Commander-in-Chief in India in 1856. In 1857 during the Indian mutiny he made a gallant attempt to go to the aid of his countrymen in Delhi, but died of cholera on the march.
2. Daniel O'Connell, MP (1775–1847) was the great Irish Catholic patriot. He was called to the Irish Bar in 1796 and soon gained a reputation in the political field, at first as a moderate nationalist and as a witty and a brilliant orator at public meetings. He championed the cause of his fellow Catholics in religious and political freedom. When elected MP in 1828 he at first met hostility, but by his good sense and wit he won many admirers.

He was largely responsible for the passing of the Catholic Emancipation Act of 1829. He inevitably became deeply involved in the tempestuous Irish political and religious struggles of the day, on which he could be tough and intransigent in his demands, particularly for the repeal of the Union. As a dedicated reformer he helped his liberal English friends by supporting them in their fight for the Reform Bill and the anti-slavery cause. Though at times a firebrand he always in the end tried to achieve his ends by constitutional methods within parliament, even though this lost him some popular support. He died in Italy in 1847. An impressive monument in Dublin commemorates his life and work.

3. Thomas Wyse, MP (1791–1862) was another Irish Catholic politician who worked for Catholic emancipation. He was MP for Tipperary and like O'Connell, he worked closely with the Liberals for the Reform Bill, for the repeal of the corn laws and for the anti-slavery movement. Above all he advocated the extension of popular education and his book *Educational Reform* in 1837 echoed and reinforced the message of the Hills at Hazelwood. He spoke eloquently all over the country on the need for educational reform and was largely responsible for stimulating Kay-Shuttleworth to establish the first Teachers' Training College at Battersea. During Melbourne's administration in 1839–41 he was made Lord of the Treasury. There is no doubt that he was a great influence on the educational reforms of the mid and late nineteenth century.

4. James Mill (1773–1836) was born in Scotland and had a difficult and hard life in his early years. He made a living in journalism while studying and working on his major work the *History of India* which won success on its publication in 1818. In 1808 he had made the acquaintance of Jeremy Bentham, the founder of *Utilitarianism* and leading philosopher of the age. He became Bentham's most devoted disciple and chief mouthpiece as his master succumbed to the infirmities of age. He was a prolific writer ranging in his interests from logic, political economy and government to education. His most famous son, John Stuart Mill, was a victim of his father's theories; he started learning Greek at three years of age and was soon seen to be an infant prodigy. He further developed his father's ideas, writing such memorable works as his *System of Logic* (1843); *Principles of Political Economy* (1848) and *Liberty* (1859). He became a Liberal MP in 1865 and was a loyal and powerful supporter of Gladstone and his reforms. The two Mills were undoubtedly significant figures in providing the philosophical basis of Liberal politics in the nineteenth century.

5. Arthur Follett Osler, FRS (1808–1903) came from a good Unitarian family in Birmingham and attended Hazelwood School from about 1818 to 1824, leaving when he was sixteen. He was interested in science and practical subjects and found the Hazelwood curriculum to be stimulating and satisfying. With Edward Lewin (George Grote's nephew who with his brother, Emilius, were taken away from Eton to attend Hazelwood) he printed the first issue of the Hazelwood Magazine in 1822.

At an early age he established a glass works in Icknield Street, Birmingham, and soon achieved a national reputation for the quality and originality of his products. He specialised in making handsome chandeliers for the great houses, and astonished the world by being the first to manufacture huge sheets of plate glass 20 feet high. When he was twenty-six he invented a much improved Anemometer, and designed and constructed ingenious clocks. It was he who gave the city of Birmingham its town clock – *Big Brum*. He was a great philanthropist and a bountiful patron of the Birmingham and Midland Institute and of the University of Birmingham. In 1855 he was elected Fellow of the Royal Society. In the Great Exhibition of 1851 in the Crystal Palace the centre-piece in the main hall was Follett Osler's *Crystal Fountain*, which strangely enough has been exactly reproduced in America in our own day. In Dallas (where else?) a six storey glass exhibition hall, closely imitating the original Crystal Palace, houses as a centre-piece a 20 foot high copy in Venetian glass of the fountain Follett Osler designed in 1851.

6. Sir William Bowman, FRS and John Dent Goodman are mentioned in some detail on page 105 of Chapter VII and on pages 154–5. The cardboard model of the Hazelwood building made by them in about the year 1828 is now displayed in the vestibule of the School of Education at the University of Birmingham. Above it is mounted the actual Hazelwood school bell which the present author acquired in 1952, and presented to the University shortly before the historic Hazelwood building was demolished.

7. George Dixon, MP (1820–98) played a major role in the educational reforms in the latter part of the nineteenth century. He was born in Yorkshire, but at eighteen years of age came to Birmingham to work with a firm of exporters, of which he later became head. After spending a few years on business in Australia, he returned to Birmingham and entered enthusiastically into its municipal life, eventually becoming Mayor in 1866. As an advanced Liberal he was keenly interested in education, and in 1867 inaugurated a series of important educational conferences in Birmingham; they were attended by leading figures from all parties and also by people like Dr Temple, then headmaster of Rugby. Resolutions urged municipal corporations to raise rates for local education, and suggested measures to safeguard the education of young children who were sent out to work. More important still, the conferences advocated compulsory education for all. All this led to the formation of the *Birmingham Education Association*, strongly supported by Joseph Chamberlain; the Association expanded nationally to become the *National Education League* in 1869 which was the popular driving force that brought about the passing of *Forster's Education Act of 1870*. George Dixon was its first national President. This was one of the most important pieces of legislation in the whole of British educational history; it established the structure of state education once and for all. George Dixon was an MP from 1867 to 1876 and his name is commemorated in some Birmingham schools.

8. William Edward Forster, MP (1818–86), was a devout Quaker and in 1841

he entered the woollen industry in Bradford, soon becoming a prosperous mill owner. He was an ardent Liberal and worked for Parliamentary reform and for other liberal causes. In 1850 he married Jane Arnold, the eldest daughter of Dr Thomas Arnold's family. He became MP for Bradford in 1861 and held the seat until his death in 1886. Colonial affairs interested him and he was a strong supporter of Disraeli's Reform Bill in 1867. In 1868 Gladstone appointed him Privy Counsellor and he played a big part in promoting educational developments, leading to his *Education Act of 1870* and the establishment of School Boards under local authority control.

9. Robert William Dale (1829–95) was an eminent Congregational divine who, as Pastor of Carr's Lane, Birmingham from 1859, had an enduring influence on the town in whose life he took a prominent part, especially in the field of education. He was a friend and supporter of Joseph Chamberlain. He travelled widely and preached and lectured abroad. His influence as a theologian extended beyond his Congregational faith and he never hesitated to indulge in vigorous controversy when the occasion demanded it. Matthew Arnold once described him as a 'brilliant pugilist'. He was instrumental in founding Mansfield College, Oxford in 1885, which absorbed the earlier Congregational Spring Hill College in Birmingham.

10. James Bryce (1838–1922) is so important to our story that he deserves a special mention. Born in Belfast and educated first at Glasgow University, he became a noted jurist, historian and politician. In 1857 he won a scholarship to Trinity College, Oxford where he distinguished himself in law and classics. He was an active member of the Old Mortality Club where he met many eminent academics and won the friendship of his contemporary George Birkbeck Hill (Rowland Hill's nephew) with whom he enjoyed many continental holidays and learnt something of the Hill family as educational pioneers. He became a Fellow of Oriel College in 1842 and was called to the Bar in 1867.

His passionate hobbies were travel and mountaineering; he climbed mountains in Switzerland, Iceland, Italy, Japan, Russia, Canada, America and in Hawaii where he nearly fell into the volcano, Mauna Loa. In 1898 the triple-peaked Mount Bryce in the Canadian Rockies was named after him.

Bryce was an authority on the American Constitution and was later Ambassador to that country. As a politician he worked tirelessly to sort out the tangled affairs of the Balkans and Ireland. Gladstone appointed him Chancellor of the Duchy of Lancaster with a place in the Cabinet in 1892 and in the following year he was invited by Queen Victoria to accompany her on a visit to Florence: she admired his scholarship and becoming modesty, as well as his ability to converse with her in German. He was always deeply interested in educational matters and by his important Bryce Report on Secondary Education in 1895 he provided the blue-print on which, in Michael Sadler's view, the new administrative structure of modern secondary education was built. More particularly, as we have shown elsewhere, his Report shaped the curriculum of secondary education as laid down in the ensuing Balfour Education Act of 1902 and which still largely survives to this day. It is no coincidence that this new pattern of secondary education followed very closely the innovations first introduced by Rowland Hill at Hazelwood and Bruce Castle schools back in the 1830s.

This very remarkable and versatile man was created a Viscount in 1914. He received honorary degrees from thirty-one universities, fifteen of which were in America. He was always close to the events of the day – from the Jameson Raid in the Boer War, to the Roger Casement episode during the 1914–18 war and to the creation of the League of Nations.

VIII *A Final Assessment* (pp. 110–31)

1. Sir Francis Baring's testimony in favour of Rowland Hill's work during his three years temporary appointment at the Treasury was made in the course of presenting Rowland's petition to the House of Commons in the summer of 1843, when he humbly prayed that the House would be pleased to institute an inquiry into the state of the Post Office, with a view to adopting his plan in its complete form etc.

The ensuing debate is recorded in the Hansard report for 27 June under the heading 'Postage Reform' and can be found on pages 400 to 446.

The proposer was Sir Thomas Wilde (1782–1855), a notable Whig reformer: he later became Chief Justice and Privy Counsellor, and in 1800 assumed the office of Lord Chancellor as Baron Truro of Bowes, Middlesex. Sir Thomas recounted in great detail the circumstances of Rowland's appointment to a temporary post at the Treasury in September 1839, and its termination in September 1842. He clearly revealed the serious shortcomings of the Post Office at the time: notwithstanding the great increase in population and the extension of trade, no improvement had occurred in the revenue of the Post Office. Sir Thomas candidly exposed the failures of the department to institute any significant improvements, and showed up its inability to produce any accurate facts on the conduct of its affairs. Though Rowland Hill's plan for a penny postage had been implemented, no effort had been made to carry out his further measures for improved management, better facilities and necessary economies. Any temporary loss of revenue, Wilde declared, was solely due to this refusal to carry through Rowland Hill's complete plan.

Sir Thomas quoted many examples of 'the most inexcusable negligence on the part of some of the Post Office officials' and declared that 'improvement after improvement suggested by Mr Hill met with resistance'. Sir Francis Baring added his weight to Rowland's causes (as we have noted earlier) and confirmed the view that the Post Office officials 'were throughout entirely hostile to Mr Hill's plans'.

In the same debate Robert Wallace, rallying to Rowland's support, saw fit to assert categorically 'that no other man living had a just claim to the invention of the penny postage but Mr Rowland Hill.' Joseph Hume, too, added his testimony, pointing out that 'whilst every department of our revenue was found to be declining, the revenue derived from the Post Office had gone on increasing progressively during the last three and a half years'. He finally declared quite bluntly that Rowland Hill 'had not been assisted as he ought to have been by the officials in the office'.

The Chancellor of the Exchequer made a lengthy and desperate attempt to defend the conduct and record of the Post Office, but his arguments lacked conviction.

As a result of the debate the Commons agreed that a Select Committee should be set up 'to inquire into the progress which had been made in carrying into effect the recommendations of Mr Rowland Hill for Post Office improvements. . . .'

In due course Rowland appeared before the Select Committee and the details of his own evidence in the face of a most thorough examination occupies 134 folio pages of the Blue Book containing the Report of the Committee. His confident mastery of the facts and the incontrovertible logic of his arguments undoubtedly helped to secure his permanent appointment as Secretary to the Postmaster General in 1846 and his eventual promotion to the post of Secretary to the Post Office in 1854.

Against the irrefutable evidence of Rowland's well-informed supporters in the House of Commons and his own testimony before the Select Committee, the gossipy twitterings of Anthony Trollope and his like, on which Dr Daunton places such credit, seem to be quite contemptible.

Bibliography

The Hills and the Hazelwood System

Brayley, E. W. The Utility of Knowledge of Nature considered with reference to the introduction of Instruction in the Physical Sciences into the General Education of Youth. Birmingham, 1831, London, 1831.

Edwards, Eliezer. Biographical and Historical sketch. London, 1879.

Fellows, Arthur. Notes on the History of Hill Top and Hazelwood Schools. Miscellaneous MSS, Bruce Castle Museum.

Goodman, John Dent. A slim leather-bound foolscap Miscellany of manuscripts, letters and documents relating to Hazelwood School; Birmingham Reference Library.

Hazelwood Magazine. Vol. 1 Sept. 1822 (No. 1) – Dec. 1823 (No. 14)

    Vol. 2 Feb. 1824 (No. 1) – Dec. 1824 (No. 10)

    Vol. 3 Missing

    Vol. 4 Missing

    Vol. 5 Feb. 1827 (No. 1) – Dec. 1827 (No. 10)

    Vol. 6 Feb. 1828 (No. 1) – Dec. 1828 (No. 10)

    Vol. 7 Feb. 1829 (No. 1) – Dec. 1829 (No. 10)

    Vol. 8 Feb. 1830 (No. 1) – Nov. 1830 (No. 9)

The above volumes are to be found in the Birmingham Reference Library, except for Vol. 5 which is in the Birmingham Library, Margaret Street.

Hill, Arthur & Albert. Sketch of the System of Education at Bruce Castle. London, 1852.

Hill, Arthur. Hints on Discipline. London, 1855.

Hill, Frederic. An Autobiography of 50 years in times of Reform. London, 1894.

Hill, George Birkbeck. Life of Sir Rowland Hill, KCB, and

Hill, Matthew Davenport Jnr. Eton and Elsewhere. John Murray, London, 1928.

Hill, Rowland. MS Diary – 5 bound Octavo Volumes – in Bruce Castle Museum in 1953.

Hill, Rowland. Sketch of the System of Education, Moral and Intellectual, in practice at the schools of Bruce Castle, Tottenham and Hazelwood, near Birmingham. Birmingham & London, 1833.

Hill, Rowland and Frederic. Laws of Hazelwood. Birmingham & London, 1827.

Hill, Rowland and Matthew. Plans for the Government and Liberal Instruction of Boys in Large Numbers, drawn from Experience. London, 1822.

Hill, Rowland and Matthew. Public Education; Plans for the Government and

Liberal Instruction of Boys in Large Numbers, as practised at Hazelwood School. London, 1825.

Hill, Rowland and Matthew. The Organisation of Hazelwood School. (Reprint of the 1825 Edition of Public Education). London, 1894.

Hill, Thomas Wright. Remains of T. W. Hill, Esq., FRAS, together with notices of his life. Privately printed, 1859.

Hill, Thomas Wright. Selections from T. W. Hill's Papers. London, 1860.

Hill Top Exercises. Birmingham, 1814.

Plimley, A. J. A Notebook on English Geography. MS Birmingham Reference Library, 1815.

Wise, M. J. An Early 19th century Experiment in the Teaching of Geography. *Geography*, 1948.

The Birmingham Background

Davies, W. J. Token Coinage of Warwickshire. Birmingham, 1895.

Dent, A. K. Old and New Birmingham. Birmingham, 1880.

Dent, A. K. The Making of Birmingham. Birmingham & London, 1894.

Gill and Briggs. The History of Birmingham, 2 Vols. Oxford, 1952.

Hutton, T. W. King Edward's School, Birmingham. Blackwell, Oxford, 1952.

Langford. A Century of Birmingham Life. Birmingham & London, 1868.

Ryland, T. H. Reminiscences. Birmingham, 1904.

Sargant, W. L. Essays of a Birmingham Manufacturer, 4 Vols. London, 1869–71.

Sargant, W. L. Life and Philosophy of Robert Owen. London, 1860.

Whitwell, T. S. Warming and Ventilating Houses and Buildings. Cambridge, 1834.

Contemporary Birmingham Newspapers – passim: Aris's Birmingham Gazette, Birmingham Commercial Herald, Bissett's Magnificent Directory, Birmingham, 1808.

Histories of Education

Adamson, J. W. English Education, 1789–1902. Cambridge, 1930.

Archer, R. L. Secondary Education in the 19th Century. Cambridge, 1928.

Barnard, H. C. History of English Education. London, 1947.

Bellot, H. H. University College, London. London, 1929.

Bentham, J. Chrestomathia. London, 1816.

Body, A. H. John Wesley and Education. London, 1936.

Bruce, P. A. History of University of Virginia, 1819–1919, 5 Vols. New York, 1920–22.

Carpenter, L. Principles of Education, Intellectual, Moral and Physical. London, 1820.

Chandos, J. Boys Together, English Public Schools, 1800–64. Oxford, 1985.

Edgeworth, R. L. and M. Practical Education. London, 1789.

Felkin, F. W. From Gower Street to Frognall. London, 1909.

Bibliography

Hans, H. New Trends in Education in the 18th Century. London, 1951.

Hansen, A. D. Liberalism and American Education in the 18th Century. New York, 1926.

Hill, F. National Education. London, 1836.

Huxley, T. H. Physiography. London, 1869.

Judges, A. V. ed. Pioneers of English Education. London, 1952.

Mack, G. ed. Public Schools and British Opinion, 1780–1860. London, 1938.

McLachlan, H. English Education under the Test Acts. Manchester, 1931.

Parker, I. Dissenting Academies in England. Cambridge, 1914.

Patten, J. S. Jefferson, Cabell and the University of Virginia. New York, 1906.

Priestley, J. Essay on a Course of Liberal Education. Cork, 1765.

Quick, R. H. Essays on Educational Reformers. London, 1868.

Salmon, D. Lancaster and Bell. London, 1932.

Spencer, H. Education; Intellectual, Moral and Physical. London, 1861.

Spencer, H. J. University College School. Hampstead Annual, 1906–7.

Stephen, L. The English Utilitarians, 3 Vols. London, 1900.

Thring, E. Education and School. London, 1864.

Turner, D. M. History of Science Teaching. London, 1927.·

Wallas, G. Life of Francis Place. London, 1898.

Wyse, T. Educational Reform. London, 1837.

The Colonisation of South Australia

Blainley, G. A Land Half-won. Melbourne, 1980.

Bunbury, H. W. Early days in Western Australia. Oxford, 1930.

Cannon, M. Who's Master? Who's Man? London, 1971.

Hasluck, A. Thomas Peel of Swan River. Melbourne, 1965.

Price, A. G. The Foundation and Settlement of South Australia. Adelaide, 1924.

Torrens, R. On the Colonisation of South Australia. London, 1835.

Wakefield, E. G. A Letter from Sydney. London, 1829.

Wakefield, E. G. A View of the Art of Colonisation. London, 1849.

The London and Brighton Railway

Bradley, D. L. Locomotives of the London, Brighton and South Coast Railway, 1839–1903. London, 1969.

Brighton Gazette. 1843–6.

Ellis, H. The London, Brighton and South Coast Railway, 1839–1922. I. Allan, London, 1960.

Gray, A. The London to Brighton Line, 1841–1977. Oakwood Press, 1943.

Turner, J. T. H. The London, Brighton and South Coast Railway, 3 Vols. Batsford, London, 1977–79.

Rugby School and The Arnolds

Bamford, T. W. Thomas Arnold. London, 1960 & 1970.

Chandos, J. Boys Together; English Public Schools 1800–1864. Oxford, 1985.
Fitch, J. Great Educators; Thomas and Matthew Arnold. London, 1899.
Hughes, T. Tom Brown's Schooldays. London, 1857.
Rouse, W. H. D. Rugby School. London, 1898.
Rowse, A. L. Matthew Arnold. London, 1976.
Stanley, A. P. Life and Correspondence of Thomas Arnold, 1844, 2 Vols. London, 9th Edition, 1875.
Strachey, L. Eminent Victorians. London, 1918.
Trevor, M. The Arnolds. London, 1973.
Wymer, N. Dr Arnold of Rugby. London, 1953.

The Postal Reforms

Daunton, M. J. Royal Mail; the Post Office since 1840. Athlone Press. London, 1985.
Hill, G. B. The Life of Rowland Hill and the History of Penny Postage, 2 Vols. London, 1880.
Hill, H. W. Rowland Hill and the Fight for Penny Post. London, 1940.
Hill, P. The Post Office of Fifty Years Ago. London, 1887.
Hill, P. The Origin of Postage Stamps. London, 1888.
Hill, R. Post Office Reform; its Importance and Practicability Jan. 1837; Feb. 1837; Nov. 1837 and 1838. London.
Lowe, R. The British Postage Stamp of the 19th Century. London, 1979.
Robinson, H. Britain's Post Office. Oxford, 1953.
Smyth, E. Rowland Hill, the Story of a Great Reform. London, 1907.

The American Connection (Appendix A)

Bazeley, E. T. Homer Lane and the Little Commonwealth. London, 1928.
Campayre, G. Johann Heinrich Pestalozzi. London, 1908.
Chamberlain, R. W. There is No Truce (Biography of T. M. Osborne). New York, 1935.
George, W. R. Citizens Made and Remade. New York & London, 1913.
George, W. R. The George Junior Republic. New York, 1910.
Heafford, M. R. Pestalozzi. London, 1967.
Holman, H. Pestalozzi; an Account of his Life and Work. London, 1908.
Lane, H. Talks to Parents and Teachers.
Neill, A. S. Hearts, not Heads. 1945. London, 1928.
Neill, A. S. Talking of Summerhill. 1967.
Osborne, T. M. Prison without Walls. New York, 1914.
Osborne, T. M. Society and Prisons. Oxford, 1916.
Wills, D. The Hawkspur Experiment. London, 1941.
Wills, D. The Barns Experiment. London, 1945.
Wills, D. Homer Lane. London, 1964.

Bibliography

Hillska Skola (Appendix B)

Bjelfvenstam, E. Hillska Skolan på Barnängen, 8pp. Stockholm, 1928.

Björling, E. G. Um Uppfostrings – Skolan på Barnängen, 51 pp. Stockholm, 1833.

Ericsson, H. Hillska Skolanpa Barnangen, 1830–1846, 164 pp. Stockholm, 1885.

(The present author is indebted to the Royal Library, Stockholm, for the loan of the above Swedish publications.)

Hazelwood Magazine, Vol. 8, No. 7 – Sept. 1830.

Opening ceremony of Hillska Skola translated from the Stockholm newspaper *Medborgaren* of 6 July 1830.

Hazelwood Magazine, Vol. 8, No. 8 – October 1830.

Count Frolich's opening speech at the ceremony translated from the Swedish.

The Adhesive Stamp and the Penny Black

Hill, H. W. Rowland Hill and the Fight for Penny Post. London, 1940.

Hill, P. The Origin of Postage Stamps. London, 1888.

Lowe, R. The British Postage Stamp of the 19th Century. London, 1979.

Index

A.H. = Arthur Hill
F.H. = Frederic Hill
G.B.H. = George Birkbeck Hill
R.H. = Rowland Hill

Index

notes and comments, 157
visited by Author, 21
Hill, Ormond (Frederic's son), 42
Hill, Pearson (Rowland's son) 1832–98, 39, 51
  investigation into adhesive stamp claims, 147
  Post Office appointment, 42
Hill, Rowland, 1795–1879, 29–39
  administration skills, 31–4
  appearance, 38
  biographical summary, xvii–xviii
  Birmingham Assay office, 31
  born Kidderminster, 29
  boyhood, 30–1
  character, 34–5, 88–101
  children, 39
  circle of friends and admirers, 36–7
  craft work, 30
  education, 33
  family tree, xix
  final assessment, 110–31, 178–9
  to France, 44–5
  Hazelwood School, headmaster, 1808–27, 1–21, 34–7, 149–57
  see also Hazelwood School breakthrough
  higher salary offers, 80–1
  Hill Top, 36
  hostility from Post Office colleagues, 33, 179
  as inventor, 28, 64–5
  Knighthood, 55–6
  left-wing views, 24, 32, 104
  London and Brighton Railway Company, 1843–46, 33, 53–63
  Director, later Chairman, 1, 62
  marked as a Jacobin, 24, 32, 104
  marriage to Caroline, 32, 39
  meticulous timekeeping and statistical records, 13, 58
  Post Office career (1839–42 and 1846–64), 32–3, 65–85
  relations with Col. Maberly, 112–14
  see also Maberly, Colonel William Leader: Postal Reforms of Rowland Hill
  retired from Post Office March 1864, 33, 84
  postage, early interest, 30
  poverty, 30
  private coaching, 31
  pupil teacher at Hill Top, 31
  relations with Trollope, 38, 117, 161
  Secretary to Post Office, 1854–64, 33, 83
  seeks Matthew's advice, 27
  South Australia colonisation, 1833–39, 33, 36, 44–52, 162–4

  see also South Australia colonisation
South Australia Commission, Secretary and Chief Executive Officer, 1
  see also South Australia colonisation
State funeral, 39
summoned back to Post Office, 76
testimonial, 76, 178–9
and Thomas Arnold, 86–102, 169–74
  see also Arnold, Thomas
timekeeping, 13, 58
working conditions for staff, 39
Hill, Sarah (sister) 1807–40, 22, 43
Hill, Thomas Wright (father) 1763–1851, 22–5
  Bruce Castle opened, 23
  Fellow, Royal Astronomical Society, 23
  Hill Top move, 23
  Lionel Street School purchased, 23
  opened private school, Lionel Street, Birmingham, 2
  Hill Top, Birmingham, 2
  sons as pupil teachers, 2–3
  Sunday school teacher, 22–3
  Unitarian conviction, 23
Hill Top (school), Birmingham, 2
  move to, 23, 25
Hill, William Howard (brother) 1805–20, 22, 43
Hillska Skola (Swedish Hazelwood), 8, 142–4
Home Colonies: a plan . . . crime, 45
Hone, William, 9
Hood, Thomas (1795–1845), 76
  notes and comments, 169
Huxley, Aldous, 20
Huxley, Sir Julian, 20
Huxley, Thomas Henry, 19

Industrial schools, 26

James, Thomas, Headmaster of Rugby, 87, 88
Jefferson, Thomas (1743–1826)
  letter from Matthew Davenport Hill, 16–17
  new education system, 132–3
  notes and comments, 156
  requests copy of *Public Education*, 25
Jullien, Marc Antoine, 8, 95, 142
Junior Republic at Freeville, 132, 134–5

Kennedy, B. H., at Hazelwood School, 16
Knight, Charles (1791–1873), 25, 94, 105, 124, 145–6, notes and comments, 158

Laleham School, notes and comments, 95–6, 171
Lancaster, Sir Ray, 20

Index

Post Office
  controlled by Board, not PMG,
      130
  jealousy, disloyalty, and frustration of plans
      during absence through illness, 100
      see also Postal Reforms of Rowland Hill
Postage, paid on delivery, 30
Postal Reforms of Rowland Hill, 64–85
  achievements, 85, 131
  adhesive stamp, 113, 145–8
  appointment by Chancellor, 71
      salaries offered, 27, 71
  background to reform, 67–70
  Blue books, 67, 69
  candling, 68
  character, 111
  charge by weight rather than distance, 120
  clerical assistance, 72
  determination and self-confidence, 111
  dismissal, 75–6
      summoned back, 76
  earlier history, 66–7
  economic forecasts by R.H., 118
  efficiency discredited, 126–8
  'fallacious return', 77–8, 123–5
  Freedoms, 84
  full salary as pension, 84
  illegal franking, 68
  illhealth retirement, 84
  injustices, 127
  internal wranglings, 78–81
  letter boxes, 69
  loyalty of some staff, 83
  misleading financial information to weaken
      Rowland's case, 77–8
  Money order accounts and embezzlement,
      75
  non-cooperation of officials, 73–4, 77–8,
      82–3
  notes and comments, 165–9
  payment by sheets, 68
  Penny Black, 73, 75, 145–8
  Penny post success, 78, 85
  Penny Postage Act 1839, 46, 70, 105
      first letters, 72
  prepayment, 119–120
  railway contracts, 82
  railway costs, 128
  registered letters, 125–6
  R.H. appointed Secretary, 33, 81, 111, 179
  rotary printing press refused, 65, 122–3
  rural services, 74–5
  single sheet regulation, 68, 119
  stages of R.H. involvement, 110–11
  success denied, 124–5
  Sunday working, 78–9

  tensions leading to delay, 122–3
  threats, 83
  Treasury error on postal returns, 123–5
  vigorous leadership from R.H., 121
  wage controls, 129–30
  weaknesses of system, 118–20
Practical Education, 154
Priestley, Dr Joseph C., 2, 22, 23, 133
  notes and comments, 149–50
  Sunday school, 22
Principles of Church Reform, 101
Printing craft at Hazelwood, 28
Printing press, rotary, 65, 122
  patented, 28
Prison Reform, 41, 42
Public Education, Plans for Government . . .
      1822, 1825, 5, 7, 25, 66, 95, 132, 136,
      151
  reactions and reviews, 5–7
  Swedish translation, 142
Public schools 1800–1900, conditions, 3–4,
  in Australia, 99
Pupil teachers, sons at Hill's schools, 2–3

Queen Victoria, 55–6
  notes and comments, 164

Rachel, 98, 171
Ragged Schools, 26
Railway Chronicle, farewell to R.H., 62
Rallis, Eustrathios, 158
(La) Revue Encyclopédique, 8
Ready-stamped envelope or cover, 145–6, 159
Reform Bill & Act 1832, 4, 23–4, 94, 104,
      163–4
Rotary printing press, 28, 51, 65, 122
Rouse, W. H. D., 15
  notes and comments, 155–6
Rousseau, Jean Jacques (1712–88), 66, 142,
      154
  notes and comments, 165
Royal Mail: The Post Office since 1840, xiii,
      110–13
Rugby football at Hazelwood, 156
Rugby School *see* Arnold, Thomas, of Rugby
      School and Chapter VI passim
Russell, Lord John, notes and comments,
      160–1

Sadler, Sir Michael, 107–8
Sala, George Augustus, 116
Salaries at Rugby, 88, 171
Sand, George (1804–76), 98, notes and
      comments, 171–2
Sandwich, Earl of *see* Montagu, Hon. George

[191]